A Roof Overhead

and

Other Plays

BY

Mahonri Stewart

For production rights to any of Mahonri Stewart's plays, contact him directly at
mahonristewart@gmail.com.

ISBN 978-0-9883233-7-7

Published by:
Zarahemla Books
869 East 2680 North
Provo, UT 84604
info@zarahemlabooks.com
ZarahemlaBooks.com

Printed in the U.S.A.

the material. These talented and sensitive actors are up for the task and are superb as they bring to life some of the most important players in our early church history . . . I am appreciative of Stewart's courage in writing this bold, candid, historically authentic work honoring Emma Hale Smith. The play is an important historical achievement."

— Nan McCulloch, *The Association for Mormon Letters*

"To his credit, playwright Stewart doesn't gloss over [the controversies] but allows them to find their own level. He lets the audience decide what to think, while lobbying for us to dwell on Lewis' incredible insights into Christianity and the souls who choose to embrace it."

— Jerry Early Johnston, *Deseret News*

"I think Mormon literature needs works [like *The Fading Flower*] that probe these unseen corners of the Mormon past, works that try . . . to get at the truth behind the mysteries and obscurities—or go mad in the attempt."

— Scott Hales, *The Low Tech World*

A Roof Overhead

Winner of the 2012 Association for Mormon Letters Award for Best Drama

"As to be expected with a Mahonri Stewart play, the title *A Roof Overhead* is thematically telling. What happens under the roof of this home full of loving but flawed people is what draws us into their lives. Most, but not all, of the interaction between family members and friends is pleasant and happy, but even when the characters steer us into uncomfortable areas that still challenge many members of the Church today (like, for instance, Blacks and the Priesthood), we are presented with multiple sides of those issues in a fair and balanced manner. No one seeing this play would consider it unbalanced. The father Maxwell Fielding is fond of saying throughout the play, 'It's about being fair.' *A Roof Overheard* is nothing if not fair.

"Stewart's skill at dialogue and characterization, mingled with just the right amount of humor, drama, and pathos, anchors us to the play—we become more than mere observers. We become members of the diverse set of characters and we, characters and audience alike, share this roof overheard. What this play says to Mormons is, 'We are not alone in the world. We need to learn to get along with others of different, or sometimes, no faith.'"

— Excerpt from the *AML Award Citation for Drama, 2012*

"Stewart's characters are all strong, all opinionated, and all delightfully quirky in ways that help the audience suspend disbelief. An audience member could come to the play over several performances and glean new insights to his various themes of diversity, family bonds, and the dimensions of maternal influence."

— Margaret Blair Young, *Dawning of a Brighter Day*

Friends of God

"Good script, good story, good actors, good Lord, go see it . . . This is a story about how the good Lord tries his friends."

— Harlow S. Clark, *AML-List*

The Prince's House

"I was quite impressed with 'The Prince's House.' It had never occurred to me to think about the day-to-day struggle of loving someone who suffers from possession (or the psychological analogue to it). I don't think I've ever seen a story that takes this seriously as a human condition (as opposed to a cheap plot device or evil to be opposed). Hats off . . ."

— Jonathan Langford, Author of *No Going Back*

White Mountain

"The dialogue seemed natural and easy . . . I loved the way dreams played a role in both the theme and the dramatic structure of the play. The verbal retelling of dreams was lovely, but best of all were the staged dreams. They are nicely written and beautifully and poignantly staged by director Brian Randall. I was invested in the characters enough that I would have liked to have seen more of their story, but this short play was self-contained enough to be satisfying on its own."

— Bianca Morrison Dillard, *Utah Theatre Bloggers Association*

Yeshua

"Mahonri Stewart's *Yeshua* tells the familiar story of Jesus, but unlike so many retellings of the Savior's life, it does not play like a highlights reel of the Gospels. At its heart, *Yeshua* is about our need for deeply personal relationships—not only with the divine, but with all of humanity. *Yeshua*, like the title character Himself, invites us to reach out in love to God and our neighbor."

— Scott Hales, Literary Critic
and Award Winning Cartoonist of *Garden of Enid*

Farewell to Eden

Published in Saints on Stage: An Anthology of Mormon Drama

*Winner of the Kennedy Center's American College Theatre Festival's
2003 National Playwriting Award (Second Place)
and the KCACTF National Selection Team Fellowship Award*

"One of the most intelligently written plays I have read in a decade."

— Gary Garrison, KCACTF Playwriting Chair/
Dramatists Guild President

"*Farewell to Eden* is a uniquely rewarding character study that is so splendidly played as to make it highly recommended."

— Blair Howell, *Deseret News*

"The depth doesn't keep it from being accessible. Witty banter, symbolism, broad range of characters, historical figures popping in and out, romantic stories that avoid clichés, and did I mention witty banter and fully fleshed out characters? Please sign me up."

— Kara Henry, *Front Row Reviewers*

"*Farewell to Eden* is brilliant. It's complicated, not very predictable, and has a lot of depth and characterization."

— Sharon Haddock, *Deseret News*

"Mahonri Stewart, remember that name . . . a tremendous debut."

Eric Samuelsen, *Irreantum Magazine*

". . . intriguing, full of plot twists and authentic character development . . . this production probably has the most pleasantly understated acting that audiences can find in Northern Utah right now . . . a thought provoking experience for anyone who catches *Farewell to Eden*."

— Russell Warne, *Utah Theatre Bloggers Association*

The Fading Flower and Swallow the Sun

"Stewart is rightly one of the leading voices in Mormon theatre right now."

— Laura Craner, *A Motley Vision*

"I personally felt that the plays spoke deeply to me as the kind of Mormon who inhabits a largely secular world . . . and views my own faith through the lens of the perpetual tensions this exacerbates: tensions between secular and sacred, insider and exile, spiritual and intellectual, narrative and history . . . That I can delve this deeply is, in my mind, a testament that the source material has real substance. That I wanted to do so in the first place, is a testament to Stewart's craft and artistry as a playwright."

— Nathaniel Givens, *Times and Seasons*

"*The Fading Flower* obviously makes use of historical studies of the Smith family and of polygamy . . . [In *Swallow the Sun*] Stewart also has a deep knowledge of the writings and biography of C. S. Lewis . . . *The Fading Flower* is both poignant and tragic . . . audience members will also be surprised with the complexity of what was assumed to be familiar territory . . . the literary qualities of the plays are real and the historical accuracy is remarkable. Stewart's drama deserves its prominent place in contemporary Mormon letters."

— David Allred, *The Association for Mormon Letters*

"As a play, *Swallow the Sun* is well-written, funny, and thought-provoking . . . *Swallow the Sun* is a captivating journey from doubt to belief."

— Scott Hales, *A Low Tech World*

"Intriguing and compelling . . . [*Swallow the Sun*] has a fascination about it that holds the audience's attention."

— Rodger L. Hardy, *Deseret News*

"Stewart is ever the writer of brilliant dialogue. [*The Fading Flower*] is so powerful and beautifully written it demands competent actors to match

Contents

Friends of God   1

White Mountain   109

The Prince's House   133

A Roof Overhead   145

Yeshua   267

Acknowledgements   389

Friends of God

A Mormon History Play in Two Acts

Production History

Friends of God first premiered at Art City Playhouse in Springville, UT on January 6, 2006. It had the following cast and crew:

CAST

Joseph Smith: Benjamin King

Emma Smith: Heather Jones

Hyrum Smith: Jordan McMillan

William Law: Adam Argyle

Jane Law: Dadre Mitchell

Eliza R. Snow: Holly Harris

John Taylor: Stephen Driggs/Mahonri Stewart[1]

Willard Richards: Kenneth Brown

Actor 1: Amos Omer

Actor 2: Penny Pendleton

Actor 3: Adam Stallard

Actor 4: Jason Fullmer

Porter Rockwell: Bryce Bishop

Leonora Taylor: Sarah Harris

Governor Ford: George Anderson

Brigham Young: Rhett Dial[2]

Mary Ann Young: Melissa Chung

---

1. Due to an emergency, I took over the role from Stephen Driggs for the last couple of performances.

2. Brigham and Mary Ann Young were characters in the original production, but in this published revision the characters have been cut out as they did not contribute greatly to the main plot, and unnecessarily lengthened the play—as much as I liked the actors who played them.

Executive Producer: Gavin Grooms/Utah Stage Artists
Director: Mahonri Stewart
Costume Designer/Construction: Amelia Schow
Lighting Design: Dadre Mitchell
Lighting Technician: Adam Harvey
Set Construction: Gavin Grooms
Set Design: Mahonri Stewart
Fight Choreography: Adam Argyle and Amos Omer
Set Painters: Heather Jones, Adam Stallard, Anne Stewart, Mahonri Stewart
Original Music: Nathaniel Drew

For my mother Joanna MacKay Stewart,
Who gave me The History of Joseph Smith by his Mother, *the first full*
volume of Mormon History I read;

And to Alex Parent,
Who accelerated that interest when he gifted me The Martyrs *by*
Lyman O. Littlefied, and lent me Truman G. Madsen's lectures on Joseph
Smith when I was in high school.

I have read higher heights and deeper depths in Church History since
then, but it was those volumes in my early life that were the tinderbox
that created this passionate fire.

"Since God had commanded it, it was necessary that I do it. Since God commanded it, even if I had a hundred fathers and mothers, even if I had been a King's daughter, I would have gone nevertheless."

— Jeanne d'Arc, Condemnation Trial (1431)

"For years I have been waiting for someone to do justice in recording in song and story and painting and sculpture the story of the Restoration, the reestablishment of the kingdom of God on earth, the struggles and frustrations; the apostasies and inner revolutions and counter-revolutions of those first decades; of the exodus; of the counter-reactions; of the transitions; of the persecution days; of the miracle man, Joseph Smith . . . "

— Spencer W. Kimball, "The Gospel Vision of the Arts" (1978)

Friends of God

Act One

ACTOR 1 walks out onto the stage and he gingerly looks out at the audience for a while, with a smiling, friendly manner.

ACTOR 1. Welcome to Missouri.

ACTOR 2 comes out as well. She is more hesitant, but initially polite.

ACTOR 2. Good to meet you, folks.

ACTOR 1. Are y'all Mormons? Or can I trust you?

ACTOR 2. Are you Missourians? Or can I trust you? (*Beat.*) The looting and capture of Far West was a terrible thing. A terrible thing.

ACTOR 1. Have you ever figured what a group can do, if they all think the same? Say they gots a leader—a "prophet"—like ol' Joe Smith. He says he talks to God and that God tells him whats all of us is supposed to do. Say that group grows and grows like mildew and that they don't stop growin'.

ACTOR 2. The Haun's Mill Massacre came first. It came after the Extermination Order was signed by Governor Boggs. Perhaps you maybe think what we believe's heretical or somethin', but I probably think that lots of what you believe is a bunch of rubbish as well. But did that justify a state order to exterminate an entire religion, if we didn't leave the state?

ACTOR 1. Whatcha gonna do when they start votin' the same? Whatcha gonna do when they start comin' from other states, from the

North, East, from Canada, from all over the place and focus themselves on one spot. A hornet is easy enough to deal with, if you only have one to deal with. But what happens when they build a whole nest of hornets right above your head? Are you just gonna to turn your rights and privileges over to them? Are you gonna let them spoil the community you tried so hard to build?

ACTOR 2. The Haun's Mill Massacre was conducted by the Missouri State Militia. Have you ever thought your own government would turn against you? They killed men, women, and children. No warning, no skirmish. They just came in and started shootin'. All with the Governor's blessing.

ACTOR 1. They said they was some chosen people and this was their Zion. We could stay here for now, but God had really meant it for them and they were goin' to buy it and build up their own community. They wouldn't buy or sell with us. They warn't friendly like. Stuck to themselves mostly, unless you was interested in their religion. A bunch of snobs, the pack of them.

ACTOR 2. I was in Far West and that was the most frightening moment in my life. People were killed, we were badgered and insulted. They sieged the city and took away the guns we had—that left them open to loot Far West for what they wanted. Including the women. I don't like to talk about that part, but my sister she was—well, what they did—well, I don't like to talk about that part.

ACTOR 1. Then they started all of that abolitionist talk. If you want to be a part of a community, you gotta act like that community, or at least not preach all your high handed ideas. Do you reckon we were just gonna let such a group get powerful? No, not for the moon and all the stars. We had our rights, just like anyone else.

ACTOR 2. 'Mong our martyrs, we seen an apostle get killed. David W. Patten. He was a good man, among the best. A man of God. Captain Fear Not, we called him. He was known for healin' people, miraculous like. Even a blind woman. Just like in the Bible. Can you imagine killing a man like that? A man of God isn't immortal or anything.

They killed the likes of Stephen or Paul or Peter. If Jews bleed, then so do Mormons.

ACTOR 1. If we could just get Smith and their other leaders, then we knew the whole blasphemous religion would stop.

ACTOR 2. I couldn't bear to think of them putting Joseph in that dank dungeon. What kind of black humor did somebody have to call that place Liberty Jail? Imagine putting a man like Brother Joseph in a place like that.

ACTOR 1. It was a real shame that ol' Joe weren't killed on the spot. You can thank the ol' traitor Doniphan for that missed opportunity.

ACTOR 2. Thank the Lord for Alexander Doniphan.

ACTOR 1. That false prophet was ready to be executed, but then Doniphan went on his self-righteous tirade. Sometimes I think some of the ridiculous laws we set up let evil thrive.

ACTOR 2. Doniphan proved that there is kindness and justice among the Gentiles yet.

ACTOR 1. That Joseph Smith, he sold his soul to the devil. That's why he could do so many miracles. I heard he was an adulterer, a liar, a conjurer, a gold digger, a counterfeiter—even a murderer. And all this time people is callin' him a prophet.

ACTOR 2. There was no man that made me feel closer to God than Joseph Smith. Joseph may have not been perfect, some may have thought him a bit rough and tumble like—but he was not a deceiver. And he was not deceived.

ACTOR 1. After we drove them out of Missouri, they went to Illinois. They started a city there. And guess who became their mayor? Joseph Smith. Guess who became the lieutenant general of their militia? Joseph Smith. Guess who then ran for the President of the United States? Joseph Smith. See a pattern?

ACTOR 2. When the government failed us, Joseph was there. He went directly to Washington to talk to the likes of Henry Clay and John Calhoun, and even President Van Buren himself. Did they ever help us? The president said to him, "Your cause is just, but I can do nothing for you. I'll lose the vote of Missouri." Is it any wonder that in Nauvoo Joseph asserted himself; sought to protect our people politically and militarily? He had seen his people persecuted so heavily—in Nauvoo he made sure that wasn't going to happen again.

ACTOR 1. If only we could have finished the job in Missouri before he did so much more damage.

Exit ACTOR 1.

ACTOR 2. In Missouri we were pressed like grapes. But we poured out like new wine, pure and unfermented, ready to be put into the new bottle of Nauvoo. In Liberty Jail, Joseph was ground to ashes. But out of those ashes he flew out a Phoenix, shiny and fiery-like, more powerful and more searching than ever. Yes, Nauvoo, there was our glory.

Exit ACTOR 2. ACTOR 3 walks out onto the stage and he gingerly looks out at the audience for a while, with a smiling, friendly manner.

ACTOR 3. Welcome to Illinois.

Blackout.

SCENE 2

WILLIAM LAW appears, addressing the audience:

WILLIAM LAW. What have the Mormons done to Illinois? This is the question which I have frequently asked of those who are busy with the tongue of slander in calumniating the Latter-day Saints. Perhaps many of them judge from rumor, not having investigated the matter for themselves. There are those who cry out, "Treason! Murder! Bigamy! Burglary! Arson!" and everything that is evil, without being able to refer to a single case that has been proved against the Mormons.

WILLIAM steps down. Enter ROBERT FOSTER.

ROBERT FOSTER. Fine oratory there, President Law. Too bad the truth of it is more slippery than water.

WILLIAM LAW. Robert Foster. I'm surprised you still show your face around here.

ROBERT FOSTER. I won't let men like Joseph Smith destroy my life.

WILLIAM. You destroyed your own life when you decided to involve yourself in the licentious practices of John C. Bennett. Hyrum and I found out all about the wife he abandoned, the women he seduced, the brothels he constructed in Nauvoo, the abortions he performed . . .

ROBERT. Yes, quite the list.

WILLIAM. You have brought the curse of God upon you.

ROBERT. The sanctified William Law. Always spouting off such holy talk, dignified speeches. Such a polished, perfect saint and gentleman. Wash all that away and you'll be revealed to be nothing but Joseph Smith's dupe.

WILLIAM. You were the one duped by Bennett, sir. You believed his lies and practiced his hellish teachings. Did you really believe that the Prophet Joseph would have taught such evil doctrines?

ROBERT. Do you really think that he didn't?

WILLIAM. Well, he's denied it, hasn't he?

ROBERT. I've been keeping my ear low to the ground lately, and I'm finding out new information all the time. Yes, President Smith has been able to avoid it in the technicalities of his talk. But he sure is hiding something. A new system of marriage.

WILLIAM. I will not believe the lies of an adulterer.

ROBERT. Whitened sephulcre. Full of dead men's bones. All manner of uncleanness.

WILLIAM. You slander me, sir.

ROBERT. Do I? Well, perhaps the stories I hear of you are wrong as well then.

WILLIAM. What libel do you refer to?

ROBERT. Are there so many that you must keep track? Let him without sin cast the first stone, William Law. An adulterer accusing me of adultery . . .

WILLIAM. Pernicious lies—I am not an adulterer!

ROBERT. Perhaps not. But when Joseph Smith starts uncovering your sins, let's see how you feel then? Let's see how you feel when you are denounced in public by a man who you know has kept hidden his own dealings. But when you reach that road, remember those who understand your plight.

WILLIAM. You are a wicked man, Robert Foster.

ROBERT. Aren't we all?

Exit ROBERT, *leaving* WILLIAM *deeply disturbed. Exit* WILLIAM.

SCENE 3

The Smith home. EMMA SMITH *is looking through some papers. Joseph enters and kisses her on the cheek:*

JOSEPH. Good afternoon, darling. What are you reading?

EMMA. The Female Relief Society minutes. I had Eliza bring them over when she came to teach the children. Some of the women had some urgent questions about something you said to us.

JOSEPH. Oh? I'm surprised they didn't nod off.

EMMA. Believe me, you were saying some—*controversial* things. Like this: ". . . the Society should move according to the ancient Priesthood, hence there should be a select Society separate from all the evils of the world, choice, virtuous and holy— Said he was going to make of this Society a kingdom of priests as in Enoch's day—as in Paul's day . . ."

JOSEPH. You're right. That's scandalous. I'll apologize to them tomorrow.

EMMA. Seriously, Joseph, what does this mean?

JOSEPH. What do you think it means?

EMMA. I dare not hope.

JOSEPH. If I am given time, Emma, I will reveal to you every key and principle the Lord has taught me. You will be able to pass the angels that stand as sentinels and become a lady of light beyond anything you could have expected. A priestess. A queen. A goddess.

EMMA. That is what I wanted to—wait, what do you mean, "If I am given time?" Of course you have time.

JOSEPH. Oh, Emma, listen! We must all prepare to receive those revelations, or else we can't have them. I could explain a hundred fold more than I ever have of the glories of the kingdoms manifested to me in vision, were I permitted, and were the people prepared to receive them.

EMMA. Am I ready to receive them?

JOSEPH. I don't know, are you? (*Beat.*) Where are the children?

EMMA. Working on their lessons with Eliza.

JOSEPH. I'm glad that you and Sister Snow are such good friends.

EMMA. She's been a great comfort to me. And so intelligent! I need that kind of conversation! There is no woman who stimulates me more than she does. And she does a marvelous job teaching the children.

JOSEPH. Just because I didn't have the opportunities of an education doesn't mean that my children won't. They'll be like their mother in that regard.

EMMA. If I needed to marry an educated man, I would have.

JOSEPH. And if you had that choice to make again?

EMMA. You don't need to ask that question, Joseph. You know my heart.

JOSEPH. Hear me out, Emma. If you had known what we have had to go through—the mobbings, the terrors, you and the children having to wander homeless in the winter storms while I lay in prison—the loss of so many of our dear, little ones. Would have you . . . ?

EMMA. Now stop it, Joseph. I love you. You mean the world to me.

JOSEPH. I love you, too, I always will. But . . .

EMMA. Then we don't need to have this conversation. Especially in the sunlight of our experience. After such a long journey, we are finally prospering.

JOSEPH. The Lord will require more of us. Our travails and pains are not over.

EMMA. The Lord has seen our sacrifices. He is pleased. He is satisfied.

JOSEPH. He will test us even as Abraham. He will wrench our very hearts strings.

EMMA. Joseph, stop it! The Lord tore out my heart strings when He took my children away! (*Beat.*) But I have submitted to that, I have submitted to Him every step of the way. He is satisfied. He must be.

JOSEPH. Emma, I know you, and I know your goodness, even when some others do not.

EMMA. I have never cared about the opinions of others.

JOSEPH. Another of your virtues. But, Emma, what you have had to endure in the name of the Lord—you must comfort yourself knowing that God is your friend in heaven, and that you have one true and living friend on earth, your husband.

EMMA. And I am your friend.

JOSEPH. (*Sober pause.*) Emma, you have borne every grief, every sacrifice—except one.

EMMA. No. We are through with that. You promised.

JOSEPH. Emma, the Lord's revelations cannot be so easily discarded. I wanted to please you, but more so I want to please God. You don't know the severity the angel put upon . . .

EMMA. We are through with it! I will no longer listen to that principle from hell! How can you . . . ? After everything, how can you still . . . ?

JOSEPH. How can you ask me to deny an angel of the Lord?

EMMA. If you value our marriage, never mention it again.

JOSEPH. Emma, please . . .

EMMA. It's not from God, Joseph. It can't be.

Enter ELIZA SNOW, initially unseen.

JOSEPH. Emma! You are forcing me into an impossible . . .

EMMA. No, you are forcing me! If you continue to press this, then there is no hope for us!

ELIZA clears her throat.

EMMA. Eliza!

ELIZA SNOW. I am sorry. I didn't mean to . . .

EMMA. No, it's all right, Eliza. This conversation is over. Isn't it, Joseph? (*Silent beat.*) How were the children today?

ELIZA. I've been sent by the children to deliver an urgent message to Joseph: they say that they have been kidnapped by Captain Kidd and his pirates who often sail upon the fish pond. If their father doesn't save them soon, they may have to walk the plank.

JOSEPH. Yes, urgent indeed. Captain Smith will go to the rescue.

Exit Joseph. Uncomfortable silence and then:

ELIZA SNOW. He's really just one of the children, isn't he?

EMMA. Yes, and sometimes children need to be disciplined.

ELIZA. Well, *your* children are very well behaved. Except perhaps that big one who just bounded out of here. He is a tough nut to crack, that is sure.

They both smile at each other.

EMMA. Joseph and I are deeply grateful for you, Eliza. Joseph is a little self-conscious about his lack of formal schooling. He doesn't want his children to suffer the same embarrassment.

ELIZA. That's only natural.

EMMA. Can you imagine a man like him doing what he's done without the aid of Heaven? He couldn't have composed a well written letter in those days, much less the Book of Mormon.

ELIZA. If the world could only see what we see. Then all the mobs would stop.

EMMA. Would they?

ELIZA. Of course.

EMMA. Perhaps it would only anger them even more. You are right about that one, the world does not know him. There are parts of him which even I don't know—they are too deep and mysterious for me.

ELIZA. Nonsense. The Lord has made you equal to your husband. There is one speech of his that I loved. I borrowed Brother Wilford's notes and committed to it memory: "The things of God are of deep import; and time, and experience, and careful and ponderous and solemn thoughts can only find them out. Thy mind, O man, if thou wilt lead a soul unto salvation, must stretch as high as the utmost heavens, and search into and contemplate the darkest abyss, and the broad expanse of eternity—thou must commune with God."

EMMA. (*Strangely affected:*) It is ironic that such a rustic man could revolutionize so much. In the first days of the Church, the things he taught were simple and—understandable. But since we've come to Nauvoo . . .

ELIZA. Hasn't he become glorious? The refiner's fire of Missouri truly made a great man out of him!

EMMA. I don't know. (*With a strained smile:*) I liked it when I was smarter than him. (*Beat.*) But, as you said—now we are to be equals.

ELIZA. Perhaps there was purpose in his supposed ignorance. It leaves so much more room for the education of God when we don't cling too tightly to fallen man's ways.

EMMA. Yes.

ELIZA. Uncluttered. No worldly theories of Babylon to block the way. No customs or . . .

EMMA. . . . traditional values . . .

ELIZA. . . . we become so open to the revelations of God . . .

EMMA. . . . the revelations of God. He preached recently: "what many people call sin is not sin; I do many things to break down superstition, and I will break it down." (*Beat.*) Purposes. God has his purposes.

ELIZA. Emma? (*EMMA begins to cry. ELIZA freezes in surprise and then rushes to embrace EMMA.*) You have friends, my dear. What's wrong?

EMMA. Am I a wicked woman?

ELIZA. What? No, of course not!

EMMA. I can be so jealous hearted.

Long pause.

ELIZA. Emma, your husband is a prophet of God.

EMMA. I know that. You think I don't know that?

ELIZA. He is a righteous man. The things he teaches are true.

EMMA. Eliza, you don't know what you are saying. You don't know what is—oh, I can't even say it! Are you so sure? Are you so sure that everything he teaches is true?

ELIZA. Well, probably not everything. I'm sure that he's not a perfect man. You of all people would know his faults. His humanity. You see that, more intimately than most do. Yet you also know his Greatness. His Calling. Don't let your familiarity with him block you from what you know.

EMMA. Oh, and what do I know, pray tell?

ELIZA. You know that God talks to him. That he is God's friend.

EMMA. (*Beat.*) I suppose I do know that.

ELIZA. Can I tell you about my first impressions of Joseph?

EMMA. Yes, I would like that.

EMMA nestles her head into ELIZA's lap. ELIZA begins stroking her hair.

ELIZA. The first time I saw your husband, he'd called at my father's with Sidney Rigdon, who had been our Campbellite pastor. Sidney was convinced that Joseph was a prophet by then and was telling everyone in his congregation. I was skeptical, to say the least. But I caught Joseph when he thought he was alone, warming himself by our fire. As I watched him from the shadows, I scrutinized his face as closely as I could without attracting his attention. He was at ease, calm—he had a peace that I have never observed in liars. I decided his was an honest face. In that firelight playing on his countenance, I could not doubt his relaxed, peaceful face.

EMMA. And doesn't he have a wonderful face?

ELIZA smiles, but then catches herself. There is a pause before she continues:

ELIZA. It took me a long time to join this Church. I was incredulous at first. Cynical. Yet the Spirit bore witness to me of the truth. When I was—when I was taught things that were very difficult for me to understand, I could stand on that Spirit which gave me so much more faith and courage in my convictions.

EMMA. You have been a true friend to me, Eliza.

ELIZA. I—I hope we can be even more than that to each other, Emma. I consider us like sisters. When all these things are worked out, I hope we can be so much more.

SCENE 4

Lights cross fade to HYRUM SMITH *and* JOSEPH *wrestling.* HYRUM *seems to have the upper hand, but then Joseph accomplishes a reversal.*

HYRUM. You're not going to pin me, you're not going to pin me . . .

JOSEPH pins HYRUM on his back.

JOSEPH. (*With a mischievous smile:*) I pinned you.

HYRUM. Little brother, you're gettin' my goat.

JOSEPH helps HYRUM to his feet.

JOSEPH. That's not difficult with a self-serious fellow like you.

HYRUM. Someday I'll be able to best you, you know.

JOSEPH. Stick to your gentleman's games. When you get a little more muscles on those bones of yours, then maybe I can have a little bit of fun with you.

JOSEPH laughs and turns away.

HYRUM. I'll show you how a true gentleman wrestles!

HYRUM tackles JOSEPH from behind.

JOSEPH. Cheater!

The two begin to wrestle again.

HYRUM. You're not going to pin me, you're not going to pin me . . .

Once again, JOSEPH pins HYRUM.

JOSEPH. I pinned you.

HYRUM. All right, my goat is got.

JOSEPH. Want to go two out of three?

HYRUM. I don't know . . .

HYRUM suddenly springs on JOSEPH. Again, they wrestle. Enter WILLIAM:

WILLIAM. Excuse me, Brethren . . .

JOSEPH. (*With a laugh:*) Can't you see we're busy, William?

HYRUM. You're not going to pin me, you're not going to pin me . . .

    JOSEPH pins HYRUM.

JOSEPH. I pinned you.

HYRUM. All right, I may have pulled something . . .

JOSEPH. We even had an audience to view your shame this time! (*JOSEPH helps HYRUM up.*) The Bible says that there must be two or three witnesses in all things, after all. (*Beat.*) Wanna wrestle, William?

WILLIAM. Joseph, do you really think it is best for people to see servants of God tussling around on the ground?

JOSEPH. Why not? Jacob wrestled with an angel. It is perfectly scriptural.

WILLIAM. And you, Hyrum! I know Joseph is sometimes—untraditional—but I wouldn't have expected to see you in such a state!

HYRUM. (*To Joseph:*) You call *me* serious.

WILLIAM. Joseph, I really must bring all of this to your attention. Not only the wrestling and the baseball and the games with that trouble making brood . . .

JOSEPH. "Suffer the little children," William.

WILLIAM. . . . but now you've also let Thomas Lyne infect Nauvoo with those pernicious plays.

JOSEPH. Wait, are you being serious? I wept during their production of *Pizarro* at the Masonic Hall.

HYRUM. I thought it was a lovely production, too. Did you see it, William?

WILLIAM. No, certainly not! But I heard the stories! To have an apostle like Brigham Young—an apostle!—dressed up like a pagan, Incan priest!

JOSEPH. (*With a subversive smile:*) Brother Lyne told me that he should have been more careful casting Brigham as the High Priest—he may get used to it!

WILLIAM. And still you joke! We are the leaders of this people. We need to set an example. We should discountenance houses of revelry and dancing, dram shops, theaters—they lead away from virtue, from holiness—they will lead us to vice and debauchery!

HYRUM. Calm down, William. As members of the First Presidency, you and I certainly have the right to counsel Joseph, but let's not get . . .

WILLIAM. We need to be cleansed, or we shall fall!

HYRUM. That is enough, William!

WILLIAM. Joseph, I want you to consider what we were talking about the other day.

JOSEPH. What *you* were talking about.

WILLIAM. You are this community's religious leader, as well as their civic leader. As mayor and prophet, so much depends on you. We ought to establish some stricter community guidelines about what is and is not allowed in Nauvoo.

HYRUM. William, really, let's talk about something more . . .

WILLIAM. (*Ignoring HYRUM.*) And we should not only focus on behavior, but the root of behavior. Belief. We need a more unified belief system. I've told you again and again, let us establish some more creeds of belief. Relate it all back into one system. There are other religions where a man must believe or be kicked out of their church. This is reasonable . . .

JOSEPH. I want the liberty to believe as I please, it feels so good not to be trammeled. It does not prove that a man is not a good man because he errs in doctrine.

WILLIAM. Joseph, there are odd beliefs, dangerous beliefs that are circulating in Nauvoo. Ridiculously, some are even saying that some of those beliefs are originating with you.

HYRUM. I am not sure if I know what is being discussed here . . .

WILLIAM. Of course we know that you are a pure man, Joseph. A prophet. Let us declare to the world pure doctrine that proves such. Let's establish what our creed truly is.

JOSEPH. (*Steely:*) The Latter-day Saints have no creed. We are ready to believe all true principles that exist, as they are made manifest to us.

WILLIAM. You can't mean that. Perhaps you have been influenced . . .

JOSEPH. Yes. By angels and the Holy Spirit.

WILLIAM. I have long questioned the choice of some of the people you surround yourself with. Their demeanor, their habits, the language they use . . .

JOSEPH. William, I love a man better who swears a stream as long as my arm, yet deals justice to his neighbors and mercifully deals his substance to the poor. I love that man much better than the long, smooth faced hypocrite.

Tense pause.

WILLIAM. I hope you'll see reason soon.

Exit WILLIAM.

HYRUM. It wouldn't hurt to use a little tact, Joseph.

JOSEPH. And William was so subtle?

HYRUM. Joseph . . .

JOSEPH. Hyrum, you have the integrity of Job. God loves the loyalty you have shown me and His Church.

HYRUM. Yes, Joseph, but . . .

JOSEPH. But God will test even your integrity, Hyrum.

HYRUM. What are you talking about?

JOSEPH. What if God were to reveal to you something that would shake even your faith?

HYRUM. I am ready to follow God in any circumstance, but . . .

JOSEPH. The rumors that William has heard—you have heard them as well?

HYRUM. (*Pause.*) Yes. And denounced them.

JOSEPH. Then keep denouncing them. We need to be careful with how we proceed with this.

HYRUM. Joseph, I don't understand. They aren't true. You would never do that. God would never condone that.

JOSEPH. But what if, in certain circumstances, He did? If He commanded it, even. Hyrum . . .

HYRUM. I don't want to hear it. Joseph, I love you too much to indulge such fancies.

JOSEPH. Hyrum . . .

HYRUM. I don't want to hear it!

Exit HYRUM.

JOSEPH. (*Calling after HYRUM:*) God will try you, Hyrum! Even a man as righteous as you.

Exit JOSEPH.

SCENE 5

Lights rise on a social gathering. HYRUM, JOHN TAYLOR, LEONORA TAYLOR, ACTOR 4 as DAN JONES, WILLIAM, and JANE LAW are among the group, in addition to the other ACTORS, who are intermingling with them. ACTOR 2 is playing Hyrum's wife, MARY FIELDING SMITH.

MARY FIELDING. (*To HYRUM:*) Darling, where's Joseph? Our host has abandoned the party!

HYRUM. Emma needed some help in the kitchen, Mary. He'll be out in a moment.

ACTOR 1. Help in the kitchen, did you say?

LEONORA. Brother Joseph does many such things for his wife. He proves himself a very thoughtful and loving husband in that.

Enter JOSEPH, unseen by the others, carrying a platter of food. Sensing that the conversation is about him, he remains quiet to overhear:

ACTOR 1. Such home habits are not in accord with my idea of a great man's self respect.

MARY FIELDING. Be careful what you say, sir, for Joseph is a great man.

ACTOR 1. And that's why I bring it up. I don't mean offense, of course.

MARY FIELDING. Then what do you mean?

ACTOR 1. All I mean is, if the prophet were here, then I would give him some good natured, corrective advice.

MARY FIELDING and HYRUM notice JOSEPH. JOSEPH puts his finger to his lips. They nod and smile inconspicuously.

MARY FIELDING. So, if the Prophet were here, what would you say to him?

Enter EMMA and ELIZA, also carrying food, drinks, utensils, etc. Joseph signals them to be quiet as well.

ACTOR 1. I would remind him of every phase of his greatness and call to his mind of tasks that were performed that were too menial for such as he. To work in the kitchen is too great a humiliation!

LEONORA. (*Also catching JOSEPH's eye:*) A humiliation, do you say?

ACTOR 1. Too terrible a humiliation! For he is the head, and he should not do it.

JOSEPH. (*Revealing himself, with platter in hand.*) If there be humiliation in a man's house, who else should or could bear the humiliation?

ACTOR 1. Oh, Brother Joseph!

JOSEPH. Well, my friend? Who should bear it?

ACTOR 1. Well, er, Brother Joseph, I just wanted you to see things in a clearer light. A woman is ennobled when she serves her husband dutifully, wouldn't you agree? Take my wife for example. You must admit, my wife does much more hard work than does your wife.

JOSEPH. Then I pity your wife.

ACTOR 1. Why—why, here now!

JOSEPH. Where is your wife now?

ACTOR 1. Doing as she ought to, finishing chores which she had neglected this afternoon.

JOSEPH. (*With a disapproving look:*) If a man cannot learn in life to appreciate a wife and do his duty to her, he need not expect to be given one in the hereafter.

There is a tense silence.

ACTOR 1. I—I'm not really quite sure what to say to that.

JOSEPH. I would suggest that you go relieve your wife of those chores.

ACTOR 1, abashed, grabs his hat and coat and then exits. JOSEPH takes this opportunity to speak to the group, and then more particularly to EMMA:

JOSEPH (CONT'D). It is the duty of a husband to love, cherish, and nourish his wife, and cleave unto her and none else; he ought to honor her as himself, and he ought to regard her feelings with tenderness, for she is his flesh, and his bones. It is not the place of the man to rule over his wife as a tyrant, neither as one who is fearful or jealous that his wife will get out of her place, and prevent him from exercising his authority.

EMMA. Amen!

DAN. Here, Sister Smith, let me help you with that.

EMMA. Thank you, Brother Jones.

JOHN. Let me give you a hand, Sister Snow.

ELIZA. I appreciate it, Elder Taylor.

JANE approaches EMMA, taking her by the arm and talking to her privately. EMMA is slightly uncomfortable with the intimacy of the gesture.

JANE. You have a mighty fine husband, Emma.

EMMA. Why, uh, thank you.

JANE. Now if only William could be so thoughtful.

EMMA. William is a good man, Jane.

JANE. Oh, he's good. I see that. We have our troubles, though.

EMMA. Truly, that's none of my . . .

JANE. He's a little strict at times. And it would be nice to get out once in a while, beyond Church and—well, you ought to count your lucky stars, Emma.

EMMA. Now, Jane . . .

JANE. The majority of women, we receive average men. Men who generally want to be good, but who suffer a bit in the faults which men seem so eager to display. Oh, but your husband. As humble as the earth, yet as bold and as expansive as the sky!

EMMA. Is it really appropriate to . . .

JANE. You have married greatness, a man whose name shall go down through the generations! I would trade places with you in an instant.

EMMA. Jane!

JANE. Have I upset you?

EMMA. "Thou shalt not covet."

JANE. Oh, don't be angry, Emma. You misunderstand me.

EMMA. I certainly hope so.

JANE. But you must admit that your husband is admirable. A true prophet.

EMMA. Your prophet. My husband.

JANE. And you are a woman who is worthy of such a man. Really, I see that I have distressed you, I am so sorry. That was not my intention. Let's upon a different subject, shall we? Let's see, well, I was just down Parley Street the other day and I found this exquisite new shop . . .

JANE's voice fades off. Enter PORTER ROCKWELL, *looking disheveled, disoriented, and ragged. His face is hidden amidst his coat, hat, etc.*

JOHN. (*Motioning to* PORTER.) Joseph . . .

JOSEPH. Who is that? A drunk?

DAN. Perhaps a Missourian, Joseph. This may be dangerous.

JOSEPH. Whoever he is, escort him out, Brethren.

JOHN, DAN, WILLARD, WILLIAM, and HYRUM go to POR- TER and try to grab him. A struggle ensues:

PORTER ROCKWELL. Let me go!

WILLIAM. You won't get near him, you rascal!

JOSEPH. Brethren, wait! (*JOSEPH comes up to* PORTER *and gets a clears view of his face.*) Port?

PORTER. Now ain't that a fine way to greet a friend?

JOSEPH. Porter Rockwell! You're out of prison!

The men let PORTER *go and* JOSEPH *embraces him.*

PORTER. Just like you prophesied I would be.

JOSEPH. I hardly recognize you!

PORTER. That was awful obvious.

JOSEPH. I swear, Port, the time will come when good men will no longer have to bend under the oppression of illegal law suits and false imprisonments. But God has delivered you!

PORTER. Yeah, a miracle, I know—but I need to talk to you alone, Joseph.

WILLIAM. Surely, Brother Rockwell, you can discuss the matter here among friends.

PORTER. (*Giving* WILLIAM *a withering look:*) I surely can't.

JOSEPH. All right, Port, let's just step outside then.

WILLIAM. Wait a minute, Joseph. (*Taking him aside:*) Are you sure it's safe?

JOSEPH. If I'm not safe with Port, then I don't know who I would be safe with. Just the sight of him scares most scoundrels away.

WILLIAM. That's not what I mean. He's just come back from the hands of your enemies, Joseph. How did he get out? Perhaps he's in league with them now. Perhaps they set him free to trap you.

JOSEPH. That man gave up his freedom to defend the Church.

WILLIAM. They say he tried to murder Governor Boggs!

JOSEPH. If so, as I said, he gave up his freedom to defend the Church. Boggs tried to kill all of us.

WILLIAM. Are you defending . . . ?

JOSEPH. Porter Rockwell puts God first and has always been a solid and true friend to me. I trust Porter Rockwell almost more than anyone else in the world.

WILLIAM. He's a rough man, Joseph.

JOSEPH. The Lord does not look on the outside appearance, William. He's been my friend since I was young in Palmyra. Porter has the pure heart of a child.

WILLIAM. Porter Rockwell is anything but a child! I'm not sure if I trust him anymore. I'm not sure if I ever did.

JOSEPH. I trust him even more than I trust you. Now excuse me. (*To* PORTER:) Come on, Port.

Exit JOSEPH and PORTER, leaving WILLIAM exasperated. HYRUM approaches WILLIAM.

HYRUM. William?

WILLIAM. Yes?

HYRUM. What you said to me and Joseph the other day . . .

WILLIAM. (*Taking HYRUM aside.*) I know it upsets you, but . . .

HYRUM. There seems to be truth in it. I have been hearing the same rumors from other sources now and—well, Joseph said something to me that could be interpreted . . .

WILLIAM. Yes?

HYRUM. We must get to the bottom of this.

WILLIAM. I knew you would come around! William Marks and I have been talking and we feel it best to bring it before the public. Especially coming from us, that will make Joseph respond.

HYRUM. Wait—publicly?

WILLIAM. I don't see any way around it.

HYRUM. I don't want to publicly go against Joseph.

WILLIAM. Do you agree with these new teachings?

HYRUM. I—I'm not sure if I understand them, but if what I hear is true . . .

WILLIAM. We must act quickly, Hyrum. This new teaching is attracting the highest men in the Church.

HYRUM. Then we may not be able to reverse it.

WILLIAM. Are we agreed?

HYRUM. I want to try to see Joseph about it first.

WILLIAM. What would that change?

HYRUM. If Joseph has a revelation on the subject—I would believe it.

WILLIAM. Hyrum, no, it can't possibly be true. A man is supposed to only have one wife.

HYRUM. But, you see, William, that is it. I have already had more than one wife.

WILLIAM. You were a widower, Hyrum. That is a completely different case.

HYRUM. I have thought a great deal about this since the conflict the other day. If I go to heaven, and if I were to be presented with that good woman over in heaven, my dear Mary, and if then I was presented with my dear Lovina, who is already there, but told that I must choose between them, am I to just abandon the one and cleave to the other?

WILLIAM. Perhaps it is as Jesus said, that we neither marry nor are given in marriage, but are as the angels.

HYRUM. No, the scripture says that in heaven they neither marry, nor are given in marriage—that doesn't mean that we are not supposed to be sealed together on earth. This is the time of our probation. Jesus said, "For this cause shall a man leave his father and mother, and cleave to his wife; And they twain shall be one flesh: so then they are no more twain, but one flesh."

WILLIAM. I think you are wresting the scriptures, my friend . . .

HYRUM. Am I? Any more so than you are? Jesus said they are *no more twain* –one flesh!

WILLIAM. Not you, too, Hyrum. The root of this is wickedness.

HYRUM. How do you know that? Has God told you anything about it?

WILLIAM. Monogamous marriage has been the bedrock of society for . . .

HYRUM. God may or may not talk to you, William. But I know he talks to Joseph.

WILLIAM. Hyrum, it can't possibly be . . .

HYRUM. Don't worry, William. We shall know all about it soon.

Lights dim and blackout on the party as JOSEPH *and* PORTER *enter alone.*

JOSEPH. So what is this about, Port? Is everything all right?

PORTER. Joseph, when they captured me they tried to make me go traitor on you. They wanted me to lead you away so that they could capture you. They told me to name my price.

JOSEPH. And?

PORTER. I told them they were barking up the wrong tree. But I got a piece of disturbin' information. They got an inside source.

JOSEPH. What do you mean?

PORTER. There are traitors. I don't know who, but it sounded like some of them were high up. Perhaps some of the apostles. Or the First Presidency. People who know you—who are close to you.

JOSEPH. It's come to that again, has it?

PORTER. Joseph, there are folks in Nauvoo who want you dead.

Lights fade and PORTER *exits.*

SCENE 6

JOSEPH *steps into a light, addressing the audience.*

JOSEPH. I calculate to edify you with the simple truths of heaven.

ACTOR 2 *as* MARY ELIZABETH ROLLINS LIGHTNER *enters another light, addressing the audience.*

MARY ELIZABETH. It is true I have been in the Church from its beginning. I have been acquainted with all those who were first members of this Church, with all those who saw the plates and handled them, with even those who saw the angel Moroni who came to them.

JOSEPH. There are but very few beings in the world who understand rightly the character of God. If men do not comprehend the character of God, they do not comprehend their own character—they do not understand their own relationship to God.

MARY ELIZABETH. There was a day when Joseph got up to speak to us. As he began to speak very solemnly and very earnestly, all at once his countenance changed and he stood mute. Those who looked at him that day said there was a search light within him. I could not take my eyes off him; he got so white that anyone who saw him would have thought he was transparent. I remember I thought I could almost see the cheek bones through the flesh.

JOSEPH. What kind of being is God? Ask yourselves! I again repeat the question: What kind of being is God? Does any man or woman know?

MARY ELIZABETH. He said, "Do you know who has been in your midst?" Martin Harris said, "It was our Lord and Savior, Jesus Christ." Joseph put his hand down on Martin and said: "God revealed that to you. The Savior has been in your midst this night and I want you to remember it. There is a veil over your eyes for you could not endure to look upon Him. You must be fed with milk, not with strong meat."

JOSEPH. Turn your thoughts in your hearts, and say, Have any of you seen him? Or communed with him? Here is a question that will from this time henceforth occupy your attention while you live.

MARY ELIZABETH. I never took my eye off his countenance. Then he knelt down and prayed. I have never heard anything like it before or since. The spirit rested upon us in every fiber of our bodies, and we received a sermon from the lips of the representative of God.

JOSEPH. The Apostle says that this is eternal life: to know the only wise God—if the declaration of the Apostle be true, he will realize that unless he knows God he has not eternal life for there can be eternal life on no other principle.

MARY ELIZABETH. Every principle that has been given in the Church by the prophet is true. He preached polygamy and not only did he preach it, but he practiced it. I am a living witness to it.

JOSEPH. If I can get you to know Him, I can bring you to Him. And if so, all persecution against me will cease. This will let you know that I am His servant, for I speak as one having authority and not as a scribe.

MARY ELIZABETH. It was given to him before he gave it to the Church. An angel came to him and the last time he came with a drawn sword in his hand and told Joseph if he did not go into that principle he would slay him.

JOSEPH. Open your ears and eyes all ye ends of the earth! If the veil were rent today and if you were to see God today, you would see Him in all the person, image, fashion, and very form of man, like yourselves. For Adam was a man formed in the very fashion and image of God.

MARY ELIZABETH. Emma may deny it, but she took the two Partridge sisters by the hand and gave them to Joseph. I asked him if Emma knew about me, and he said, "Emma thinks the world of you." I was not sealed to him until I had a witness. I had been dreaming for a number of years I was his wife. I thought I was a great sinner. I prayed to God to take it from me, for I felt it was a sin; but when Joseph sent for me he told me of all these things.

JOSEPH. You have got to learn to make yourselves Gods in order to save yourselves and be kings and priests to God. I want you to know that God in the last days, while certain individuals are proclaiming His name, is not trifling with you nor me.

MARY ELIZABETH. "Well," said I, "don't you think it was an angel of the devil who told you these things?" "No," said he, "it was an angel of God. God almighty showed me the difference between an angel of light and Satan's angels. They called me a false and a fallen prophet, but I am more in favor with my God this day than I ever was in all my life before."

JOSEPH. God is glorified in the salvation and exaltation of his creatures. This is good doctrine. It tastes good. You say honey is sweet and so do I. I can also taste the spirit and principles of eternal life, and so can you. You taste them and I know you believe them. I rejoice more and more.

MARY ELIZABETH. Well, I talked with him for a long time, and I finally told him I would never be sealed to him until I had a witness. Said he, "You shall have a witness." Said I, "If God told you that, why does he not tell me?" He asked me if I was going to be a traitor. "I have never told a mortal I had such a talk with a married man." And I a married woman.

JOSEPH. I have intended my remarks to all—to all the rich and poor, bond and free, great and small. I have no enmity against any man. I love all men—I love you all, but I hate your deeds. I am their best friend, and if persons miss their mark it is their own fault. If I reprove a man, and he hate me, he is a fool; for I love all men, especially my brethren and sisters.

MARY ELIZABETH. Well, Brigham Young was with me. He said if I had a witness he wanted to know it. "Why should I tell you?" said I. "Well," said he, "I want to know for myself. Do you know what Joseph said? Since we left the office the angel appeared to him and told him he was well pleased with him and you should have a witness." I made it a subject of prayer and I worried about it because I did not dare to speak to a living being except Brigham Young. I knelt down and if a poor mortal ever prayed, I did.

JOSEPH. You don't know me—you never will. You never knew my heart. No man knows my history. I cannot do it. I shall never undertake it. I don't blame you for not believing my history. If I had not experienced what I have, I could not have believed it myself. I never did harm any man since I have been born into the world. My voice is always for peace. I never think evil, nor think anything to the harm my fellow man. When I am called at the trump and weighed in the balance, you will know me then. I add no more. God bless you. Amen.

Exit JOSEPH.

MARY ELIZABETH. A few nights after that an angel of the Lord came to me. I gazed upon the clothes and figure but the eyes were like lightning. I was frightened almost to death for a moment. The angel leaned over me and the light was very great, although it was night. When my aunt woke up she said she had seen a figure in white robes pass from our bed to my mother's bed and pass out the window. Joseph came up the next Sabbath. He said, "Have you had a witness yet?" I told him, "No." "Well," said he, "the angel expressly told me you should have." Said I, "I have not had a witness, but I have seen something I have never seen before. I saw an angel and I was frightened almost to death. I did not speak." He studied a while and put his elbows on his knees and his face in his hands. He looked up and said, "How could have you been such a coward?" Said I, "I was weak." "Did you think to say, 'Father, help me?'" "No." "Well, if you had just said that, your mouth would have been for that was an angel of the living God. He came to you with more knowledge, intelligence, and light than I have ever dared reveal." I said, "If that was an angel of light, why did he not speak to me?" Then Joseph said, "You covered your face and for this reason the angel was insulted." I went forward and was sealed to him. I know he had other wives and I have known some of them from childhood up. I knew he had three children. They told me. I think two are living today but they are not known as his children as they go by other names. These things I can testify as the living truth.

Blackout on MARY ELIZABETH.

SCENE 7

JOHN TAYLOR enters. He looks distraught. He goes over to a table and sits in it, placing his face into his hands. LEONORA calls from offstage:

LEONORA. (*Offstage:*) John, is that you? (*JOHN doesn't respond.*) John?

33

JOHN. Yes, Leonora, it's me.

LEONORA. (*Offstage:*) How was your meeting with the Prophet?

JOHN. It was—Leonora, please, come in here.

LEONORA enters, drying a tea cup.

LEONORA. Yes, John, I'm . . .

JOHN looks up and LEONORA immediately recognizes that something is amiss.

LEONORA (CONT'D). What's wrong?

JOHN. Sit down, dear.

LEONORA. Did somebody die?

JOHN. Please, Leonora, sit down.

LEONORA sits across the table from JOHN.

LEONORA. Now what's the matter?

They freeze, or lights dim on them, while ACTOR 4 as HEBER KIMBALL enters on another part of the stage, in a similar distressed situation as JOHN, albeit more disheveled. ACTOR 2 as VILATE KIMBALL enters as well:

VILATE. Come, Heber, tell me what is the matter. You have been like this for days.

HEBER. I—I can't. My heart can't stand it.

VILATE. Is it something I have done?

HEBER. No! Never think that. You are my precious, precious friend. You are the wife of my youth—the love of my heart. Vilate, I love you more than I can say.

VILATE. Then why can you not tell me how to help you? You have never kept your thoughts from me before.

HEBER. And that is why this so painful for me. It is so painful *because* I love you.

VILATE. Heber . . .

HEBER. Oh, I can't! I can't!

HEBER exits. JOHN and LEONORA unfreeze/lights raise, and their scene now overlaps with VILATE and HEBER's:

LEONORA. John, that's impossible!

JOHN. It's true—it's true. How I wish it wasn't!

VILATE goes into a praying position.

VILATE. Oh, dear Lord, please, please, hear this prayer of mine. Heber and I, we may not be perfect, we may not be as refined and polished as perhaps we ought to be—but I know that thou dost love us and that thou dost hear and answer our prayers.

LEONORA. It's reprehensible!

VILATE. Dearest God in Heaven, there's something wrong with Heber . . .

JOHN. I know, I know. I don't know how to handle it . . .

VILATE. He's not eating. He's not sleeping. He's been going on like this for days.

LEONORA. You don't know how to handle it? You're not considering this?

JOHN. He's a Prophet, Leonora.

LEONORA. It's horrible! (*She throws the tea cup to the ground. It shatters:*) It's inconceivable!

JOHN. It's not my word—I did not make it!

LEONORA. Could it not be that Brother Joseph is wrong in this? That he is deceived? That he is deceiving?

JOHN. I will not call Joseph a fallen prophet. I will not allow that same temptation overcome me that overcame Parley in Kirtland!

LEONORA. Will you allow yourself to be made a lecherous fiend?

JOHN. Leonora, you know that I have always entertained strict ideas of virtue. This is appalling to me. The idea of going and asking a young lady to be married to me when I already have a wife? It's a thing calculated to stir up feelings from the innermost depths of the human soul!

VILATE. If you could help me understand what is troubling him. If you could open to my mind how to get around this thing which is driving a wedge into his heart—and between us . . .

JOHN. I have never in my life seen a time when I have known a man deceiving a woman and not thought him to be a scoundrel. It is often done in the world, where the man is received into society and the poor woman is looked upon as a pariah and an outcast . . .

VILATE. Thy will be done.

JOHN. I have always looked upon such a thing as infamous, and upon such a man as a villain.

VILATE. I wish to understand. God, I will trust you. I will be loyal. I will submit to thee.

A bright light suddenly flashes on VILATE and she puts her hands up to shade her eyes. The lights blackout on VILATE while the scene continues with JOHN and LEONORA.

JOHN. Hence, with the feelings that I have entertained, nothing but a knowledge of God, and the revelations of God, and the truth of them, could have induced me to embrace such a principle as this. God sent me from England to Canada because I prayed for the truth. And it was there that Parley Pratt preached the Gospel to us, it was there that I saw him heal a blind woman, and it was there that the Spirit of God wrought upon me and told me this was the truth! I will not abandon God, nor His prophet. I will trust, I will be loyal, I will submit to the Lord even if it kills me!

LEONORA looks at him, stunned. Tears come suddenly to her eyes.

LEONORA. Oh, John . . .

JOHN. Leonora . . .

JOHN goes to LEONORA and embraces her. Blackout on JOHN and LEONORA, while lights raise again on HEBER, weeping and praying. Enter VILATE.

VILATE. Darling?

HEBER. Vilate, I'm sorry. I didn't mean for you to see me so . . .

VILATE. Shh. Heber, I understand.

HEBER. No, Vilate, you don't understand. I am . . .

VILATE. Heber, what you have kept from me, the Lord has shown me.

HEBER. What?

VILATE. I prayed and the Lord has shown me. He has shown me in a vision the order of Celestial Marriage. It has been made very clear to me, in its details. I also saw in my vision your—your other wife. Sarah Noon.

HEBER. Is it possible?

VILATE. I know what you have had to do, and the Lord shall transform it into something glorious. It is all right, Heber. It is all right.

HEBER. (*Crying, he embraces VILATE:*) Oh, you lovely, lovely woman! God has told you! He has told you! I have been suffering as if in hell, Vilate. I didn't know—I didn't know how . . .

VILATE. (*Also crying:*) Now we know. We know.

HEBER. I thought I might lose you. How could have I expected you to accept this?

VILATE. I am yours. And when we are sealed, I will be yours forever. I covenant to stand by you and honor the principle. I covenant!

HEBER. I haven't lost you. I haven't lost you . . .

VILATE. Shhh—oh, Heber, this is going to be hard.

Lights dim to blackout.

SCENE 8

WILLARD enters. HYRUM enters running behind him.

HYRUM. Brother Richards. Brother Richards!

WILLARD. Brother Hyrum, good afternoon.

HYRUM. I want to talk to you.

WILLARD. All right. Let's talk then.

HYRUM. I have a question to ask you . . .

WILLARD. Yes?

HYRUM. I do know that you and the Twelve know something that I do not know. I know that there is something or other which I do not understand that is revealed to the Twelve. Is this so?

WILLARD. I do not know anything about what you know, but I know what I know.

HYRUM. I've mistrusted for a long time that Joseph had received a revelation that a man should have more than one wife—and he has hinted as much to me, but I would not bear it. I am convinced that there is something that has not been told me.

WILLARD. Brother Hyrum, I will tell you about this thing which you do not know if you will swear that you will never say another word against Joseph, and his doings, and the doctrines he is preaching to the people.

HYRUM. With all my heart. I want to know the truth.

Lights cross fade immediately to JOSEPH and WILLIAM entering.

WILLIAM. Please, Joseph, there must be some mistake.

JOSEPH. There is no mistake.

WILLIAM. Please . . .

JOSEPH. William, there is no mistake in this. Whatever mistakes we perpetuate in its practice, the principle was taught to me from God.

WILLIAM. How can you force us to do this? Your enemies will see this as further signs of religious corruption.

JOSEPH. Have I ever exercised any compulsion over any man? Have I not given him the liberty of disbelieving any doctrine I have preached, if he saw fit? That which is wrong under one circumstance, may be, and often is, right under another. God said, 'Thou shalt not kill'; at another time He said, 'Thou shalt utterly destroy.' This is the principle on which the government of heaven is conducted—by revelation adapted to the circumstances in which the children of the kingdom are placed. Whatever God requires is right, no matter what it is, although we may not see the reason of it until long after the events transpire.

WILLIAM. How can it be?

JOSEPH. The Lord's thoughts are not our thoughts, his ways are not our ways. Whatever God requires is right, no matter what it is, although we may not see the reason until long after.

WILLIAM. This will certainly not be popular with the people. Does God want a nation of apostates?

JOSEPH. I'm not concerned about what will be popular with the people. I am concerned about the commandments of God.

WILLIAM. Joseph, have we not been faithful? Would God require such a horrible thing? Have we not done enough, sacrificed enough? Have we not become a righteous people?

JOSEPH. Men may preach and practice everything except those things which God commands us to do, and we will be damned at last. We may tithe and mint and rue, and still not obey the commandments of God. It matters not whether the principle is popular or unpopular, I will always maintain a true principle, even if I stand alone in it.

WILLIAM. How do you know?

JOSEPH. If the angel had conversed with you, William, then you might understand.

WILLIAM. If you will not do just this one thing, then this will become the greatest Christian Church.

JOSEPH. That may be true, but God has commanded me.

WILLIAM. Joseph, if you do this, you'll be damned.

JOSEPH. If I don't do this, I'll be damned.

WILLIAM. I can't follow you on this.

JOSEPH. Then you have no interest in the Kingdom of God.

JOSEPH exits, leaving WILLIAM distraught. WILLIAM exits.

SCENE 9

The Smith household. WILLARD is at a desk writing. EMMA is upstairs in her room, reading. Enter DAN JONES.

WILLARD. Brother Jones?

DAN. Willard. Eliza said that I could find Joseph here.

WILLARD. He stepped out for a moment. He'll be back soon. Have a seat, Dan.

DAN. What's that you're doing, Brother Richards?

WILLARD. Work.

DAN. What kind of work?

WILLARD. Important work.

DAN. What kind of important work?

WILLARD. Work that requires focus.

DAN. You're a fountain of information.

WILLARD. You won't leave me alone until your curiosity is satisfied, will you?

DAN. Nope.

WILLARD. I am looking over Joseph's history.

DAN. (*Rummaging through the papers:*) You have nice handwriting.

WILLARD. (*Grabbing the papers back:*) I need to have legibility. Joseph's history is very important. He dictates, I write.

DAN. I hear that you're here quite a lot—some say you see more of Joseph than even his own family.

WILLARD. I don't know about that. What I do know is that Joseph believes writing the history of this people is pivotal.

DAN. Will you write my history someday?

WILLARD. Well, that depends if you ever do anything worth writing about, Dan.

DAN. I suppose that may not be likely, eh?

WILLARD. I'd say not very likely at all.

DAN. You're a very big man, Brother Richards.

WILLARD. Pardon me?

DAN. I like Sister Richards. You have a very pretty wife.

WILLARD. I agree with you very much.

DAN. How did such a big man get such a pretty wife?

WILLARD. I got such a pretty wife because I went on a mission. We met in England. The Lord blesses those who go on missions. Remember that.

DAN. You met in England? How did you know she was for you?

WILLARD. Well, I knew before I even met her, I suppose.

DAN. How's that?

WILLARD. Heber Kimball was on a mission with me and he was in one part of England and I was in another at the time. Then I get this letter from him which says, "Willard, I baptized your wife today."

DAN. Yeah, I've heard of Heber's funny knack. Prophesying all over the place! He's more comfortable prophesying than I am singing! So how did you dupe her into agreeing? Buy her pearls and presents, promises that you couldn't keep—moderately sized bribes?

Enter WILLIAM *and* JANE, *unnoticed.*

WILLARD. Why did you say you needed to see Joseph?

DAN. Can't seem to remember, I'm having too much fun with you.

WILLARD. This really is important work.

DAN. How did you ask her? To marry you, I mean.

WILLARD. Her first name is Jennetta and her last name was Richards— just like mine, you see.

DAN. Your first name is Jennetta?

WILLARD. Do you want to hear this story or not?

DAN. I'll behave.

WILLARD. When we met, we were both mutually attracted. Soon enough I said, "Richards is a good name. I never wanted to change it. Do you, Jennetta?" "No, I do not," she replied. And she never did.

WILLIAM. So are you still in love with Jennetta then, Willard?

WILLARD. My love for Jennetta has only increased, William.

WILLIAM. Even with . . . (*Glancing at* DAN:) . . . recent developments?

JANE. William, please.

WILLARD. Especially with recent developments. She has proved as true as gold. I admire her all the more for being able to withstand its weight.

DAN. You know, perhaps I'd better go. I'll drop by when there is less of a crowd.

WILLARD. I'll tell Joseph you dropped by, Dan.

DAN. Then I'll see you folks later.

Exit DAN.

WILLIAM. Now it's a wonder how people are still a little squeamish about the subject!

JANE. William, you promised.

WILLARD. Why are you here, William?

Enter JOSEPH.

JOSEPH. Good afternoon, William. Good afternoon, Jane.

JANE. Good afternoon, Brother Joseph.

JOSEPH. Can you leave us alone for a moment, Willard?

WILLARD. Of course. If you need anything . . .

JOSEPH. I'll let you know.

Exit WILLARD.

JOSEPH (CONT'D). Have a seat. What can I do for you?

WILLIAM. Well, Jane and I have been discussing a great many things . . .

JANE. And we wish to be sealed together, Brother Joseph.

WILLIAM. I know we've had our differences, Joseph, but this is important to us. The chance for us to be together—always. That is the part of the doctrine I do like.

JOSEPH. (*Pause, considering.*) I wish I could help you.

WILLIAM. What do you mean?

JOSEPH. I cannot seal you together.

JANE. Brother Joseph . . .

WILLIAM. Why? Why can't you seal us together? Aren't I coming to you? Aren't I proving that I believe that you have the sealing power?

JOSEPH. I'm sorry. You may not believe me, but I really am sorry that it must be like this.

WILLIAM. I'm coming to you, Joseph. I want God's blessings. Give me your reasons.

JOSEPH. Perhaps it would be best if you and I discussed this alone, William.

WILLIAM. No, Jane and I will hear it together.

JOSEPH. You don't know what you're saying.

WILLIAM. We will hear it together!

JOSEPH. (*Pause.*) You are an adulterer, William.

> WILLIAM *appears stunned. He then collects himself and turns to leave.*

WILLIAM. Truly? Is that how you want to play this?

JANE. (*Shocked:*)William?

WILLIAM. Let's go, Jane.

JOSEPH. William, with time this can be worked through, and then we can . . .

WILLIAM. You crafty hypocrite, I will have none of it!

JOSEPH. Be careful, William.

JANE. Is it true?

WILLIAM. Will you take this man's word over mine?

JANE. Is it true?

WILLIAM. What if it were? Would that man be able to sit in judgment? (*To JOSEPH:*) I saw how you treated John Bennett, Robert Foster, the Higbees—you tell a man he can have another wife, but you condemn a different man for mistakes with those same human passions!

JOSEPH. I am married to my wives. I am responsible for them. I am sealed to them. I have been commanded by God.

WILLIAM. All under the guise of religion! A fallen prophet!

> EMMA *stands atop the stairs, unnoticed.*

JOSEPH. Be careful, William!

WILLIAM. What, you don't like to be crossed? Contradicted?

JOSEPH. When you condemn me, you condemn Abraham. You condemn Jacob. You condemn Moses. You condemn the holy prophets.

WILLIAM. That was another time! Another place!

JOSEPH. It is this time! This place! The Lord has revealed it! And He has not only revealed it to me. He has revealed it to the Twelve. To their wives. To Hyrum.

WILLIAM. Is Hyrum in this now?

JOSEPH. Yes.

WILLIAM. Your corrupting influence is astonishing. Has the Lord "revealed" it to Emma too then?

JOSEPH. Emma is—coming around. She has given me wives at times, but then the fear comes back. She still struggles, but that's natural. But we must make our flesh and our limited reason bend to God. We must prove to be worthy friends to Him.

WILLIAM. Is that how you're putting it? It makes it sound so nice and pure and correct. While I am the wicked one! Me!

JOSEPH. Pray about it. The Lord will reveal it to you.

WILLIAM. Only the devil would reveal such a thing.

JOSEPH. Just pray about it. Pour out your soul. Wrestle with God until you have an answer.

JANE. William, please, let's listen to what he has to say before we make rash judgments.

WILLIAM. Don't be duped into this, Jane.

JANE. No, hear me out. You've gotten upon your high moral horse about plural marriage, and yet you've hid this from me? Who is the hypocrite here, William?

WILLIAM. Jane, you're not understanding what's happening here.

JOSEPH. We can all work this out. With a little bit of patience and forgiveness . . .

WILLIAM. No, Joseph, I don't want you touching my personal affairs. You think that everyone revolves around you, that everything must go through you. Well, this is my territory now, and I don't want you trespassing on it.

JOSEPH. All right, if that's how you want it.

JANE. William . . .

WILLIAM. We are leaving!

Exit WILLIAM *and then, reluctantly,* JANE. EMMA *reveals herself.*

EMMA. Must it really be this way, Joseph?

JOSEPH. You know my answer to that.

EMMA. "When God commands, do it." I know.

JOSEPH. There is purpose in this.

EMMA. What if God bends us so much that we break?

JOSEPH. You won't break.

EMMA. Won't I?

JOSEPH. Emma, you're getting there. You've met the fury of men and devils. You've proven your worth. Don't let this stop you.

EMMA. (*Beat.*) Good night, Joseph.

EMMA exits. Exit JOSEPH.

SCENE 10

Enter ROBERT FOSTER *and* ACTOR 3 *as* FRANCIS HIGBEE.

FRANCIS. I've never been so embarrassed in my whole life! Joseph Smith is a monster to abuse us such! Bringing out all our . . . our . . .

ROBERT. Adulteries? Let's name them for what they are.

FRANCIS. While he sits there and pretends to all of Nauvoo that he's only bedded one woman in his life! When Bennett brought me into his circle—I thought there was Church approval!

ROBERT. From my discussions with him, John Bennett taught something different. Bennett, with the whore houses he was building on the edge of Nauvoo and the more—"free" relationships his spiritual wifery constituted, it wasn't the plural marriage that Joseph's circle has been practicing.

FRANCIS. Well, it's just lovely that you can be so philosophical about it!

ROBERT. Bennett was doing his own thing, that much is obvious. Maybe building on the rumors he was hearing as part of the First Presidency. But his version is more like the Cochranites . . .

FRANCIS. Now you've completely lost me.

ROBERT. I've been comparing the two—trying to connect where one ends and the other begins—well, anyway, what does it matter now? Joseph's not going public with his version anytime soon. The Church has cut us off, "Brother" Higbee.

FRANCIS. Keep to Francis now. It's a farce. Nobody's my brother in this place, Doctor Foster.

ROBERT. Leave off the Doctor. Just Robert to you now. We have common scars.

FRANCIS. Yes, but I'm still so—agh, Joseph Smith is a monster!

ROBERT. Not a monster. An angel.

FRANCIS. An angel?

ROBERT. An angel. An angel of light. He blinds the eyes of this people with his high positions and alleged visions. He sanctifies himself, scrubs his skin until it absolutely glows and people think they see beams of light exuding from his face, his eyes, his hair, and his very toes. An angel—no, like a god he has set himself up as. But angels of light can be counterfeits, just as gods can be false.

FRANCIS. I will shoot him and all that pertains to him; and before ten suns shall go over our heads, the Temple, the Nauvoo House and the Mansion House shall all be destroyed. All I want is to see this city sunk down to the lowest hell, and I shall!

ROBERT. Do you mean that?

FRANCIS. Of course I do. (*Beat.*) Would you?

ROBERT. (*Beat.*) I'm not proud of what I've done. That young woman I got pregnant—she's ruined because of me.

FRANCIS. It's not about what *we've* done.

ROBERT. Isn't it?

FRANCIS. He's pulling the wool over everyone's eyes, Robert! Condemning men like us while he pretends that he and his inner circle are the exceptions!

ROBERT. What can we do about it?

FRANCIS. We can't give up. We fight back. He wants to expose us to the world? Well, let's see how he feels about it when it's his turn!

Enter ACTOR 1 as JOSEPH JACKSON, with PORTER following him.

PORTER. Joseph Jackson!

JACKSON. I will not submit! I will not submit to a corrupt law!

PORTER. Assault is a law that is recognized anywhere. Come with me.

JACKSON. Make me.

PORTER. (*Motioning to the FRANCIS and ROBERT.*) Gentlemen, Marshal Greene has deputized me so that I can help take this man into custody. I'd appreciate your help in bringing him in. (*FRANCIS and ROBERT don't move.*) Ain't you goin' to help me?

ROBERT. You obviously don't know us very well, Mr. Rockwell.

PORTER. Ain't you gonna be loyal to Nauvoo's laws? To the mayor?

FRANCIS. The mayor! I would consider myself favored of God for the privilege of shooting and ridding the world of such a tyrant.

ROCKWELL. Why, you stinkin' demon from a mudpit . . .

Enter JOSEPH.

FRANCIS. And here's the Emperor himself!

PORTER. Shut it, you canal rat!

ROBERT. Oh, save the indignation. You don't impress us with your talk of laws and government. You profane the words by associating them with Nauvoo and Joseph Smith.

JOSEPH. Robert, Francis, haven't I strived to settle this with both of you?

ROBERT. We won't be caught up in your web. You've got the whole law twisted up in your favor. Just look at your use of habeus corpus! They can't arrest you, they can't bring you out of this city! You just cite that blasted Nauvoo Charter and you are tried in Nauvoo. As if any court in Nauvoo would convict you!

JOSEPH. I do everything within the law, Doctor Foster. I will no longer submit myself to those whose only purpose is to destroy me.

ROBERT. What about justice?

JOSEPH. Justice? You call Missouri mobs justice? That's where they've been trying to put me on trial, you know. Or perhaps you think I would get a fair trial in Carthage or Warsaw?

FRANCIS. It's hasn't been about God or angels or golden plates—it's been about power all along.

JOSEPH. It's been about God. But, yes, it's also been about power. The power to protect my people.

FRANCIS. And your political career? Such a divine disinterestedness there as well? Not only God's mouthpiece, but God's king! A regular David incarnate! I don't buy it.

JOSEPH. Persecution has rolled upon our heads like peals of thunder; and no portion of the government as yet has stepped forward for our relief. You know that, Francis—it was your father who went with me when we petitioned Washington about the murders, and the rapes, and the theft, and the beatings our people received in Missouri!

ROBERT. And we didn't contribute to that tenseness, Joseph? Your Danites weren't meeting insult with injury?

JOSEPH. You know nothing of what we all endured there, Robert. But, Francis, your father did. Elias Higbee was a true friend to me until the day he died. Why are you so set against me?

FRANCIS. Don't bring my father into this. Our troubles were no excuse for the wrangling of power that we have seen under your hand.

JOSEPH. I feel it my right to obtain what power and influence I can— lawfully—for the protection of injured innocence. We have not broken or fought the law, we have joined with it! We have sought its aid and protection.

ROBERT. Then the law shall be betray you.

JOSEPH. It hasn't been the only one. (*Resigns arguing with them.*) What is the trouble here, Port?

PORTER. Marshal Green deputized me to take in Jackson because he attacked Orson Spencer, after Orson tried to defend your reputation. These men won't assist me in his arrest.

JOSEPH. Then arrest them as well for refusing to assist you in the charge of your duty.

ROBERT. Wait, that's not fair!

PORTER. Do as he says.

> JOSEPH *lays his hands on* JACKSON. JACKSON *takes out a gun, pointing it at* JOSEPH.

JACKSON. Back off, Mayor, or I'll shoot.

JOSEPH. You would not scare an old, setting hen.

JACKSON. I swear, I'll do it!

> JOSEPH *charges* JACKSON *and wrenches the gun away from his hand and tosses it away.* FRANCIS *and* ROBERT *move to*

assist, but PORTER *takes out his own gun and points it at the attackers, stopping them in their tracks.* JOSEPH *and* JACKSON *continue to struggle until* JOSEPH *is able to throw him into* FRANCIS *and* ROBERT, *where* PORTER *has his gun leveled at them.*

ROCKWELL. Are you all right, Joseph?

JOSEPH. I'm fine, Port. I've wrestled stronger twelve years olds.

FRANCIS. My father was a fool to follow you.

JOSEPH. You and Robert and Joseph Jackson and your brother and all the other apostates combined are not half the man your father was.

PORTER. What should we do with them, Joseph?

JOSEPH. Let them go for now.

PORTER. What? Are you sure?

ROBERT. You won't trick us with false charity.

JOSEPH. We'll let the courts settle it. (*Picking up* JACKSON's *gun and giving it to* PORTER.) But confiscate this. Let me walk off a ways before you let them loose.

Exit JOSEPH.

PORTER. I coulda blown your brains out for that, you disloyal mutts. (*Checking* JOSEPH's *distance.*) Y'all can go then. (ROBERT *and* JACKSON *exit, but* FRANCIS *stays.*) You waiting for a written invitation?

FRANCIS. Did you know my father, Mr. Rockwell?

PORTER. (*Putting away his gun.*) Your father was a good man. Too bad his son is such a cotton brained rascal.

FRANCIS. I didn't mean what I said about my father. I know that he was a good man.

PORTER. Are you finally making some sense?

FRANCIS. I know that I haven't always done right by people . . .

PORTER. And the Prophet?

FRANCIS. (*Hardening:*) I'll go to my death against him.

PORTER. But you just said . . .

FRANCIS. My course may be wrong; but if I stop I shall get hell, and if I go on I shall get hell. I will do what I intend to do at the risk of my very own life, and I will destroy Joseph Smith, if possible. Am I not a brave man to tell you so?

PORTER. You're a coward.

> *FRANCIS lunges toward PORTER and the two grapple. POR-TER knocks FRANCIS down and a piece of paper falls out of the hat in which FRANCIS had concealed it. PORTER picks it up.*

FRANCIS. Give that back.

PORTER. What is it?

FRANCIS. Give it back. It is mine and you have no right to it.

PORTER. You seem to think it's mighty important. Are you ashamed of it?

FRANCIS. Give it back!

PORTER. There ain't no way in hell or high heaven that I'm givin' this back. We've known for some time there is a conspiracy in Nauvoo against Joseph. By how you're actin', I reckon this here paper will shed some light on the subject of who may be involved in that conspiracy. Good day, Francis.

> *Exit PORTER.*

FRANCIS. Come back here! You don't understand! Give it back!

> *Blackout.*

SCENE 11

> *JOSEPH enters and sits, reading. Enter EMMA.*

EMMA. Willard is here for you, Joseph. I'll be out in the garden.

JOSEPH. Do you want some help after I talk to Willard?

EMMA. Are you joking? Whenever you help me in the garden, it's not long until we have half of Nauvoo on our doorstep, all wanting time with you, tearing up my plants with their crowded, clumsy feet.

JOSEPH. Emma, I'm sorry. I . . .

EMMA. It's not your fault, Joseph. I just wish that we were normal, average people for once. That we could live a peaceful life.

JOSEPH. The time will come, Emma.

EMMA. I'm not sure that I can wait for the next life.

JOSEPH. It may come sooner than that, Emma. There may come a time when you are to go on without me.

EMMA. Don't talk like that. I can't bear that kind of humor.

JOSEPH. You and our children will be in the hands of God, and God will take care of you. *(JOSEPH goes over to EMMA and kisses her. She embraces him fervently.)* You are an elect lady.

EMMA. I wish I could be a better wife to you.

JOSEPH. I never asked for a better wife. Never think that God gave me others because there was a lack in you.

EMMA. Let's not talk about that.

JOSEPH. All right. Then just know that I adore you. Oh, what a commingling of thought fills my mind when I hold you. Again you are here, even in the seventh trouble. Undaunted, firm and unwavering. Unchangeable, affectionate Emma!

EMMA. I love you.

JOSEPH. I love you, too. Now you better go and get Willard. He must think that we have forgotten him.

EMMA. (*With a laugh.*) I had.

JOSEPH. Oh, what is that? Is that a laugh?

EMMA. I guess it is.

JOSEPH. I missed your laugh.

EMMA. I missed it too.

EMMA kisses JOSEPH softly.

JOSEPH. Now, if any of the apostles come by, if you can just let them right in, I would appreciate it. I'm expecting them to drop in before they leave on their missions to the East.

EMMA exits. Enter WILLARD.

WILLARD. Good morning, Joseph.

JOSEPH goes over to WILLARD, takes him by the shoulders and stares him in the eyes, searching. WILLARD is caught off guard, but locks eyes with JOSEPH and says nothing.

JOSEPH. I'm glad to see you, Willard.

WILLARD. Joseph?

JOSEPH. I'm sorry. I hardly know who are my friends and who are my enemies anymore.

WILLARD. Were you searching my soul?

JOSEPH. You could look me in the eyes, Willard.

WILLARD. I hope that I have pleased you, Joseph. That I have served you well.

JOSEPH. Willard, you are one of the best friends that I've ever had. Remember that. I have been able to keep you close to me and trust you with my history—what of it that I can give, at least.

WILLARD. I will be true to you, Joseph.

JOSEPH. (*Pausing, once again searching him.*) The day will come, Willard, when a literal hailstorm of bullets shall pass you, and you shall see friends fall on your right hand and on your left, and you shall not even receive a hole in your robe. (*Beat.*) Do you believe it?

WILLARD. Is that a prophecy?

JOSEPH. Do you believe it?

WILLARD. I'm afraid I may not.

JOSEPH. When it comes to pass, you shall believe.

Enter JOHN.

JOHN. Joseph, I've heard about the other apostles stumping for your bid to the presidency. Why haven't you called me?

WILLARD. John is an excellent orator, Joseph . . .

JOSEPH. I thought about sending you off with the rest of them, John, but I need you to run the *Times and Seasons* and *The Nauvoo Neighbor.* Your service to those papers is invaluable. With all the trouble that *Warsaw Signal* is brewing up, I need you here behind that press. I would have sent Willard off as well, but he and I need to finish my history.

JOHN. Finish?

JOSEPH. Nothing gets past you, John.

JOHN. Joseph, do you feel your life is in danger?

JOSEPH. (*Picking up a pamphlet.*) John, I've had William Phelps help me with this pamphlet, but I would like your opinion on it . . .

JOHN. Joseph, if you feel that your enemies . . .

JOSEPH. "If I were the President of the United States, I would walk in the tracks of the illustrious patriots who carried the ark of the Government upon their shoulders with an eye single to the glory of the people . . ."

JOHN. Joseph, are you listening to me?

JOSEPH. John, this is important: ". . . when the people petition to abolish slavery in the slave states, I would use all honorable means to have their prayers granted, and give liberty to the captive by paying the Southern gentlemen a reasonable equivalent—that we may break off the shackles of the poor black man and that the whole nation might be free indeed!"

JOHN. Why are you sending out the apostles, if you need to be protected here . . .

JOSEPH. "And when the people petitioned to possess the Territory of Oregon, or any other contiguous Territory, I would lend the influence of Chief Magistrate, that they might extend the mighty efforts and enterprise of a free people from the east to the west sea—and, when we have the red man's consent, we will make the wilderness blossom as a rose."

JOHN. Joseph! You won't be any good to them, if you're dead. What is going on?

JOSEPH. What is going on? This nation is in turmoil, and if they are not corrected, the time will come that war will be poured upon all nations, beginning at this place. Beginning at a rebellion in South Carolina, which will eventually terminate in the death of many souls.

WILLARD. Are you prophesying, Joseph?

JOHN. I don't care about any prophecy right now, except this: prophesy to us that you will live. For, if not, I suspect that you are sending as many of the Twelve away as you can—so that you can protect us.

JOSEPH. If your faith can alter the will of God, John, then pray away. But also pray for our Brethren in the Eastern States who will be stumping for my election.

JOHN. Tell me that you'll live a long life.

JOSEPH. If I live a long life, we would all see the Savior's coming together.

JOHN. That's not answering the question.

JOSEPH. Do you believe I'm a prophet of God?

JOHN. Of course I do!

JOSEPH. Then understand this: God has told me to send our Brethren to the Eastern States and to keep you and Willard with me. Will you obey this revelation? Will you stay with me, John?

JOHN. Until the very end. Unto death.

JOSEPH. I knew you would. What can man do if God is our friend? I shall not be sacrificed until my time comes; then I shall be offered freely.

WILLARD. We still need you, Joseph. Surely the Lord understands that.

JOSEPH. Something is going to happen. I don't know what it is, but the Lord has bid me and hastened me to give you and the rest of the 12 the keys and powers which rest upon me. And now you have got all the keys, and the hosts of Satan will not be able to tear down the kingdom, as fast as you will be able to build it up. On your shoulders will be the responsibility of leading this people right, for the Lord is going to let me rest a while. *(Beat.)* That's enough of such somber thoughts for one day!

WILLARD. You shall live a long life, Joseph. My faith will make it so.

JOSEPH. I cannot lie down until my work is finished. That I prophesy freely. I defy all the world, and I prophesy they will never overthrow me until I am ready. Now, Willard, get out that quill, ink and paper, and we shall proceed!

Enter ELIZA.

ELIZA. Joseph?

JOSEPH. Yes, Eliza?

ELIZA. May I talk to you?

JOSEPH. Yes, go ahead.

ELIZA. Alone?

JOSEPH. *(Nods.)* Willard, I guess we'll have to postpone it just a little bit longer. Can I call you back in a moment?

WILLARD. Of course.

Exit WILLARD and JOHN.

JOSEPH. Are the children finished with their lessons?

ELIZA. Yes.

JOSEPH. Did they behave today? If one of them needs some discipline
. . .

ELIZA. There's nothing wrong with the children.

JOSEPH. What is it then?

ELIZA. It's Emma. She has been very volatile about—about the principle lately. She still struggles with it, Joseph.

JOSEPH. She talks to you about it?

ELIZA. No. But I understand the subtext. She still doesn't know that I'm your wife, correct?

JOSEPH. She will when she's ready. She had enough struggles giving me the Partridge and Lawrence sisters—and she chose them. She's gone back to her old attitude.

ELIZA. You must tell her.

JOSEPH. She won't let me. She won't hear anything about it.

ELIZA. Deceit is not the way to go about this. There have been too many lies. Too many denials.

JOSEPH. Didn't Abraham deny that Sarah was his wife? To protect them?

ELIZA. And look at the mess it got them into!

JOSEPH. Do you think I like this, that this doesn't weigh on me? I argued with that angel, I quoted scripture at him! But I was commanded to do this!

ELIZA. Yes, an angel came to you with this principle. But are you telling me he also told you to lie about it?

JOSEPH. (*Beat.*) Honestly, I think they have left me to figure a lot if it out on my own. Maybe there's some lesson in it, but you don't know what a lonely and difficult position that puts me in.

> EMMA *is about to enter, but hearing* ELIZA*'s voice, stops at the door frame and remains unnoticed.*

ELIZA. I believe you received this principle, Joseph. But, as you've reminded us time and time again, we can't expect perfection from you. You are only a prophet when you are prophesying. You err like other men. You've told us this . . .

JOSEPH. I know I have made mistakes in this, but—but she threatened to divorce me, Eliza. The angel Moroni directed me to Emma, do you understand? He said I would need her to do the work and I—I love her. I don't want to lose her. But I can't disobey this commandment.

ELIZA. Perhaps Hyrum can convince her. He always has a powerful effect on her. His gentleness brings her to tears.

JOSEPH. Hyrum already tried. He brought her the written copy of the revelation. She tore it up.

ELIZA. I know you feel as if you have been put into an impossible situation, but there must be a way through this honestly.

JOSEPH. I wish I could see it.

ELIZA. I wrote a poem to comfort you. Can I share it?

JOSEPH. Yes, I would like that.

ELIZA. (*Taking the poem from her apron and reading it:*)
"I feel thy woes—my bosom shares thy spirit's agony:
How can I love a heart that dares suspect thy purity?
I'll smile on all that smile on thee as angels do above,
All who in pure sincerity will love thee, I will love.
Believe me, thou hast noble friends who feel and share thy grief;
And many a fervent pray'r ascends to heav'n, for thy relief."

EMMA. That is quite enough of that!

ELIZA. Sister Smith!

EMMA. Apparently I'm not the only Sister Smith in this place!

EMMA charges up the stairs to confront ELIZA. The lights blackout, except for lights on the ACTORS, who are gossiping with each other.

ACTOR 1. I hear that Emma attacked Eliza with a broomstick.

ACTOR 3. I heard that Emma pulled Eliza down the stairs by the hair.

ACTOR 1. No, she was pushed down the stairs.

ACTOR 2. Sister Eliza was really hurt.

ACTOR 4. No, she walked out that night—but in the rain.

ACTOR 3. Eliza was pregnant.

ACTOR 2. With Joseph's son.

ACTOR 3. The injury inadvertently killed the unborn child.

ACTOR 4. There was no child. You're all wrong.

ACTOR 3. And you have the truth about it?

> EMMA *and* ELIZA *enter from opposite sides, and the* ACTORS *become hushed.* EMMA *and* ELIZA *connect, pause, and stare intensely at each other. Blackout.*

END ACT ONE

Act Two

SCENE 1

JANE LAW is sitting alone on one half of the stage. EMMA is sitting alone on the other half. Enter WILLIAM on EMMA's half.

EMMA. Well, you wanted to meet with me, William?

WILLIAM. Thank you for seeing me. I know things have been tense.

EMMA. My whole life has been "tense."

WILLIAM. I wanted you to know that you have friends.

EMMA. Friends? Oh, I think not. I haven't had too many trustworthy friends lately.

WILLIAM. Even your husband?

EMMA. What is it that you really want?

WILLIAM. I know about Celestial Marriage, Sister Smith.

EMMA. William . . .

WILLIAM. And there are those of us who oppose it.

Enter JOSEPH on the other half of the stage. As the scenes play simultaneously, the actors in the separate scenes are unaware of each other.

JANE. You came!

JOSEPH. Good evening, Sister Jane. Where is your husband?

JANE. I'm the one who called you here.

EMMA. I have been a very vexing woman to my husband, William. I wish to do the Lord's will and to humble myself.

WILLIAM. Humble yourself to what? To that man's self exaltation?

EMMA. That man, Brother Law, is my husband. And he once considered you his friend and counselor.

JANE. It is about my husband, Brother Joseph. It is about William.

WILLIAM. Is it the mark of a true friend to follow a man to his death? No, I'm not the sort of friend to charge into the face of folly and wickedness.

JANE. I know that he is a wicked man.

EMMA. And this is the kind of "friendship" you want to extend to me now?

JANE. I understand why you couldn't seal us together.

WILLIAM. My loyalties lie with my own thoughts, my own beliefs.

EMMA. What about God's thoughts, God's beliefs?

WILLIAM. He has you convinced that all this polygamous nonsense is from God, does he?

EMMA. And you think it isn't.

WILLIAM. It is more than possible.

EMMA. No. I don't think it is. Whatever you may believe, William, this religion is not a hoax. Do you know the witnesses I have had? The gold plates from which the Book of Mormon was translated from—I felt them.

JANE. I want you to know that I still believe you are our prophet. I understand the power that exists within you.

EMMA. They were under a cloth in our house all those years ago. Even though Joseph left them out covered, out in the open I dared not look under the cloth to see them. But I wanted some sort of witness, so I touched them under the cloth, I felt the pliable gold sheets and heard the metallic rustle. There were indeed metal plates under that cloth. Gold plates given to him by an angel. I believe the Church to have been established by divine direction.

WILLIAM. And I believe the same. When I joined this Church, it was because I knew the Book of Mormon to be true—I knew that the revelations of God flowed through Joseph. But David was called by God, was he not? And Solomon? But they went after false gods and false lusts.

JANE. My husband thinks you are a fallen prophet. But I do not. I believe you to be an exalted prophet—an exalted man!

WILLIAM. Plural marriage will be the death of all the good work that has been done through Joseph, unless we stop him.

EMMA. What do you mean by "stop him"?

WILLIAM. Do you think this Church can progress through time, if we go through with this? We must rise and take Joseph's place, to lift up his stumbling feet. If we can't, we must carry on God's work without him. Establish our own Church.

JOSEPH. I appreciate your loyalties, Sister Law.

EMMA. Brother Law, do you truly expect me to betray my husband?

JANE. I can give you so much more than my loyalties, Joseph.

JOSEPH. What do you mean?

WILLIAM. What is the condition between you and your husband?

EMMA. It is good.

WILLIAM. That's not what I hear. Are you in the habit of quarreling?

EMMA. No. There is no necessity in quarreling. He usually gives heed to what I have to say. It is quite a grievous thing to many that I have such an influence with him.

WILLIAM. Many wonder where your true loyalties lie.

EMMA. I have never forsaken the faith I at first accepted.

JANE. Brother Joseph, I understand my situation. I understand that I am married to a man who will never be able to be sealed to me and who will never be able to accompany me to the Celestial Kingdom.

JOSEPH. Sister Law, I think that you ought to try to use your persuasions on him. I hope and pray that William will be able to come back to us. Perhaps you can have such an influence on him.

JANE. I have tried to urge him back into loyalty to you, but I cannot!

WILLIAM. Emma, you don't need to put on such a front of strength. It is all right that you struggle against such a principle as plural marriage. Does not the Book of Mormon say it is an abomination in the sight of God?

EMMA. There is more to that scripture. In that very same chapter it says that if the Lord desires to raise up a righteous seed . . .

WILLIAM. Look into the scars of your own heart. Look at your own personal feelings and treasured beliefs.

EMMA. Aren't I supposed to look up, not in? Look up to God?

WILLIAM. The kingdom of God is within you. God is in our hearts!

JANE. I no longer want to be with one who will tear me down. (*Embracing JOSEPH:*) If you can't seal me to my husband, seal me to you!

JOSEPH. Sister Law!

JANE. I know you have taken other wives—even the wives of men who have fallen away.

JOSEPH. (*Separating himself from JANE:*) God must direct it.

EMMA. I will be honest, William. You have touched upon the most tender and painful chords of my heart. I want to believe that what you say is true, that I don't have to submit to this . . .

WILLIAM. Then don't submit! Fight for your husband's virtue!

EMMA. What if my heart has been tainted? What if my rebellion is all just jealousy and pride?

WILLIAM. Do not call a virtuous independence tainted, nor fidelity jealousy.

JANE. Don't leave me in my pitiable station, please. I and my husband are not one. His independence is estranging himself from God.

JOSEPH. I understand your feelings, but . . .

JANE. Will you leave me tethered to a fallen angel? For that is who I am married to, a son of the morning fallen from grace! A regular

Lucifer focused on his own plans, his own ideas, his own ambitions. He leaves no room for that which is beyond himself. Will you leave me with a man who rebels against God?

EMMA. I will consider your ideas—but I will not betray my husband.

WILLIAM. Even after he has betrayed you? Polygamy!

EMMA. I hate it! I will destroy it, if I can. But I will remain with my husband. There have been times when I wanted to separate, to leave him, leave the Church, but a fierce loyalty dominated my fear and my flight. I will remain with this Church as long as he is a part of it, for I love him and I love the God he has introduced me to.

WILLIAM. But, Sister Smith . . .

EMMA. I have told you that I will consider your ideas! That is enough. Now leave.

> WILLIAM *nods and exits.* EMMA *sits, steeling her nerves against the emotions that are storming within her.*

JANE. Please, Joseph, don't make me follow him.

JOSEPH. You don't have to follow him. There's another choice. Follow God.

JANE. I need someone to uphold me. I want you to uphold me.

JOSEPH. God can uphold you.

JANE. Please, don't leave me to myself . . .

JOSEPH. I leave you to God. Prove true to Him, Jane, and what you have asked for and more can be yours.

JANE. Joseph . . .

JOSEPH. Stay true to God, Sister Law. He will be your friend. Stay loyal to him, no matter what winds or storms may come.

> *Exit* JOSEPH. JANE *sits, back to back with* EMMA, *steeling her nerves against the emotions that are storming within her. Lights dim on both of them.*

SCENE 3

Enter ACTORS 1, 2, and 3.

ACTOR 2. May 10, 1844.

ACTOR 1. After gaining a printing press, William Law, along with others who had risen against Smith, published a prospectus and announce their intentions to publish a newspaper.

Enter WILLIAM.

WILLIAM. We have a knowledge of the gross abuses exercised under the "pretended" authorities of the Charter of the city of Nauvoo. We deem it a sacred duty to advocate the Unconditional REPEAL of the NAUVOO CITY CHARTER.

Enter JOSEPH.

JOSEPH. My life is more in danger from some little dough head of a fool in this city than from all my numerous and inveterate enemies abroad.

WILLIAM. And advocate unmitigated DISOBEDIENCE to POLITI-CAL REVELATIONS, and to censure and decry gross moral imperfections wherever found, whether in Plebeian, Patrician, or self constituted MONARCH.

ACTOR 3. Friday, June 7.

ACTOR 2. One thousand copies of the first edition of the Nauvoo Expositor are published and distributed.

ACTOR 1. Its first edition—its only edition.

WILLIAM. Happy will it be with those who examine and scan Joseph Smith's pretensions to righteousness. How shall he who drank of the poisonous draft, teach virtue?

Enter ACTOR 4 as DENNISON HARRIS.

DENNISON. In the spring of 1844, I was invited by Austin A. Cowles, who was at the time a member of the High Council, to attend a secret meeting. The meeting was to be held on the following Sunday, at William Law's brick house. There was another young man by the name of Robert Scott who was also invited by William Law to attend the same meeting—being intimate friends we found out during the week that both of us had been invited to attend the same meeting. When Sunday morning came Robert Scott and I went and saw Brother Joseph. After telling him about receiving the invitation, he instructed us to go to this meeting and pay strict attention and do the best we could to learn, and remember all the proceedings. We went. At that meeting they were counseling together and working up the system and planning how to get at things the best. They were opposed to the doctrine of plurality of wives, which was the cause of their conspiring against Joseph.

WILLIAM. Polygamy! Spiritual wives! Such women are told that God Almighty has revealed it to him that she should be his spiritual wife; for it was right anciently, and God will tolerate it again. The Prophet and his devotees in this way are gratified.

DENNISON. As near as I can recollect, William and Wilson Law, Austin Cowles, the Higbees—Francis and Chauncey—Robert Foster and Brother, and two of the Hickes. William Marks was not present at all. I think Jason W. Briggs was there; also Finche and Rollinson, merchants and enemies to the Church, were there. This was the first meeting. They were plotting how and what they could do against Joseph.

JOSEPH. If I can escape from the ungrateful treachery of assassins, I can live as long as Caesar might have lived, were it not for a right handed Brutus.

WILLIAM. It is absurd for men to think that all is well, while wicked and corrupt men are seeking our destruction, by a profession of sacred things. For all is not well.

DENNISON. They worked this up considerably that Sunday, and still gave us an invitation to attend the following week. Joseph told us to go again, and was desirous that we should see and learn all that took place this day, for, said he, "this will be your last meeting; this will be the last time they will admit you into their council, and they will come to some determination. But be sure," he continued, "that you make no covenants nor enter into any obligation whatever with that party. Be strictly reserved, and make no promise either to conspire against me or any portion of the community. Be silent and do not take any part in their deliberations. They may shed your blood, but I hardly think they will, as you are so young, but they may. If they do, I will be a lion in their path. Don't flinch, if you have to die, die like men. You will be martyrs to the cause, and your crown can be no greater. But," said he, "again, I hardly think they will shed your blood."

JOSEPH. All the enemies upon the face of the earth may roar and exert all their power to bring about my death, but they can accomplish nothing, unless some who are among us and enjoy our society, have been with us in our councils, participated in our confidence, taken us by the hand, called us brother, saluted us with a kiss, but then join with our enemies.

DENNISON. We went. There was a great deal of counseling going on with each other. And every little while Austin Cowles would come and sit by me side and put his arm around my neck to ascertain how I felt with regard to their proceedings, and at the same time William Law would do the same thing with Robert Scott. They talked about Joseph, denouncing him, and accusing him. We told them that we did not know anything against Joseph or about the things they were charging him with, that we were only young men, and therefore had nothing to say. They would then try to convince us by relating things to us against him, but we told them that we knew nothing about them, and did not understand them, that we had been reared in the Church and always esteemed Brother Joseph highly. They continued to persuade us, we being the only ones who did not sympathize with their proceedings, but they failed to convert us.

WILLIAM. Many of us have sought reformation in the Church, but our petitions have been met with contempt.

JOSEPH. They turn our virtues into faults, and, by falsehood and deceit, stir up their wrath and indignation against us, and bring their united vengeance upon our heads.

DENNISON. Finally they went on to administer the oath to those present. Each man was required to come to the table and hold up the Bible in his right hand. When Brother Higbee would say, "Are you ready?" The man being sworn answered, "Yes." He would say, "You solemnly swear before God and all holy angels and these your brethren, by whom you are surrounded, that you will give your life, your liberty, your influence, your all for the destruction of Joseph Smith and his party, so help you God!"

WILLIAM. The next important item which presents itself for our consideration, is the attempt at political power and influence which we verily believe to be preposterous and absurd.

DENNISON. There were also three women brought in who testified that Joseph Smith and others—Hyrum among them—had tried to seduce them into this spiritual marriage and wanted them for their wives and also wanted to lie with them. They also made oath before this Justice, after which they were escorted out of the room, by way of the back door.

WILLIAM. Joseph may plead he has been injured, abused, and his petitions treated with contempt by the general government, and that he only desires an influence of a political character that will warrant him redress of grievances—but we care not.

DENNISON. After all in the room had taken the oath but Robert and me, we were labored with by those two brethren, William Law and Austin Cowles. Their arguments were to try to convince us that Joseph was wrong; that he was in transgression, that he was a fallen prophet, and that the Church would be destroyed except action be taken at once against him. We told them that we were young, and that we knew nothing at all about their charges. After laboring with us in this way with a view of trying to get us to take the oath, we told them we could not do it.

WILLIAM. He should not seek redress from this world. Although a frowning world may have crushed him to dust; although unpitying friends may have passed him by . . .

DENNISON. They then told us that if we refused to take the oath they would have to kill us. They could not, they said, let us go out with the information that we had gained, because it would not be safe to do so. And someone spoke up and said, "Dead men tell no tales." They gathered around us and after threatening they perceived that we could not be frightened into it. They again commenced to persuade and advise us in this way: "Boys, do as we have done. You are young, you will not have anything to do in this affair, but we want that you should keep it a secret and act with us."

WILLIAM. . . . although hope, the great comforter in affliction, may have burst forth and fled from his troubled bosom . . .

DENNISON. They then walked us off with one man on each side of us, armed with sword and bowie knife, and two men behind us with loaded guns, cocked, with bayonets on them. We had not gone more than about fifteen feet when someone cried out, "Hold on, let us talk this matter over." We were stopped, when they commenced to counsel among themselves, one of them saying that our fathers knew where we were, and that if we never returned it would at once cause suspicion and lead to trouble. They became very uneasy about it, for if they shed our blood it would be dangerous for them, as it was known where we were. Finally they concluded to let us go if we would keep our mouths shut.

WILLIAM. . . . yet in Jesus there is balsam for every wound.

DENNISON. They took us toward the river, and still cautioned us about being silent and keeping secret everything we had heard, for, said they, if we opened our mouths about it, they would kill us anywhere—that they would consider it their duty to kill us whenever or wherever the opportunity afforded, either by night or by day. I told them it would be in our interest and to our peace and safety never to mention it to anybody. They said they were glad we could see that, and after warning us in strong terms, and before the guard left us, I saw Brother Joseph's hand from under the bank of the river. He was beckoning us to him.

WILLIAM. We would be among the last to provoke the spirit of the public abroad unnecessarily, but we have abundant assurance, in case of emergency, that we shall all be there.

DENNISON. They turned back, but were yet watching us and listening to us, and one of us said, "Let us go toward the river." The guard made answer and said, "Yes, you better go to the river." With this we started off on the run, and we ran past where Brother Joseph was, and Brother John Scott was with him—he was one of his bodyguard. They slipped around the bank and came down to the same point where we were, and these men, the guard, went back. We got in a little kind of wash, where Joseph was. Joseph said, "Let us sit down here." We sat down. Joseph said, "Boys, we saw the danger you were in. We were afraid you would not get out alive, but we are thankful that you got off."

WILLIAM. We confidently look to an enlightened public for aid in this great and indispensable effort.

DENNISON. We told him all that had happened. We also told him the names of those who were there. After Joseph heard us he looked very solemn indeed, and he said, "Oh brethren, you do not know what this will terminate in." He looked very solemn, and not being able to control himself he broke right out. Brother Scott rose, and putting his arm around Brother Joseph's neck, said, "Oh Brother Joseph, Brother Joseph, do you think they are going to kill you?" And they fell on each other's necks and wept bitterly for some time. We all wept.

JOSEPH. All the hue and cry of the chief priests and the elders against the Savior could not bring down the wrath of the Jewish nation upon his head, and thereby cause the crucifixion of the Son of God, until Judas said unto them, "Whomsoever I shall kiss, he is the man; hold him fast."

DENNISON. After Joseph recovered himself, Brother John repeated the same question. Brother Joseph lifted Brother John's arms from off his neck and said, "I fully comprehend it." But he would not say that he was going to be killed. But he said in the conversation, "Brethren, I am going to leave you. I shall not be with you long; it will not be many months until I shall have to go." Brother John said, "Brother Joseph, are you going to be slain?" He never answered, but he felt very sorrowful.

JOSEPH. Judas was one of the Twelve Apostles, even their treasurer, and dipt with their Master in the dish, and through his treachery, the crucifixion was brought about . . .

DENNISON. Finally he said, "I shall go to rest."

JOSEPH. We have a Judas in our midst.

Blackout.

SCENE 4

Lights raise up on the city council, their voices raised: some arguing, some trying to pacify, some at a loss and all in general chaos. Among the group is JOSEPH, JOHN, WILLARD, HYRUM and four council members, played by the ACTORS.

ACTOR 4. Order, gentlemen—order! (*Silence.*) Now sit down. (*Everybody does so.*) Now, Willard, get out your pen and ink again and we shall resume. Now what to do about the *Nauvoo Expositor* . . .

ACTOR 1. What to do? We can't interfere with the press!

ACTOR 2. They are maligning our people . . .

ACTOR 3. Not all of us are part of your people, sir. Not all of us are part of your church.

HYRUM. No, he is right. *Our* people. It effects all of us. Latter-day Saint, Jew, Catholic, Protestant, Atheist, Muslim—all of us. We all live in Nauvoo.

JOHN. Remember what this paper says . . . (*Taking up the copy of the* Expositor's *Prospectus which they have before them:*) . . . these men demand "the **UNCONDITIONAL REPEAL OF THE NAUVOO CHARTER.**" They are not being subtle—there it is, in capital letters and bold print.

ACTOR 1. I don't see how that . . .

JOHN. Consider it. The Nauvoo Charter and the Nauvoo Legion have been the only things that have protected us from the mobbings that plagued us in other states. If the Charter were taken away from us, Nauvoo's protection under the law would be withdrawn. They would strike down the giant that has protected us from returning to those fiery days in Missouri. And all of Nauvoo, no matter your religious persuasion, will be affected by that.

ACTOR 1. It's bluff and hot air.

JOHN. Is it? Are you willing wager you safety on it? The safety of your neighbors? The safety of your wife and children?

ACTOR 1. They can't tamper with the law.

HYRUM. If that Charter is chopped down, the winds that will come upon the people of Nauvoo will be terrible. Those who weren't with us in Missouri don't know what will have to be endured.

ACTOR 3. This isn't Missouri. We aren't among Missourians.

JOHN. Don't think that all devils reside in Missouri.

ACTOR 2. You don't have to travel much farther than Carthage and Warsaw to find that out.

JOHN. Or Nauvoo.

JOSEPH. The press needs to be removed.

ACTOR 3. Removed!

JOSEPH. The consequences have been shown to me, if we don't.

ACTOR 3. We need not be rash here. I've trusted you, I've even admired you—but we can't do that!

ACTOR 1. Remember the Constitution!

JOSEPH. You know I won't act outside the law.

ACTOR 1. Then how do you propose . . . ?

JOSEPH. John?

JOHN. Joseph is right. It's within the law. We've studied it out.

ACTOR 3. But . . .

JOSEPH. Willard?

> WILLARD *rises from his desk, where he has been recording the proceedings.*

WILLARD. The Nauvoo Charter gives us the power to remove all public nuisances . . .

ACTOR 3. That's a pretty broad word: "nuisance."

WILLARD. Sir William Blackstone's writings on law are the measuring stick in both Britain and America. He is the most respected authority on law in all national courts. He states that . . . (*Reading from a book:*) ". . . a libelous and filthy press may be considered a nuisance and abated as such."

JOSEPH. And our own charter, given to us by the legislature of this state, gives us the power to remove nuisances; and by ordering that press to be abated as a nuisance, we conceive that we are acting strictly in accordance with law.

ACTOR 4. But, Joseph, the American people's feelings about the press . . .

ACTOR 2. The people! Well, the people of Nauvoo are indignant. The people have been threatening its annihilation. The people see that these men are conspiring on the life of their prophet and the lives of their families!

ACTOR 3. Or have they just placed down the facts?

HYRUM. Would you offend us to our faces, sir?

ACTOR 3. Is this paper so offensive to you because it finally brings polygamy out into the open? Not all of us have fallen for your denials of the practice.

HYRUM. There is more to it than that.

ACTOR 3. Is there?

JOHN. We have gone over story after story of their attempts on Joseph's life. These men do not, as they claim, have truth and righteousness as their chief aim.

ACTOR 3. Perhaps they would say the same about you.

JOHN. Those men have made veiled death threats against Joseph in that paper of theirs! They have laid a blue print for the destruction of the people of Nauvoo. Do you disagree or deny that this has, at least in part, been their intention?

ACTOR 3. (*Beat.*) No.

JOHN. (*To* COUNCIL MEMBER 1:) And you?

ACTOR 1. That has been their obvious intention.

JOHN. Then there is no disagreement.

ACTOR 1. No, you don't get to simplify it like that, John. We are in a critical position. Any move we make for the abating of that press will be looked upon, or at least represented, as a direct attack on the freedom of speech. They will see it as one of the best circumstances to assist them in their murderous goals.

ACTOR 4. That's true. So they have us if we do, and they have us if we don't. They have put us in check mate.

ACTOR 2. It's quite the knot.

ACTOR 3. It is a hard case.

> *There is a silence as the reality of their danger comes upon them.*

JOSEPH. Well, gentlemen—brethren. My friends. Do you think they will be satisfied with my destruction? I tell you as soon as they have shed my blood they will thirst for the blood of every man and woman who dares believe the doctrines that God has inspired me to teach to this generation.

ACTOR 3. They can't be as hateful as you say.

JOSEPH. Will you have to lose your children as I have, to understand the ultimate designs of such men? Will you, too, have to have bayonets pointed at your necks, be thrown in cold dungeons, and be offered the flesh of a man before you realize they will use any weapon at their disposal to destroy us, whether that be dagger, pistol, or printing press?

ACTOR 1. It is an attack on a press!

JOSEPH. And they have made an attack upon my people! No man is a stronger advocate for the liberty of free speech and the press than I am. You must remember that we had our own press destroyed and scattered in Missouri. Do you think I relish in returning that action? It's abhorrent to me! Yet when this noble gift is utterly prostituted and abused, it loses all claims to our respect. When it is used as an instrument for death, then it must be accountable to us, not us to it. It then becomes as great an agent for evil as it can possibly be for good.

ACTOR 3. It is a hard case. A hard case!

JOSEPH. Notwithstanding the apparent advantage we should give our enemies by this act, it behooves us, as men, to act independent of all secondary influences. We must perform the part of men of enlarged minds, and boldly and fearlessly discharge the duties devolving upon us by declaring as a nuisance, and removing this filthy, libelous and seditious sheet from our midst.

> JOSEPH *sits and there is a considerable pause in which everyone seems to wait for someone else to speak.*

JOHN. The mayor has expressed himself frankly. He is a man who has made himself very vulnerable throughout his life for such honest expressions. He has exposed himself to fire, slander, and hate.

ACTOR 1. There is more to this, John.

JOHN. Can you doubt his honesty? Or the truth of his statements?

ACTOR 3. You are telling me that he hasn't his secrets? That all of you Mormons haven't been willing to keep some of us in the dark?

JOHN. I, for one, shall not abandon him, nor the safety of the people of Nauvoo on the account of cowardice.

ACTOR 2. Nor I.

ACTOR 4. Nor I.

ACTOR 3. Legal or not, this isn't right!

JOHN. I move for a vote. I move that we order, for the safety of Nauvoo and its members, that we destroy the Nauvoo Expositor on account of it being a nuisance and a libelous and vexatious press. All in favor?

ACTOR 4. Aye.

ACTOR 2. Aye.

JOSEPH. Aye.

ACTOR 1. (*After a considerable pause:*) Aye.

JOHN. Aye. All opposed? (*There is no response from* ACTOR 3.) All opposed?

ACTOR 3. History will not smile on us for this decision.

JOSEPH. I am willing to take upon all the slander and hate of the world, I am willing to even lay down my own life, if it means that I can protect my people from being ruled by mobs and tyrants again.

ACTOR 3. I vote nay.

JOHN. For what reason?

ACTOR 3. This is a decision motivated by fear.

JOSEPH. It is a decision motivated by faith and protective justice.

JOHN. In either case, with just one dissenting vote, the motion has carried.

Exit all.

SCENE 5

THOMAS FORD sits in an office. Enter WILLIAM LAW, ROBERT FOSTER, ACTOR 1 as JOSEPH JACKSON, and ACTOR 3 as FRANCIS HIGBEE. Enter JOHN TAYLOR, who is astounded at the group assembled at what he thought was going to be a private meeting.

THOMAS FORD. Mr. Taylor, thank you for coming.

JOHN. If this isn't an infamous group!

WILLIAM. Are you startled, John?

JOHN. Governor, what are these men doing here?

THOMAS FORD. To give their part of the story, as you are here to give yours.

JOHN. The council have already been acquitted by Judge Wells on the matter of the Expositor.

FORD. There have been some questions raised about Judge Wells' ruling.

JOHN. Why? The honorable judge is not a Mormon, so you can't say he's prejudiced . . .

WILLIAM. Everyone knows that the Church has Dan Wells in your pocket.

JOHN. Why, William, because he hasn't made oaths to kill us like you have? (*Back to FORD:*) These are men of questionable character, Your Excellency. Criminals, adulterers and murderers . . .

JACKSON. Watch yer mouth, you puke faced . . .

JOHN. If I were here on private business, I would turn to depart. Governor, do you think it proper to associate with such questionable characters?

FORD. I will hear all sides.

JOHN. Well, normally I would beg to be excused . . .

ROBERT. Then why don't you, sir?

JOHN. . . . but as I am not coming on private business, I cannot consult my private feelings.

WILLIAM. Yes, quite the gentleman. How many wives do you have now, John?

FORD. Gentlemen, please. Let's get through this. Well, Mr. Taylor, I have been discussing with these gentlemen their very valid concerns. Now I would like to hear Nauvoo's side.

JOHN. Well, Governor, as you can see, I'm ready to do just that. General Smith has sent me as part of the committee of conference to see you. I am well acquainted with the circumstances that have transpired in Nauvoo lately. Here in my possession are testimonies and affidavits confirming what I will say, which General Smith has forwarded to you.

FRANCIS. Don't believe a word of it, Governor.

JOHN. These documents and testimonies bring in question the character of the men standing about you . . .

ROBERT. They're lies, all of them!

JOHN. They also, in brief, relate an outline of the difficulties, and the course we have pursued from the commencement of the troubles up to the present. I submit them to you in whole.

WILLIAM. Governor, you must understand that . . .

JOHN. You have already had your hearing, William. Why are these men still here, Governor?

FORD. I need their counsel in relation to you.

JOHN. Their counsel! Robert Foster here is guilty of dishonesty, fraud, falsehood, and is a lewd and vulgar man towards women . . .

ROBERT. That's a lie.

JOHN. Joseph Jackson is a thief, counterfeiter, and a cut throat, who has already attempted to assassinate Mayor Smith . . .

JACKSON. A damned lie!

JOHN. William Law is a counterfeiter, dishonest in his business transactions, and has conducted meetings in which he has threatened Joseph's safety . . .

WILLIAM. Infernal falsehoods!

JOHN. And Francis Higbee is a gambler and adulterer of the first rate!

HIGBEE. Prove it!

JOHN. It's all there in the testimonies and documentation, Your Honor. Are these the men you have set up to be our judges?

WILLIAM. Now, Mr. Taylor . . .

JOHN. They evidently wince at an exposure of their acts . . .

WILLIAM. And who winced when we exposed the Church's secret acts?

JOHN. . . . and have vulgarly, impudently, and falsely repudiated them . . .

WILLIAM. John Taylor, I will be heard!

JOHN. My business at this time is with Governor Ford, Mr. Law! We have submitted to this country's laws, not yours. You have no authority over us in this matter.

FORD. Come now, gentlemen, come now. Mr. Taylor, I want Mayor Smith and all those associated to come to Carthage.

JOHN. What?

FORD. However repugnant it may be to your feelings, I think it would have a tendency to allay public excitement, and prove to the people that you wish to be governed by the law.

JOHN. In these papers you'll find all our court proceedings. We have been acquitted by non-Mormon judges! We have fulfilled the law in every particular. It is our enemies who are breaking the law, and, having murderous designs, are only making use of this as a pretext to get us into their power.

FORD. The people view it differently. Notwithstanding your opinions, I recommend that the people should be satisfied.

JOHN. If Joseph Smith complies to your request, it will be extremely unsafe in the presently excited state of the country to come without an armed force.

FORD. I recommend that you do not come with an armed force.

JOHN. Carthage is vehement against us. They will raise up a mob. We have a sufficiency of men and are competent to defend ourselves. We have about five thousand men in the legion now, if we only brought a thousand we'd be safe, but there might be a danger of collision should our forces and the forces of our enemies be brought into such close proximity . . .

FORD. I said do not bring a force. Do not bring any arms.

JOHN. They'll kill us, Governor!

FORD. I pledge my faith as Governor, and the faith of the State, that you should be protected. I guarantee your perfect safety.

Blackout.

SCENE 6

A light appears on JOSEPH.

JOSEPH. Governor Ford, writs, we are assured, are issued against us in various parts of the country. For what? To drag us from place to place, from court to court, across the creeks and prairies, till some bloodthirsty villain could find his opportunity to shoot us. Sir, we dare not come, for our lives would be in danger, and we are guilty of no crime.

Exit JOSEPH, lights raise. PORTER enters, moving in a determined direction, when EMMA also enters and frantically catches up to him.

EMMA. Port!

PORTER. Excuse me, Emma, but I'm on an errand for your husband, and must . . .

EMMA. Where is he, Port? Where is my husband?

PORTER. He's safe.

EMMA. But why isn't he in Nauvoo? Why isn't he complying to the Governor's request?

PORTER. You know as well as I do, ma'am, the Governor's promise of safety ain't no stronger than a corn dodger.

EMMA. Without Joseph in their custody, they'll attack the city!

PORTER. Joseph says that the Lord has revealed to him that ya'll will be safe.

EMMA. He can't know that.

PORTER. You of all people should know that he can. He's takin' us to the Rocky Mountains to prepare a place for all of the Church. We have a plan to smuggle you and the children out of the city as well.

EMMA. The Rocky Mountains! Our home is here.

PORTER. You've heard the prophecy like I have, Emma. It's the Rocky Mountains for us.

EMMA. He needs to be here. He needs do what the law tells him to do. I've been meeting with President Marks and we both agree . . .

PORTER. Stake President of Nauvoo or not, William Marks ain't no friend to your husband.

EMMA. Why? Because he hates plural marriage as much as I do? He's not the Laws nor the Higbees nor the Fosters. He's still loyal to the

Church. He's assured me of that. But we all know that the Church needs to be cleansed of iniquity.

PORTER. And Joseph's blood will cleanse it, you think?

EMMA. No, no, he'll be safe. The Lord has always protected him. He has always come back to me. If the Missourians couldn't kill him, neither can Warsaw, nor Carthage. We just have to have faith.

PORTER. Joseph said that they will kill him.

EMMA. Port, please, I know you know where he is. President Marks and I wrote this letter to him. Will you at least deliver it to him for us?

PORTER. (*Eying the letter.*) I don't know. Joseph knows what he's doing.

Enter ACTOR 1 as REYNOLDS CAHOON, and ACTOR 3 as HIRAM KIMBALL.

CAHOON. Port, we've tied up the horses Joseph asked for. We'll be ready to go whenever you want.

PORTER. Thank you, Reynolds. Thank you, Hiram.

EMMA. Brother Cahoon, Brother Kimball, please, tell Porter to bring Joseph back here.

HIRAM K. She's not wrong. The whole city is in agitation, Port.

CAHOON. Has Joseph abandoned Nauvoo?

PORTER. No, no, he's going to prepare a place for us . . .

HIRAM K. That's little consolation if the mobs exterminate us first!

PORTER. None of you understand the danger Joseph's in!

EMMA. (*To HIRAM K. and CAHOON:*) Will you two deliver my letter to Joseph? He's got to come back.

CAHOON. (*Taking the letter.*) I will be glad to.

PORTER. (*To EMMA:*) I hope you know what you're doin'. It's a high stakes game now.

EMMA. Joseph needs to be with his people. He needs to be with me. All is well.

Exit EMMA. Lights change to indicate a change of location, with JOSEPH, JOHN, WILLARD, and HYRUM now on stage at a campsite. PORTER, CAHOON, and HIRAM K. approach them.

JOSEPH. Reynolds, Hiram, it is wonderful to see you, Brethren.

PORTER. You may not be so happy to see 'em after you hear what they have to say.

CAHOON. Joseph, you need to go to Carthage and stand trial.

HYRUM. What? Would you have him killed?

CAHOON. It's a bailable case. There is no danger.

WILLARD. Then you don't understand the agitation of the countryside right now. They are calling for his blood and extermination.

CAHOON. All of our extermination as well!

HIRAM K. This chaos will lessen the value of our property—it will ruin a number of men, if Joseph leaves us.

HYRUM. Men like you?

HIRAM K. If Joseph doesn't come back the Governor will put the city under Martial Law, and then nothing can be brought into the city, neither can anything be taken out, and then what will anything in the city be worth?

HYRUM. We should not for the sake of a little property, be so selfish as to push him into the very jaws of death!

JOSEPH. Gentlemen, I know my own business.

CAHOON. Emma and President Marks wrote a letter for you.

CAHOON hands the letter to JOSEPH. Joseph reads it and hands it to HYRUM, who also reads it.

JOSEPH. I know my own business.

HIRAM K. You can't leave!

WILLARD. What are you trying to do, kill him?

CAHOON. They are threatening to destroy Nauvoo. They have cannons!

JOSEPH. They only want Hyrum and me. The Lord has told me that you will be safe.

CAHOON. You always said if the church would stick to you, you would stick to the church, now trouble comes and you are the first to run.

HIRAM K. You're a coward. Mobs will destroy all of our property and we will be homeless!

PORTER. Why, you damned, disloyal sons of Perdition!

JOSEPH puts his hand on PORTER's shoulder, calming him:

JOSEPH. (*Pause.*) If my life is of no value to my friends, it is of no value to me. (*Beat.*) Porter, what do you think?

PORTER. As you make your bed, I'll lie in it.

JOSEPH. Hyrum, you're the oldest. What shall we do?

HYRUM. Let's go back and give ourselves up and see the thing out.

JOSEPH. If you go back I will go with you, but we will be butchered.

CAHOON. No, it'll work out.

PORTER. Shut up, you.

HYRUM. No, Porter, it'll be all right. I feel good about it.

JOSEPH. I am going like a lamb to the slaughter; but I am as calm as a summer's morning; I have a conscience void of offense towards God, and towards all men. I shall die innocent, and it shall yet be said of me, he was murdered in cold blood.

PORTER. We'll go with you all the way.

JOSEPH. No, you mustn't go, Porter.

PORTER. But, Joseph . . .

JOSEPH. Do not come to Carthage after me. Stay in Nauvoo. Do not suffer yourself to be delivered into the hands of our enemies or to be taken prisoner by anyone. Your loyalty shall be rewarded with a life as long as your hair. (*PORTER reluctantly nods*). Hyrum, you can't come to Carthage either.

HYRUM. Joseph . . .

JOSEPH. If I must die, that doesn't mean you have to.

HYRUM. Emma's letter said that the Governor still promises his protection.

JOSEPH. Stay behind. I want you to lead the Church in my place. I want you to avenge my blood by leading the Saints to safety. You can fix all of this.

HYRUM. I'm not leaving you, Joseph.

JOSEPH. Hyrum, please . . .

HYRUM. We'll go through this together.

JOSEPH. Hyrum, you don't understand. We won't . . .

HYRUM. (*Taking him by the arms and looking him straight in the eyes.*) Joseph, I covenant in the name of Israel's God, that where you live, I will live, and where you die, I will die.

JOSEPH. I . . .

HYRUM. I covenant.

JOSEPH. (*With reluctant emotion.*) Amen.

    Blackout.

SCENE 7

Enter JOSEPH to EMMA. There is a tense pause, but then JOSEPH goes to her and embraces her, which she welcomes warmly.

EMMA. Joseph, you're shaking.

JOSEPH. Oh, Emma . . .

EMMA. We've gone through this before.

JOSEPH. This is different, Emma.

EMMA. No, it's not. Don't say that.

JOSEPH. Emma, I need you to listen right now. Can you train my sons to walk in their father's footsteps?

EMMA. Joseph, you are coming back.

JOSEPH. Emma, can you train my sons to walk in their father's footsteps?

EMMA. Stop it. You are coming back.

JOSEPH. Can you train my sons to walk in their father's footsteps?

EMMA. You are coming back!

JOSEPH. (*Resigned.*) Well, if they do not hang me, I do not know how they will kill me.

PORTER. Joseph, we've alerted the Saints like you wanted. When do you want to speak to them? They'll be anxious to hear from you.

JOSEPH. Port, I've changed my mind. It's late. Tell them that I'm going to spend tonight with my family.

PORTER. Understood. Do you need anything else?

JOSEPH. Just guard the door, Port. I don't want anyone else here. I want privacy with my family.

PORTER. Yes, Joseph.

Exit PORTER.

JOSEPH. Now, it's just you, me, and the children tonight.

Lights fade on EMMA and JOSEPH.

SCENE 8

Lights rise on FORD *and* ACTOR 3 *as* COLONEL GEDDES.
Enter JOHN.

JOHN. Governor Ford!

FORD. Good day, Mr. Taylor. This is my associate, Colonel Geddes. Colonel, this is John Taylor.

GEDDES. A pleasure.

JOHN. It is ridiculous! Absolutely illegal!

FORD. What is it, Mr. Taylor? As you can see, the Colonel and I are busy.

JOHN. Not too busy to get Joseph out of the fire you put him into, I hope.

FORD. Mayor Smith made his own fire.

JOHN. He has been thrown into prison!

FORD. Trials can result in that consequence.

JOHN. There has been no trial yet and we have already paid bail.

FORD. Is there another charge leveled against him?

JOHN. Have you been apprised of it?

FORD. Shouldn't I have been?

JOHN. How much are you in league with these people, Governor?

FORD. I am in league with no group, except for the state of Illinois. As its Governor, I will make no other alliance.

JOHN. The exemplar of honor, I'm sure.

FORD. I must satisfy the people, Mr. Taylor.

JOHN. Or get lynched, I suppose? Or, even worse, fail in your re-election!

FORD. You came here for a reason other than to condemn me, I presume?

JOHN. These "people" you fervently represent are intent on confining Joseph. Why is that? After he was set loose on bail, affidavits were made on him for treason. The men who have made them are known scoundrels. Their intent should be clear, Governor.

FORD. I hear as many slanderous things from them about you.

JOHN. Robert Smith has ordered Joseph and Hyrum into prison without a hearing! When Judge Smith made the mittimus, he had no legal right to do so. The statute of Illinois expressly provides that "all men shall have a hearing before a magistrate before they shall be committed."

FORD. Now, let us be reasonable about this.

JOHN. They have had no such hearing!

FORD. What do you expect me to do, Mr. Taylor?

JOHN. It's an outrageous charge and an indignity offered to men who stand in a position such as yours. You know very well that it is a false and vexatious proceeding. They are not guilty of any such crime.

FORD. I did not say that I believed the charges. I'm sorry that the thing has occurred, but the best thing to be done is to let the law take its course.

JOHN. Law! What law? This is against the law!

FORD. You must bend to the law.

JOHN. At your request we are here. At your insistence we have paid bonds, which we could not by law be required to do so, but which we have been required to do so to satisfy a prejudiced people. Your request was that we should come unarmed. It has become a matter of serious importance to decide how far your promises can be trusted, and how far we are safe from mob violence.

GEDDES. Governor, it certainly does look from all I have heard, from the general spirit of violence and mobocracy that here prevails, that it was not safe for them to come unprotected.

FORD. Do you want a civil war on my hands?

JOHN. You are asking too much! Too much to require gentlemen to suffer the degradation of being immured in a jail at the instance of such worthless scoundrels as those who have made this affidavit! We are innocent.

FORD. It looks very hard, but it is a matter over which I have no control, as it belongs to the Judiciary.

JOHN. No control! You had control when you manipulated Joseph in coming to Carthage. Why weren't you so concerned about the proper role of the Executive branch then?

FORD. I cannot interfere with the proceeding.

JOHN. You have already interfered!

FORD. I have no doubt that they will be immediately released.

JOHN. I certainly have my doubts.

FORD. Mr. Taylor . . .

JOHN. We have complied with all of your requests, although extra-judicial, and not within your powers as an Executive. Can we not ask you to put the same restraints upon them?

FORD. I will detail a guard, if you require it, and see you protected.

JOHN. If we are to be subject to mob rule, and to be dragged, contrary to law, into prison at the instance of every infernal scoundrel whose oaths can be bought for a dram of whiskey, your protection avails very little indeed. We have miscalculated your promises.

JOHN goes to leave.

FORD. Mr. Taylor, wait . . .

JOHN. Can you give us at least this satisfaction? Joseph wants to know that if you leave Carthage or go to Nauvoo, whether he can accompany you. That you won't leave him alone in this place.

FORD. He has my word as a gentleman.

JOHN. Well, he will be comforted to know that at least.

Exit JOHN.

FORD. Oh, it's all nonsense. You will have to drive these Mormons out yet.

GEDDES. Your Excellency?

FORD. I mean it, Colonel.

GEDDES. If we undertake that, Governor, when the proper time comes, will you interfere?

FORD. No, I will not.

GEDDES. Is that a promise?

FORD. I will not interfere—until you are through.

Exit GEDDES and FORD.

SCENE 7

JOSEPH, HYRUM, JOHN, WILLARD, and ACTOR 4 as DAN JONES are all in a room in Carthage Jail. HYRUM is reading from the Book of Mormon by candlelight, WILLARD is writing, while the others are scattered about the room listening to HYRUM, or preoccupied with their own thoughts.

HYRUM. "And Alma and Amulek came forth out of the prison, and they were not hurt; for the Lord had granted unto them power, according to their faith which was in Christ. And they straightway came fort out of prison; and they were loosed from their bands; and the prison had fallen to the earth, and . . ."

JOSEPH. Hyrum, I feel more like Abinidi right now than Alma and Amulek.

HYRUM. We are not martyrs yet. Have hope, brother. God is with us.

JOSEPH. God was with Abinidi. (*Beat.*) Hand me The Book of Mormon, please. (*HYRUM does so and JOSEPH slips to a section and begins reading.*) "And it came to pass that I prayed unto the Lord that he would give the Gentiles grace, that they might have charity.

And it came to pass that the Lord said unto me: If they have not charity it mattereth not unto thee, thou hast been faithful; wherefore thy garments shall be made clean. And because thou hast seen thy weakness, thou shalt be made strong, even unto the sitting down in the place which I have prepared in the mansions of my Father. And now I . . . bid farewell unto the Gentiles; yea, and also unto my brethren whom I love, until we shall meet at the judgment seat of Christ, where all men shall know that my garments are not spotted with your blood."

HYRUM. You mustn't despair.

JOSEPH. Hyrum, if you could be but liberated, it would not matter much about me. There is so much that will be required of the Church and they need . . .

HYRUM. You will be back to lead the Church.

JOHN. Perhaps it is best that we get some sleep now. Have you finished with your writing, Willard?

WILLARD. I can take it up later. Let's go to bed.

   WILLARD blows out the candle and moonlight pours into the jail.

JOHN. You will sleep on the bed, Joseph. There's no need to argue the point, we've decided upon it.

JOSEPH. Thank you. For the most intelligent dream tonight, brethren. (*There is a momentary silence as they all recline into sleeping positions. A GUNSHOT is heard. JOSEPH crawls out of the bed and makes his spot by DAN under the window.*) I think I am safer on the floor. (*Pause. There are no more gunshots.*) Dan, are you afraid to die?

DAN. Has that time come think you? (*He pauses to consider it.*) Engaged in such a cause, I do not think that death would have many terrors.

JOSEPH. (*Prophetic:*)You will yet see Wales and fulfill the mission appointed you ere you die.

Lights fade on the group in jail, except a light on DAN, *who addresses the audience.*

DAN. Dan Jones would live to fulfill Joseph's prophecy to go on a mission to Wales. He would become one of the most successful missionaries in Latter-day Saint history, being responsible for the conversion of thousands in his homeland.

It is now morning and the lights rise. JOSEPH *hands* DAN *a letter.*

JOSEPH. Get this to Orville Browning. He's been a good lawyer to me in the past. I'll need his expertise.

DAN. No fear, I'll get it to him.

DAN *descends the stairs to overhear a talk among the militia group, the* CARTHAGE GRAYS, *among whom are* ACTORS 1 *playing* JOSEPH JACKSON *and* ACTOR 3 *playing* SERGEANT WORREL.

JACKSON. I don't think they'll prove a thing against him, but we have eighteen accusations against him, and if one fails we will try another to detail him here.

DAN. Joseph Jackson? (*Going directly to* ACTOR 3, *who is playing* SERGEANT WORREL.) Sergeant Worrel, please, sir, are Joseph's guards supposed to be conspiring with one of his most known enemies? I don't see Governor Ford's reasoning in stationing the Carthage Grays to guard the very man they earlier said that they wanted to kill.

JACKSON. We have worked too hard to get ol' Joe to Carthage to let him get out alive. (*Patting his pistols.*) The balls are in here that will decide the case.

WORREL. And unless you want to die with him, you'd better leave before sundown. You are no better than him for taking his part.

DAN. Please, sir, cool down. You do not mean that.

WORREL. You'll see that I can prophesy better than ol' Joe—neither he nor his brother nor anyone who is with them will see the sun set today.

JACKSON. (*Cocking a pistol at* DAN.) I would love to bore a hole through ol' Joe.

Upstairs JOSEPH, HYRUM, WILLARD, *and* JOHN *are trying to cool themselves in the heat.* JOSEPH *has two pistols, he hands one to* HYRUM.

JOSEPH. These were left for us.

HYRUM. I don't like to see such things used.

JOSEPH. Neither do I. But we may have to defend ourselves.

HYRUM. (*Reluctantly placing the pistol in his pocket.*) Give us a song, John.

JOHN. A song? What would you like to hear?

JOSEPH. "A Poor Wayfaring Man of Grief." You sing that one so beautifully.

JOHN. (*Singing:*)
A poor wayfaring man of grief,
Hath often crossed me on his way,
Who sued so humbly for relief,
That I could never answer nay . . .

As JOHN *continues to sing softly, the scene below continues. Enter* FORD. JACKSON *uncocks his pistol and goes back to the* GRAYS.

JACKSON. So the discharged militia will make a sham discharge in obedience to orders, and the McDonough troops will leave for Nauvoo with the Governor, where he'll give them a good speech about what is required of them, if they wanna live . . .

DAN. Governor!

JACKSON. Then the militia will return to town, boys, and tear down the prison and have those Smiths' lives before sundown. All you have to do is shoot over their heads.

DAN. Are you hearing this, Governor? Are you hearing this!

FORD. I have heard nothing.

DAN. They are loud enough for even your deaf ears! They're going to kill our men, sir!

FORD. You are unnecessarily alarmed for your friends' safety, sir. The people are not that cruel.

DAN. You need to place better men than professed assassins to guard Joseph and Hyrum. They are American citizens who have surrendered to your pledged honor! Is it true that you're leaving to Nauvoo?

FORD. I need to take care of some things among your people.

DAN. You promised that you would not leave Joseph alone, that you would take him with you, if you left.

FORD. I'm afraid that is not possible. I will be back.

DAN. Then I have but one request to make, if you will leave their lives into the hands of these men to be sacrificed.

FORD. What is that, sir?

DAN. That the Almighty will preserve my life to a proper time and place to testify that you have been timely warned of their danger.

ACTOR 1. We will hang Joe and Hyrum as soon as the Governor is out of the way.

FORD. Goodbye, Mr. Jones.

Exit FORD.

DAN. (*Calling after FORD:*) How can you not do anything?

As JOHN sings the last two verses, he becomes louder and the words are clear and distinct again.

JOHN. . . . In pris'n I saw him next condemned,
To meet a traitor's doom at morn.

The tide of lying tongues I stemmed,
And honored him mid shame and scorn.
My friendship's utmost zeal to try,
He asked if I for him would die.
The flesh was weak; my blood ran chill,
But my free spirit cried, "I will!"

DAN. (*Approaching the Carthage Grays.*) I will not let you kill innocent men.

JOHN. Then in a moment to my view,
The stranger started from disguise;
the tokens in his hands I knew;
The Savior stood before my eyes.

WORREL. Second thoughts, we'd better get you out of the way right now.

The CARTHAGE GRAYS begin to encroach upon DAN.

JOHN. He spake and my poor name he named,
"Of me thou hast not been ashamed."

JACKSON. What's that in his hand?

JOHN. "These deeds shall thy memorial be;
Fear not, thou didst them unto me."

WORREL. They must be orders for the Nauvoo Legion! Joe's sending for them!

JACKSON. Don't let him get away!

They grab DAN, but he struggles free. DAN exits. Exit JACKSON after him.

WORREL. (*Calling after JACKSON:*) He's getting on his horse! It's too late!

HYRUM. Sing it again, John.

JOHN. Brother Hyrum, I don't feel much like singing.

HYRUM. Never mind that. Commence singing, and you will get the Spirit of it.

JOHN. Oh, Joseph, this is impossible! It's a legal farce and a flagrant outrage. If you will permit it and say the word, I will go to Nauvoo and have you out of this prison in five hours, if the jail has to come down to do it.

JOSEPH. No, John, you mustn't do that. (*Changing the subject:*) It has been very kind of the jailer to let us use this room, but we may be safer in the cell, since this door lock is faulty. (*To WILLARD:*) If I go in the cell, will you go with me?

WILLARD. Brother Joseph, you did not ask me to cross the Mississippi with you. You did not ask me to come to Carthage with you. So do you think I would forsake you now? But I will tell you what I will do: if you are condemned to be hung for treason, I will be hung in your stead, and you shall go free.

JOSEPH. You cannot.

WILLARD. I will.

JOHN, seated by the window, cries out.

JOHN. They are coming! They are coming!

JOSEPH. Everyone against the door!

The four of them pin themselves against the door. The mob enters and pour up the stairs. Among them we see JOSEPH JACKSON, ROBERT FOSTER, FRANCIS HIGBEE, and, prominently in the front, WILLIAM LAW.

The mob try to push the door open, but, being unable to do so, one of them fires at the key hole. JOSEPH, JOHN, and WILLARD spring aside, but HYRUM remains, pushing against the door.

HYRUM. (*Sensing his fate.*) I am a dead man.

Another shot is fired and hits HYRUM in the face. HYRUM falls to the floor, killed instantly. JOSEPH goes to the floor, cradling his brother's lifeless body. WILLARD *tries to keep the door closed while* JOHN *parries the muzzles of the guns, which are trying to push into the room, with a walking stick.*

JOSEPH. Hyrum! Oh, my dear brother Hyrum . . .

Suddenly steeling himself, JOSEPH *rises, takes out the pistol from his vest pocket. He fires the gun several times at those behind the door, injuring some of the mob. He then drops the pistol, it being empty now.* JOHN *continues to use his cane to parry and push back the guns that keep trying to emerge into the door.*

JOSEPH (CONT'D). That's right, John, parry them the best you can.

JOHN *continues to parry until he is unable to anymore.* JOHN *drops the cane and rushes to the window but is fired at by those outside the window and those behind him. Shattered glass is heard.* JOHN *is shot several times.*

JOHN. I'm shot!

JOHN *crawls under the bed to protect himself from further injury.* JOSEPH *looks at* WILLARD *and then calmly walks to the window and calls out a Masonic cry for help:*

JOSEPH. Is there no mercy for the widow's son?

The door bursts open and WILLARD *is pinned behind it. As* JOSEPH *reaches the window, he is shot from behind and from below.* WILLIAM LAW *prominently shoots the fatal blow.*

JOSEPH. O Lord, my God!

JOSEPH *falls out the window, out of view to the mob below. More shots are heard, until there is a shout:*

MOBBER. The Mormons are coming, the Mormons are coming!

The jail is emptied as the mobbers flee an imaginary enemy. Silence. WILLARD *goes to the window to see his dead friend's body below. He is in shock. He turn to leave, but* JOHN *reaches out a hand from under the bed.*

JOHN. Stop! Take me along, Doctor.

WILLARD. Oh, John! You are alive!

> WILLARD *takes* JOHN *from under the bed.* JOHN *groans in pain.*

JOHN. (*Wincing.*) Careful. Careful, now.

WILLARD. This is going to be a hard case for you, John, but if your wounds are not fatal, I want you to live to tell the story. (*JOHN groans again.*) Oh Lord, our God, spare us!

> *Blackout.*

SCENE 8

> *Lights appear on* JOHN TAYLOR, THOMAS FORD, ELIZA SNOW, EMMA SMITH, WILLIAM LAW, *and* ROBERT FOSTER, *as they address the audience.*

JOHN. The testators are now dead, and their testament is in force.

FORD. Thus fell Joe Smith, the most successful imposter in modern time.

ELIZA. Once more the "prophet's free":
Your ill directed fury
Brought forth a "Jubilee."

FORD. A man who, though ignorant and coarse, had some great natural parts, which fitted him for temporary success.

EMMA. It was improbable a learned man could do produce the Book of Mormon; and, for one so ignorant and unlearned as he was, it was simply impossible.

FORD. But which were so obscured and counteracted by that inherent corruption and vices of his nature, that he could never succeed in establishing a system of policy which looked to permanent success in the future.

WILLIAM. I was annoyed very frequently by receiving letters from parties asking for interviews and items about Nauvoo and Mormons. I got tired of it all and said no man or woman should interview me on that subject, and none ever shall. I am heartily sick of it all.

ROBERT. You Saints are going to the West. I wish I was going among you, but it can't be so, I am the most miserable wretch that the sun shines upon. If I could recall eighteen months of my life I would be willing to sacrifice everything I have upon earth, my wife and child not excepted. I did love Joseph Smith more than any man that ever lived.

JOHN. I was acquainted with Joseph Smith for years. I was with him living, and was with him when he died. I testify before God, angels, and men, that he was a good, honorable, virtuous man. That he lived and died as a man of God and a gentleman.

ROBERT. I know that I was accessory to his murder, and I have not seen one moment's peace since that time. I know that Mormonism is true, and the thought of meeting Joseph and Hyrum at the bar of God is more awful to me than anything else.

ELIZA. Thou hast found a seclusion—a lone solitude
Where thy foes cannot find thee—where friends can't intrude;
In its beauty and wildness, by nature design'd
As a retreat from the tumult of all humankind,
And estrang'd from society: How do you fare?
May the God of our forefathers comfort you there.

JOHN. The Book of Mormon, and this book of Doctrine and Covenants of the church, cost the best blood of the nineteenth century to bring them forth for the salvation of a ruined world.

WILLIAM. I have forgotten many things which I once knew; cannot bring them to my mind and it is exceedingly painful to me to try to remember anything connected with Mormonism; I do not wish to be discourteous; but I cannot be interviewed. I have denied many others and must deny you.

JOHN. They lived for glory, they died for glory and glory shall be their eternal reward. From age to age shall their names go down to posterity as gems for the sanctified.

EMMA. Though I was an active participant in the scenes as they transpired, and was present during the translation of the plates, and had cognizance of things as they transpired, it is marvelous to me, "a marvel and a wonder," as much so as to anyone else.

JOHN. (*Quietly, a man's last words:*) Joseph . . . Joseph . . . Joseph . . .

EMMA. Joseph . . . Joseph . . . Joseph!

Enter JOSEPH SMITH.

JOSEPH. How good and glorious it has seemed to me, to find pure and holy friends, who are faithful, just, and true, and whose hearts fail not; and whose knees are confirmed and do not falter, while they wait upon the Lord, in administering to my necessities, in the day when the wrath of mine enemies was poured out upon me.

Blackout.

THE END

Heather Jones as Emma Smith, Benjamin King as Joseph Smith, and Holly Harris Anderson as Eliza R. Snow. Photo by Michelle Argyle.

Benjamin King as Joseph Smith and Heather Jones as Emma Smith. Photo by Michelle Argyle.

Benjamin King as Joseph Smith and Adam Argyle as William Law. Photo by Michelle Argyle.

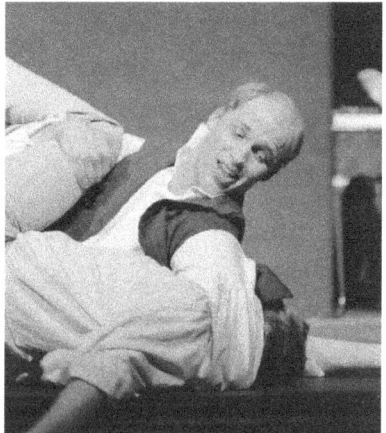

Benjamin King as Joseph Smith and Jordan McMillan as Hyrum Smith. Photo by Michelle Argyle.

Benjamin King as Joseph Smith and Jordan McMillan as Hyrum Smith. Photo by Michelle Argyle.

Holly Harris Anderson as Eliza R. Snow and Heather Jones as Emma Smith. Photo by Michelle Argyle.

Holly Harris Anderson as Eliza R. Snow and Heather Jones as Emma Smith. Photo by Michelle Argyle.

Penny Pendleton as Vilate Kimball. Photo by Michelle Argyle.

Amos Omer as Heber C. Kimball. Photo by Michelle Argyle.

Bryce Bishop as Porter Rockwell and Benjamin King as Joseph Smith. Photo by Michelle Argyle.

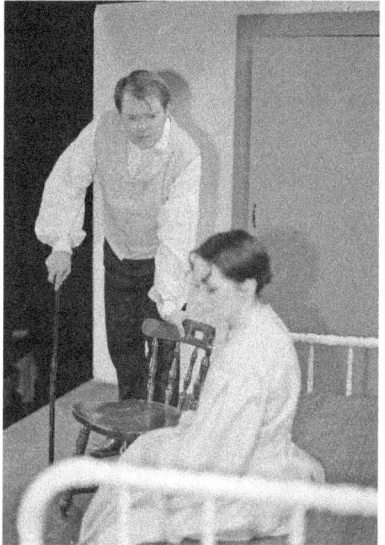

Mahonri Stewart as John Taylor and Sarah Harris as Leonora Taylor. Photo by Michelle Argyle.

Dadre Mitchell as Jane Law, Adam Argyle as William Law, and Benjamin King as Joseph Smith. Photo by Michelle Argyle.

Jason Kelly Fullmer as Dan Jones and Kenneth Brown as Willard Richards. Photo by Michelle Argyle.

Mahonri Stewart as John Taylor, Jason Kelly Fullmer as Robert Foster, George Anderson as Governor Thomas Ford, and Adam Argyle as William Law. Photo by Michelle Argyle.

Amos Omer, Adam Stallard, Bryce Bishop, and Jason Kelly Fullmer as mob members; Benjamin King as Joseph Smith, Jordan McMillan as Hyrum Smith, Kenneth Brown as Willard Richards, and Mahonri Stewart as John Taylor. Photo by Michelle Argyle.

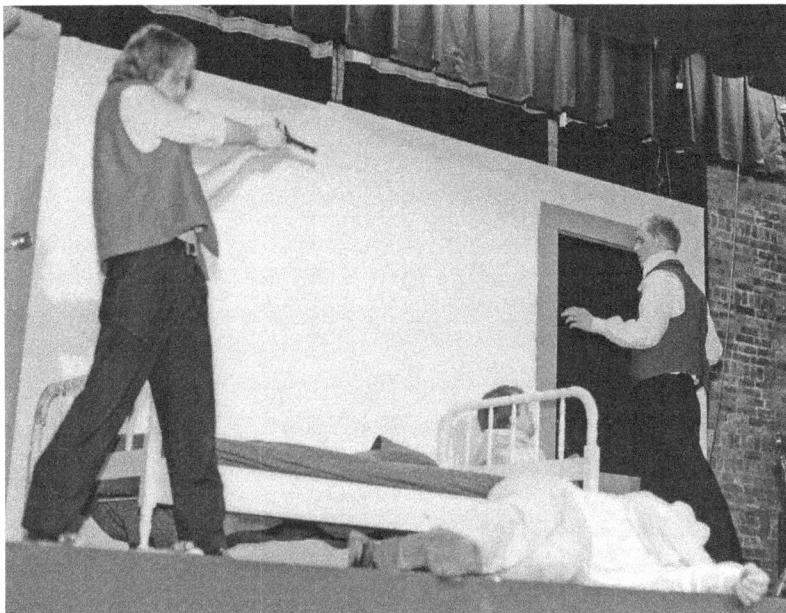

Amos Omer as Joseph Jackson and Benjamin King as Joseph Smith. Photo by Michelle Argyle.

The entire cast of *Friends of God*. Photo by Michelle Argyle.

White Mountain

A One Act Play

Production History

"White Mountain" originated as a student project at Timpview High School in late 1999. Over a decade later, Zion Theatre Company performed "White Mountain" at Provo Theatre Company in Provo, UT, as part of the set *Immortal Hearts and Other Short Plays* on July 16, 2010. Alterations to the text were very minor and it is more or less the same play that Stewart wrote in high school. It had the following cast and crew:

CAST

Ruth: Bryn Dalton Randall

Abraham: Amos Omer

Mercy: Jamie Denison

Jacob: Alex Barlow

CREW

Director: Brian Randall

For the Wilson family, especially Krista, Janel, and Danielle.

Visiting your family's house in high school, where you often invited me to participate in your Spirit filled family prayer and scripture study, was a deeply meaningful experience for me. Your home was a spiritual sanctuary.

"And it shall come to pass afterward,
that I shall pour out my spirit upon all flesh;
and your sons and your daughters shall prophesy,
your old men shall dream dreams,
your young men shall see visions:
And also upon the servants and upon the handmaids in those
days shall I pour my spirit."

— Joel 2:28–29, KJV

White Mountain

A cabin in Frontier America, 1830s. Enter ABRAHAM WAIN-WRIGHT and MERCY KIMBALL.

MERCY. Now, Mr. Wainwright, I will not hear another maligning word about your dancing. You were superb.

ABRAHAM. I think your toes will tell you a different story later tonight.

MERCY. Truly, stop! False humility does not become you. You stepped on my toes once, I'll grant you that, but after that, well . . .

ABRAHAM. Yes?

MERCY. Stars were trailing from your feet.

ABRAHAM. You have a poetic turn to you, Miss Kimball.

MERCY. Hardly. I'm afraid I'm rather rough on my beaux. Or so I'm told.

ABRAHAM. Is that what I am? Your beau?

There is a brief, tense pause.

MERCY. I do not mean to . . .

ABRAHAM. No, I'm sorry, I spoke out of turn. Perhaps I should not have brought you here . . .

MERCY. No! I mean, I liked that you did. I still like it. Well, I . . .

ABRAHAM. You do?

MERCY. I thought I was perfectly, well, plain . . .

ABRAHAM. Plain about what?

MERCY. Mr. Wainwright, I know I have a reputation for over-zealousness, and if I have said anything unbecoming . . .

ABRAHAM. I'm getting mighty confused here, Miss Kimball. Are you or aren't you . . . ?

MERCY. I like you!

ABRAHAM. You—"like" me? And by that you mean . . . ?

MERCY. You have shown me many kindnesses . . .

ABRAHAM. And that means?

MERCY. You're not letting me pass through this with any sort of dignity, are you?

ABRAHAM. I am so sorry, I don't speak a woman's language very—prettily. When a woman tells me she wants to be my friend, it has meant that she wants nothing to do with me and when she's treated me miserably, she's apparently tried to tell me she's interested in starting something and when . . .

MERCY. Do I have to spell it out to you?

ABRAHAM. I'm afraid my spelling is pretty shoddy, too.

MERCY. Well, then I guess I have to give a crack at the only language you may understand then. (*MERCY urgently kisses ABRAHAM. After a moment, she draws away and can't look at ABRAHAM, regretting the impulse. ABRAHAM is slightly shocked.*) I—I am so, so—well, I don't what I am—but sorry. I apologize for such an impetuous temperament. It gets me in all sorts of . . .

Having fully recovered, ABRAHAM comes over to MERCY and touches her lightly on the cheek, which silences her. They gaze at each other for a moment and then slowly, gently, ABRAHAM kisses MERCY.

ABRAHAM. Mercy.

MERCY. Abraham.

ABRAHAM. Do we understand each other?

MERCY. Perfectly.

They kiss again. ABRAHAM withdraws abruptly, to MERCY's confusion.

ABRAHAM. Mercy . . .

MERCY. Did I do it wrong?

ABRAHAM. No. You are doing everything right, believe me.

MERCY. Then . . .

ABRAHAM. There's something I have to know first, before we continue with any of this.

MERCY. All right.

ABRAHAM. My Pa wasn't around, but my Ma, she was something mighty special and she brought us up right. The Bible was meat and drink to us . . .

MERCY. I could tell. That's one of the reasons I have been so—admiring.

ABRAHAM. It wasn't a regular education by any means, but it was special to me . . .

MERCY. I know what you mean.

ABRAHAM. Hear me out a bit, please. People, well, people have been saying strange things about you . . .

MERCY. Not you, too! I am utterly sick to death of all the backbiting and the gossip in this town!

ABRAHAM. No, no, hear me out . . .

MERCY. Please, Mr. Wainwright, if that's what I can expect from you, perhaps I've misjudged . . .

ABRAHAM. (*Warmly; gently touching her face again.*) Mercy.

MERCY stops and looks up with some hope again.

MERCY. Go on.

ABRAHAM. People talk, and you can't really stop them from talking, even when they're saying outright lies. A reputation is a fragile thing, and the slightest mistakes are misinterpreted and re-misinterpreted—they get distorted and fabricated out of their original shape. I understand all that.

MERCY. Thank you, Abraham.

ABRAHAM. But I have picked up on what they've said, and I just wanted to clear something up, before we keep going with this.

MERCY. All right . . .

ABRAHAM. People say—well, they say that you're a—visionary woman.

MERCY looks away, she does not want to answer to this.

ABRAHAM (CONT'D). How do you respond to that, Mercy?

MERCY. How do you expect me to?

ABRAHAM. The most honest way you know how.

MERCY. Well, I have dreams and the like, much like other people.

ABRAHAM. Except not like any other people. Folks say that your dreams come true. That you get—messages and the like, and that—that you've even seen the future, and then seen that future come to pass. And your dreams are just the beginning of your experiences, aren't they?

MERCY. And what if it was true? As you know, I was engaged to Mr. Palmer last year, but when he got whiff of those stories he made his position perfectly clear. Oh, he was very religious himself, he said. But he didn't want to marry a fanatic. He said it was just one stride away from witchcraft.

ABRAHAM. So it's true?

MERCY. (*Painfully:*) Yes.

ABRAHAM. Praise the Lord.

MERCY. Pardon me?

ABRAHAM. You're like me. You're just like me.

There is a KNOCK.

MERCY. Oh—I'm rather dizzy, may I sit?

ABRAHAM nods and answers the door to find RUTH, with a suitcase. ABRAHAM is stunned.

ABRAHAM. Ruth?

RUTH. Good evening, brother.

ABRAHAM. Ruth! Come in, come in! Where's Jacob?

RUTH. (*Looking at MERCY tentatively, but then decides to throw it all out there:*) Jacob—Jacob left me.

ABRAHAM. What?

RUTH. He's gone. And he's not coming back.

Long pause as this sobering piece of news settles in.

ABRAHAM. Oh, Ruth . . .

MERCY. Perhaps I should go . . .

ABRAHAM. Mercy, I'll get Jeremiah next door—perhaps he can accompany you home, while I talk to . . .

RUTH. By all means, Abraham, walk her home.

ABRAHAM. You're certain?

RUTH. I've traveled this far by myself, haven't I? Anyway, I would relish just a bit more solitude right now, if you don't mind.

ABRAHAM. As soon as I get Mercy home, I will be right back.

RUTH. Whatever you feel is best.

Exit ABRAHAM and MERCY. Still repressing her emotions, RUTH gets down to business and places her suitcase on a table and starts unpacking her things. Before long she gets to a man's shirt. She is surprised to see it in there. RUTH pokes her finger through a hole in it, laughing sadly. She looks at it in her hands and, almost against her own will, she smells it with longing. She sits in a chair and looks around bewildered. She caresses the shirt softly and then places her head upon it, wrapping it like a pillow in her arms. Exhausted, she sleeps. There is a

*change in the lights indicating a change in the time and place.
JACOB appears. JACOB is dream-like, not dressed in period
specific clothing like the rest, but rather seems timeless. JACOB
takes away the luggage and then comes back to RUTH and
starts caressing her hair softly, as she continues to sleep softly.*

JACOB. What are you dreaming, my dear one? Are they the stressful
dreams of re-living trauma? Of deep seated fears revealing themselves? The dreams of the bizarre interactions of seemingly random
pieces of your life? Or are they fantasies of wishes certain never to
reveal themselves in this life, so they must find place in your rest?

RUTH. (*Stirring:*) Hmmm . . .

JACOB. Am I a dream?

RUTH. Jacob?

JACOB. Good morning, Love.

RUTH. Good morning.

JACOB. Sorry to interrupt your dreams.

RUTH. There's no vision that could replace you.

JACOB. Or am I made of the same substance as dreams?

RUTH. No. You're real.

JACOB. Am I?

RUTH. Yes. (*Taking his hands:*) See? Tangible.

JACOB. I love you, Ruth.

RUTH. I'm very lucky.

JACOB. What should we do today?

RUTH. Do? You have to manage the shop and I have to get the house
organized, not to mention mend this shirt of yours . . .

JACOB. All of that can wait, can't it? I'll just close the shop for today
and you can leave the house until tomorrow. As for my shirt . . .
(*JACOB takes the shirt:*) . . . we'll use it as our banner!

RUTH. Banner?

JACOB stands on the chair and starts waving the shirt like a flag.

JACOB. Our banner! It will be the symbol of our freedom, the flag of our revolution!

RUTH. And what is it exactly that we're revolting against?

JACOB. Against this whole rigid city. These stale people.

RUTH. Now, Jacob . . .

JACOB. I'm becoming cramped in that shop.

RUTH. Jacob, we've been here less than a year . . .

JACOB. And I'm already discontent with it.

RUTH. You'll settle into it.

JACOB. I don't want to settle into it. Let's go to the edge of the wilderness!

RUTH. We just got back from the edge of the wilderness.

JACOB. Not as far as I would have liked to have gone.

RUTH. Now listen, please, Jacob. We've finally got something steady here. There's stable commerce here, there's culture, respectable people, and wealth to be had. We're doing well, aren't we? We're happy, aren't we?

JACOB. You're happy.

RUTH looks at JACOB with a level gaze, having an internal debate. She then smiles.

RUTH. Then let's take the day off. We'll run away from our cares—for a day.

JACOB. Don't say that unless you mean it.

RUTH. I mean it.

JACOB strides over to RUTH and take her hands.

JACOB. Oh, Ruth, I love you! Just wait a minute, I'll get my hat!

Exit JACOB. An anxious fear comes over RUTH.

RUTH. So when do I wake up?

Blackout.

SCENE 2

ABRAHAM is asleep in a chair, snoring slightly, his head back, his hands up. RUTH enters and smiles affectionately at her brother. An idea then occurs to RUTH and she smiles mischievously. She enters again with a jar of molasses and a feather. She then pours the molasses into ABRAHAM's right hand, pondering the risks involved. She decides to go forward with it, and brings the feather to ABRAHAM's nose. ABRAHAM snorts, but there is no other effect. RUTH brushes the feather under his nose again. ABRAHAM brushes his face his left hand. Undaunted, RUTH pours the molasses in ABRAHAM's empty hand as well. She is about to bring the feather back to his nose when there is KNOCK, which wakes up ABRAHAM.

ABRAHAM. What in tarnation . . . (*He sees the molasses in his hands and then looks up at RUTH:*) You little sprite—you mischievous imp!

ABRAHAM stands and approaches RUTH with his molasses covered hands.

RUTH. Now, Abraham, remember how much you love me . . .

ABRAHAM. This isn't about love, this is about revenge!

RUTH. Don't you dare . . . (*Another KNOCK.*) The door . . .

ABRAHAM. They can wait . . .

A chase ensues, as ABRAHAM tries to cover RUTH with the molasses. There is squealing, yelling, and screaming. They exit momentarily. MERCY enters, with a basket.

MERCY. Abraham? Is everything all right? I heard . . .

RUTH and ABRAHAM re-enter, this time RUTH trying to fend ABRAHAM off with a mug of water.

RUTH. You wouldn't dare! You wouldn't dare!

ABRAHAM. Wouldn't I? Wouldn't I!

MERCY. Oh my!

Both of them laughing and shrieking, ABRAHAM smears the molasses on RUTH's face, and RUTH tries to fend him off with her hands, covering her hands with the molasses as well. They then both look up and see MERCY for the first time.

ABRAHAM. Mercy?

RUTH throws the water into ABRAHAM's face. Pause.

MERCY. (*With a smile.*) Good morning, Abraham.

ABRAHAM. (*Dripping.*) Good morning. I would offer my hand, but . . .

MERCY. That's quite all right.

RUTH. I'm going to clean up.

ABRAHAM. What about me?

RUTH. You can wait.

RUTH goes back to a pitcher of water and basin, with which she washes up.

MERCY. I apologize for barging in. I heard the screaming and I thought there was—trouble.

ABRAHAM. Not too far off, I reckon. So what can I do for you?

MERCY. I made some bread and I thought to bring some over for you. And some jam.

MERCY hands the basket to ABRAHAM.

ABRAHAM. Mercy, that's so kind . . .

MERCY. I thought you could use some cheering up . . . (*Glancing over at RUTH.*) . . . both of you.

RUTH. You needn't have gone to the trouble.

MERCY. Oh, it was my . . .

RUTH. No, really. You should just let us be.

ABRAHAM. Ruth . . .

RUTH. I am not the subject for charity.

MERCY. That was not my intent.

There is an awkward pause.

ABRAHAM. Mercy, I'm . . .

MERCY. It's all right. I have some other errands to do in town. Will I see you soon?

ABRAHAM. Count on it.

MERCY. (*A happy smile.*) Good. Then good morning to you both.

ABRAHAM. Thank you again.

Exit MERCY.

RUTH. A little forward, don't you think?

ABRAHAM. You should know that Mercy and I have—an understanding.

RUTH. I don't think that is wise, Abraham.

ABRAHAM. Do you have a quarrel with Mercy?

RUTH. She's trouble.

ABRAHAM. I don't like you flapping your tongue with gossips.

RUTH. Do you know that she's moving to Missouri?

ABRAHAM. Missouri?

RUTH. Honest truth. I heard it from her own sister.

ABRAHAM. Why hasn't she told me?

RUTH. Because there's more to the story. I imagine she's working up to it. She's going to Missouri because her prophet told her so.

ABRAHAM. Now I know you're talking nonsense.

RUTH. Joe Smith! He's had some sort of vision or revelation or something that Zion's in Missouri.

ABRAHAM. Mercy's not a Mormon.

RUTH. Not yet. But she was very intent upon those traveling missionaries the other day. Lapping every word, like a cat to cream. She's being discussing it with her family, but they'll have none of it. I suppose you're next.

ABRAHAM. Well, you can't blame a woman for being curious.

RUTH. This goes well beyond curiosity.

ABRAHAM. Well, I won't bring it up until she does.

RUTH. So that's it?

ABRAHAM. Her beliefs are her business. I didn't understand any of what those fellows were saying about gold scripture or angels, but I do understand that I love Mercy, and if that means following her to Missouri or back, then I'll do it.

RUTH. Don't be impulsive, Abraham.

ABRAHAM. I know my heart.

RUTH. You don't know anything! You don't think I loved Jacob? He was a true poet, his soul was expansive, but people like Jacob, like Miss Kimball, like this Joseph Smith—they capture people's hearts like other people capture butterflies.

ABRAHAM. My relationship with Mercy has nothing to do with your relationship with Jacob.

RUTH. Don't you think I know why you've fallen in love with that starry eyed religionist? You're filled with all that religion Ma and Pa put on us when we were children and then a girl like that comes along she knocks you off your scripture shod feet!

ABRAHAM. I know you have had it tough, Ruth, but I'm not going to let your bitterness poison my happiness.

RUTH. Take it from someone who's traveled down that road of idealistic dreams: it's all a sham. Settle down with someone sturdy, pretty enough, but reliable. Someone who will clean for you, cook for you, raise your children, and help build a life with you. I married the poet, I married that dreamer, and here I am, the product of a cooled passion.

ABRAHAM. Ruth . . .

RUTH. If she is going to abandon her whole life for these visions and prophets, do you think she'll value you anymore than she has her security? (*A KNOCK.*) Don't answer it.

With a defiant glance to RUTH, ABRAHAM *answers the door.* MERCY *enters.*

MERCY. I am sorry, but I left a book of mine in the basket . . .

RUTH *retrieves the book from the basket, before anyone can reach it. It's the Book of Mormon.*

RUTH. The Gold Bible. So this is the kind of tom foolery you're tracking to Missouri for, Miss Kimball?

MERCY. (*Looking at* ABRAHAM, *probing his feelings.*) I—I was hoping to tell you soon.

RUTH. The whole town's talking about how you've joined up with Ol' Joe Smith.

MERCY. Have some respect talking about the Prophet.

RUTH. The imposter deserves no respect from me, and if you're throwing in with his lot, you don't either.

ABRAHAM. Ruth, that is enough!

MERCY. It's all right . . .

ABRAHAM. I'm not going to let you go defenseless.

MERCY. I'm not defenseless.

ABRAHAM. You need an advocate.

MERCY. The Lord is my advocate.

RUTH. Oh, get off your mountain, Mercy.

ABRAHAM. What's that supposed to mean?

RUTH. That's the dream she's been spreading around lately. Her glorious vision from God! A big, white mountain.

ABRAHAM. Mercy?

MERCY. She is right. (*Turning her attention fully on* ABRAHAM:) In my dream, I saw myself climbing a mountain. It was rough terrain, and I was carrying a heavy load. I had to discard my precious things as I climbed up it—in the end I had to even discard my heart. But every time I sacrificed a new item, a new burst of energy came to me. And then I approached the summit . . .

RUTH. And then she saw the very face of God!

ABRAHAM. Truly?

MERCY. Almost. I knew I would see God, if I could only reach the top. But right before I was able to reach over the last hill, I woke up.

RUTH. Do you want to know what her mountain really is, Abraham? It is a snow covered wilderness. And she is a hermit, cutting herself from the rest of us. I have figured you out, Mercy.

MERCY. Have you.

RUTH. You're as human as the rest of us.

MERCY. I've never claimed otherwise.

RUTH. Oh, yes you have! You've established yourself as the Holy of Holies, the sole defender of righteousness! Trudging through that snow, a lonely wanderer in that frozen wasteland. I don't begrudge you your human faults. We all have those. It's your discontent with the rest of humanity that offends me.

ABRAHAM. So you want to drag her down with the rest of us?

RUTH. Why do you say that with such contempt? We're not the ones on the freezing peaks, dying of cold and loneliness.

ABRAHAM. And what do you have to offer?

RUTH. Company. The knowledge that you're never alone.

MERCY. The Lord offers the same thing.

RUTH. Well, I'm sorry if I don't find the company of invisible angels and Gods who don't show their faces very comforting.

MERCY. What do you think, Abraham?

RUTH. Don't fall for her pretty words.

ABRAHAM. You're the one waxing eloquent, Ruth, not her. Pray with me tonight, Ruth, we can discover the truth of this for ourselves.

RUTH. God doesn't talk to me.

MERCY. Or maybe you don't talk to God.

RUTH. Don't.

Exit RUTH.

ABRAHAM. I'll give you my answer tomorrow.

MERCY. I'm going—you do realize that? With or without you.

ABRAHAM. I know.

MERCY. I know it doesn't sound very loyal.

ABRAHAM. Loyal to who? Your ultimate loyalty does not belong to me.

MERCY kisses ABRAHAM softly.

MERCY. We will talk tomorrow.

Blackout.

SCENE 3

RUTH is asleep with her head on the table again. JACOB appears. RUTH awakes.

RUTH. Jacob . . .

JACOB. Hello, Ruth.

RUTH. Where have you been?

JACOB. Oh, it was wonderful! I went off into the woods—I was delightfully lost!

RUTH. What time is it? (*Looking out the window:*) Why, it can't be more than an hour before dawn!

JACOB. You should have seen the moon over the lake I found! Never have I felt more alive, more free . . .

RUTH. Did you even hear what I said?

JACOB. I have to take you there . . .

RUTH. Jacob!

JACOB. Ruth it's magic, it's a dream . . .

RUTH. Yes, a dream, it's all been nothing but a dream!

JACOB. A glorious vision . . .

RUTH. And I just woke up!

JACOB. Ruth, don't you understand?

RUTH. Only too clearly. I was worried to death over you.

JACOB. I didn't think about that . . .

RUTH. Then maybe you should start thinking. You're uprooted!

JACOB. Uprooted?

RUTH. Like a tree in a tornado, torn from all security, from all life giving earth. And some day you'll crash back to the ground, devastated!

JACOB. Don't do this . . .

RUTH. You didn't even go the shop, did you?

JACOB is silent.

RUTH (CONT'D). How do you expect we're going to survive? You think manna is just going to fall from heaven?!

JACOB. Oh, we'll do all right. But, Ruth, what's the point of living, if we have nothing to live for?

RUTH. I'm living for you. When are you going to start living for me?

JACOB. Ruth, where's the woman I married? The woman who understood what I needed from life?

RUTH. She grew up.

JACOB. Well, that's it, isn't it?

JACOB goes towards the door.

RUTH. Where are you going?

JACOB. To my imaginary kingdom.

RUTH. Where are you going!

JACOB. I'm leaving.

RUTH. When will you be back?

JACOB. I am not going to be back.

RUTH. What? Are you serious?

JACOB. Goodbye, Ruth. I loved you.

RUTH. No—no! Don't leave, Jacob. I am sorry, please, please, don't go . . .

JACOB. I can't give you the security you want. I'm no mountain.

RUTH. Jacob . . .

JACOB. Just a dream, that's all I've been.

RUTH. Wait.

JACOB. You want to be rooted? Find the rock to build on. I've been built on the sand.

RUTH. This didn't happen. You had left by now, you didn't say any of this.

JACOB. Is this another dream then? Or is it something else?

RUTH. No, I won't be fooled again!

JACOB. Do you have faith in your God?

RUTH. Another illusion, another vision, another foolish, selfish dream!

JACOB. Don't be confused. Don't be afraid. Understand what this is.

RUTH. I've already been abandoned.

JACOB. I Am calling for you, Ruth.

RUTH. Who are you?

JACOB. I Am calling.

JACOB disappears as ABRAHAM enters, gently shaking RUTH.

ABRAHAM. Ruth . . . Ruth . . .

RUTH. Ah! Abraham? I was dreaming?

ABRAHAM. You were on your feet—talking—I thought you were wide awake at first. Are you all right?

RUTH. What's wrong with me?

ABRAHAM. Ruth, I need to talk to you. I have made a decision.

RUTH. A decision? About what?

ABRAHAM. I'm going. With Mercy.

RUTH. What? No . . .

ABRAHAM. I'm leaving you the house. The farm. You can sell it, keep it, do whatever you wish with it.

RUTH. This is nonsense—you're tired. We'll talk about this in the morning.

ABRAHAM. It is morning. I've had a full night's rest and I know what I'm supposed to do. I love you, Ruth. I hope that you prosper.

RUTH. Your charity abounds. When Jacob abandoned me, he wasn't nearly so gracious. (*Hurt, ABRAHAM turns to leave.*) I'm sorry, Abraham. You have to understand—this is all very hard.

ABRAHAM. I know.

RUTH. Is it your love for her?

ABRAHAM. I do love her, but no.

RUTH. God—did He give you your answer?

ABRAHAM. He gave me a dream. A vision.

RUTH. I envy all of you your visions.

ABRAHAM. It was like Mercy's dream, I was climbing a white mountain. Like her, I was required to discard precious things, things I thought I needed, but in their place I filled the Eternal Need. As I reached the top, I realized why the mountain was white. It wasn't snow or ice at all.

RUTH. What was it then?

ABRAHAM. Lilies. The mountain was white because it was covered with lilies.

RUTH. Go away.

ABRAHAM. Ruth . . .

RUTH. Just go away!

ABRAHAM exits. RUTH is struggling with an onslaught of emotion. She sits on a chair, struggling against her tears when she sees Jacob's shirt, where it had been left underneath the table. She picks it up and places her finger through the hole. An unexpected emotion comes over her. The tears fade. She then kneels.

RUTH (CONT'D). God, have you abandoned me? Or . . . or . . . I don't want to be alone . . . I want . . . I want . . .

Suddenly RUTH has a sudden intake of breath and she looks up, the light becoming brighter. After the brightest point, the lights blackout.

THE END

Photo 1: Alex Barlow as Jacob, Bryn Dalton Randall as Ruth, Amos Omer as Abraham, and Jamie Denison as Mercy. Photo by Greg Deakins.

Photo 2: Amos Omer as Abraham, Bryn Dalton Randall as Ruth, and Jamie Denison as Mercy. Photo by Greg Deakins.

Photo 3: Amos Omer as Abraham and Bryn Dalton Randall as Ruth. Photo by Greg Deakins.

Photo 4: Alex Barlow as Jacob.
Photo by Greg Deakins.

Photo 5: Bryn Dalton as Ruth. Photo
by Greg Deakins.

Photo 6: Amos Omer as Abraham and
Jamie Denison as Mercy. Photo by
Greg Deakins.

The Prince's House

A Short Play

Production History

Zion Theatre Company premiered "The Prince's House" at the Provo Theatre as part of the set *Immortal Hearts and Other Short Plays* on July 16, 2010. It had the following cast and crew:

CAST

William: Jason Kelly Fullmer
Margaret: Rebecca Minson

CREW

Director: Mahonri Stewart

Dedicated to Christopher Clark:

A Shakespearean scholar, an extremely effective teacher, a brilliant direc-tor, a gifted playwright, a believer in ghosts and demons, a man of God.

FAUSTUS. Come, I think hell's a fable.

MEPHASTOPHILIS. Ay, think so still, till experience change thy mind.

— Christopher Marlowe, *Doctor Faustus*

The Prince's House

Enter WILLIAM.

WILLIAM. These dark demons, what do they that we fear?
    Why do we quake at mere shadow's contort?
    They bear no swords, they shake no awful spear
    Their whisperings we can always retort
    Even famed Legion at their frightful worst
    Were brought down without army's shield or blade
    Mere words sufficient to dispel accurs'd.
    From man's house draw out dark and shade
    They twist their shape, they darken mortal eyes
    Blaspheme holiness in their insolence.
    Just jesters are they in mere scarlet dyes
    Mere asses when rid of their opulence.
    Yet at their sight great men fall helplessly
    And courage is smothered in black, tainted sea.

Enter MARGARET.

WILLIAM (CONT'D). Ah, Margaret William's wife!

MARGARET. Aye, my lord—thy wife.

WILLIAM. Thou art no wife of mine, but thou wouldst be William's wife, if Prince William occupied his house.

MARGARET. You speak of houses?

WILLIAM. Aye, he kept his house swept, and it is now clean for his guests.

MARGARET. How dost thou, my lord?

WILLIAM. Well, well.

MARGARET. Well, my lord?

WILLIAM. Aye. Doth it not appear so?

MARGARET. I suppose.

WILLIAM. Then thou dost suppose upon appearances.

MARGARET. What else does one suppose on?

WILLIAM. I would not dare suppose. Do take care, Lady Margaret, lest thou art plagued with locusts.

MARGARET. I do not care for locusts, sir.

WILLIAM. Locusts are but playful bedfellows compared to what plagues me when I'm covered.

MARGARET. What ails thee, William?

WILLIAM. Women ail me, but that is not what I spoke of. Get thee hence, thou art like them.

MARGARET. Like who, sir?

WILLIAM. Do not call me sir when they are about, lest they tear thy hair for jealousy. Dost thou not see them? Or have they covered thy eyes in addition?

MARGARET. Lord William, art thou not well?

WILLIAM. Well! As well as one can be when his eyes are scaled and his mind is trembling. Yet it is not madness that afflicts me so, but a greater portion of sight.

MARGARET. If I mistake not, thou dost not need a doctor, but a priest.

WILLIAM. Oh, the father that we possess would be made an ass by such as these.

MARGARET. Then in the name of the Holy Christ, cast them out thyself. Thou art trembling.

WILLIAM. And why dost thou not tremble when they are about?

MARGARET. I do not see them, so in my ignorance I am safe.

WILLIAM. They would prefer thee to tremble, as in times past.

MARGARET. And yet I stand firm.

WILLIAM. Waves cast me about in their awful grip
Winds do tie me down in the midst of storms . . .

MARGARET. Lord, my lord, calm thyself . . .

WILLIAM. Salt chokes my aching throat on trembling ship . . .

MARGARET. Do not listen to them, Sir William, they are but wisps of dreams, no more dangerous than a woman's hair in thy face.

WILLIAM. While on the planks I spy their shadowed forms
I cry, I cry for them to tear my eyes . . .

MARGARET. William, be still!

WILLIAM. To still these bloody visions they decree
I cry, I cry for witlessness, not wise
That I sense them not, that I may not see . . .

MARGARET. O what madness should possess thee—what dark arts make thee so wild, but wise?

WILLIAM. Yet they tarry in their ceaseless track
I cry, I cry . . .

MARGARET. Cease, my lord!

WILLIAM. Lady Margaret? Dost thou dwell here in the woods?

MARGARET. We are not in the woods, but the chambers of our home.

WILLIAM. The woods, my lady. I see the forms of trees casting their clocks upon the ground.

MARGARET. If these be woods, my lord, then let them be holy.

WILLIAM. Nay, not holiness.

MARGARET. Aye, holy. Let Oberon and Titania be not full of mischief and malice here, but of holy prayers and angelic hymns.

WILLIAM. Nay, not so!

MARGARET. Art thou so easily troubled by holy words?

WILLIAM. No, for they are but fanciful fiction made to ease man's troubled mind; and man does not believe them even when they are uttered by his deceiving tongue.

MARGARET. Glory be to the God of Abraham. Glory be to the God of Isacc. Glory be to the God of Jacob, of Israel, and his mighty son Joseph!

WILLIAM. Cease, thou foolish woman, thou babbling tongue!

MARGARET. Glory be to the God of Saint Peter, of Saint James, of Saint John, of Saint Paul, the God of the Holy Martyrs . . .

WILLIAM. Cease!

MARGARET. I fear thee not.

WILLIAM. Thou dost love the man that we claim? We can kill him.

MARGARET. He was a righteous man, so he shall die in Christ.

WILLIAM. We can kill him!

MARGARET. Glory be to the God of Abraham, of Isaac, of Jacob, the God of . . .

WILLIAM. No praise me first!

MARGARET. What hast thou that I should praise thee, demon?

WILLIAM. We shall be first.

MARGARET. Thou shalt not even be last.

WILLIAM. Then praise him, praise William, praise the man you love!

MARGARET. He is secondary in my love. The primary is God. Glory be to the God of Abraham, the God of Isaac, the God of Israel . . .

WILLIAM. I cry, I cry that their power may dim
That I may be released from painful wrack . . .

MARGARET. . . . the God of his mighty son Joseph!

WILLIAM. My body withers, it is aching slim
Thus I drown in devil's madness and screams
And am but a doll in their plans and sche . . .

MARGARET. William, my love, listen to me. It is thy Margaret. Block out their voices, my lord. Thou hast thy own voice, a bell separate from their vile music. It rings true, rings with a will and a choice bestowed upon thee. They may inherit thy body, but thou dost still gain control of thy spirit.

WILLIAM. Margaret—no, Margaret, my spirit is broken, helpless on the floor.

MARGARET. Do not give way to madness.

WILLIAM. Margaret . . .

MARGARET. Ignore their rhymes and their chants and their rhythms. Thou dost not need be so bound. Their forms are frighteningly beautiful, their voices charmingly dark, but heed them not, and banish the fear that rules thy kingdom and ascend to thy throne!

WILLIAM. Throne? This mortal man has no throne! Earthly thrones are but vanities when the Prince of this World comes to inhabit.

MARGARET. Glory be to the God of Abraham . . .

WILLIAM. Thou whore of Christ, I shall kill thee!

MARGARET. Glory be to . . .

> WILLIAM *attacks* MARGARET. *A struggle ensues.*

WILLIAM. O, thou who was fearless, art now gripped by fear, its hand upon your throat!

MARGARET. Sir William, hear me! (*MARGARET scratches at* WILLIAM's *face and she breaks free.*) My lord, my husband, it is not thee that speaks thus, it is not thy heart that feels such, it is not thy hands that commit such! Hear my words and join the fray against Beezlebub's fools, that godly reason may take action!

WILLIAM. Sluttish woman, it shall require more than . . .

MARGARET. William, look upon thy wife! Look upon the woman who has so often waited upon thee with tenderness—draw strength from the God of our fathers!

WILLIAM. I care not for tenderness, nor for thee, nor for thy father's God!

MARGARET. But William doth care for me and our God. Glory be to the God of Saint Peter, the God of Saint James, the God of Saint John . . .

WILLIAM. Still thy filthy tongue!

MARGARET. In Christ's name be gone, demon!

WILLIAM screams and collapses on the floor. MARGARET goes to him.

WILLIAM. I—I am in my halls again.

MARGARET. True, my lord, the chambers of our home.

WILLIAM. I feel faint, my lady.

MARGARET. Then lay here in my lap and rest.

WILLIAM. I saw myself, or what appeared to be, as if I were a bird above my body, or a crab separated from his shell.

MARGARET. Yet thou art not bird, nor crab, but a body and a spirit married, as husband and wife. But thou shalt be able to distinguish from what was once blurred by evening's wood. There will be light to separate spirits into their separate spheres. But rest now, my lord, for not even locusts trouble thee now.

THE END

Rebecca Minson as Margaret and Jason Kelly Fullmer as William.

Rebecca Minson as Margaret and Jason Kelly Fullmer as William.

A Roof Overhead

A Contemporary Drama in Two Acts

Production History

A Roof Overhead premiered at the Little Brown Theatre in Springville, Utah, on April 16, 2012. It had the following cast and crew:

Binary Theatre Company then performed a revised version of *A Roof Overhead* in Tempe, Arizona, on February 3, 2012, with the following cast and crew:

CAST

Sam Forest: Noel Miller

Abish Fielding: Sarah D'Agostino

Daisy Fielding: Ivy Gambier

Maxwell Fielding: Peyton Scott Geery

Naomi Fielding: Kendra Schroeder

Joel Fielding: Seth Ephraim Scott

Tyrell Howard: Zachary Figures

Ashera: Victoria Murray

Jenny Pond: Alana Gordon

CREW

Director: Mahonri Stewart

Assistant Director: Bethanne Abramovich

Stage Manager: Jeremy Leung

Scenic Designer: Jessika Watson

Lighting Designer: Hailey Featherston

The play is dedicated to my family:
My parents,
My sisters,
My brothers.
Under their roof was genuine happiness,
Which I now realize is a rare thing indeed.

"Mock them, ridicule them in public, don't fall for the convention that we're far too polite to talk about religion. Religion is not off the table. Religion is not off limits. Religion makes specific claims about the universe, which need to be substantiated. They should be challenged and ridiculed with contempt."

— Richard Dawkins, *The Rally for Reason*

"It's natural to have questions—the acorn of honest inquiry has often sprouted and matured into a great oak of understanding. There are few members of the Church who, at one time or another, have not wrestled with serious or sensitive questions. One of the purposes of the Church is to nurture and cultivate the seed of faith—even in the sometimes sandy soil of doubt and uncertainty."

— Dieter F. Uchtdorf, "Come Join with Us"

"Joseph Smith was a fraud. A con artist. A brilliant story teller, but ultimately, a liar and an awful historian. His cult should not be taken seriously, should have no power over the world, and should not be knocking on my door unless they're willing to answer the most fundamental questions about their cult without finishing with 'Yeah, I don't know much about this.' The Book of Mormon though, is no more or less ridiculous or and more or less a work of fantasy, than the Bible, the Koran, the Torah and every other 'Holy' dogmatic fairy tale the World has had to endure, books that for centuries demanded the suspension of reason on pain of death. The Book of Mormon simply amplifies and emphasizes the stupidity and dangerous dogma of all organized religion."

— Jamie Smith, "The Mormon Delusion"

"The Lord created us in His image and likeness, and we are the image of the Lord, and He does good and all of us have this commandment at heart: do good and do not do evil. All of us. 'But, Father, this is not Catholic! He cannot do good.' Yes, he can . . . "The Lord has redeemed all of us, all of us, with the Blood of Christ: all of us, not just Catholics.

Everyone! 'Father, the atheists?' Even the atheists. Everyone!" . . . We must meet one another doing good. 'But I don't believe, Father, I am an atheist!' But do good: we will meet one another there."

— Pope Francis, Mass in Rome, March 2013

"There is something infantile in the presumption that somebody else has a responsibility to give your life meaning and point . . . The truly adult view, by contrast, is that our life is as meaningful, as full and as wonderful as we choose to make it. And we can make it very wonderful indeed."

— Richard Dawkins, *The God Delusion*

A Roof Overhead

Act One

SCENE 1

The play is set in a moderately sized home in an undetermined state in America, 2012. There is a set of stairs that go up into the top floor of the house, and also a door that leads to the basement. Another door leads into the kitchen. There are things which one might expect in a typical living room. The home shows a pleasant, if not somewhat predictable, scene. It is evidently a home of a religious family, in this case Latter-day Saints (Mormons). There are pictures of Jesus Christ, Mormon temples, perhaps even Joseph Smith and the current LDS First Presidency on the walls.

There is also a prominent picture, taken recently, of the Fielding family. In the portrait there is MAXWELL FIELDING, *the father. In his late forties or early fifties, Maxwell looks sufficiently conservative in his clothing, down even to the tie he is wearing, which has boring, vertical stripes in boring colors, with a traditional two button suit coat. His appearance is clean, organized and meticulous. Yet something in his soft smile does not allow for him to come off as cold, or even imposing. He has an evident gentleness, even though he does not have an evident charisma.*

Close to him is his wife, DAISY FIELDING. *Similar in age to* MAXWELL, *she also appears the part of the Mormon housewife, but there is something slightly off about Daisy that allows her to narrowly escape the stereotype that otherwise may have been imposed upon her. She doesn't quite wear her hair the same, or dress the same as other women her age, although she would never dare do anything too outrageous or out of step . . . she is definitely not out to get attention. But she does have marks of individuality placed in a graceful and subtle self-design.*

Standing close together in the picture, although not close enough to be mistaken as spouses, are NAOMI and JOEL FIELDING. In her twenties, NAOMI conforms to the basic standards of Mormon modesty, but she has some evident spunk in her style and demeanor, which is warm and welcoming rather than attention starved. Apt to wear soft Spring colors, light material which can breath and subtle touches of bright color, she has the rare talent of seeming warmly appealing, without resorting to being flagrantly modern or fashionable. Even when NAOMI is in her most formal attire, she seems absolutely relaxed and easy going. JOEL, on the other hand, looks more bookish and intellectual, even down to his spectacles. He has an endearing mixture of the awkward and the sophisticated in his appearance. He's not without fashion sense, when he decides to pay attention to it, but generally doesn't care enough to go at it full force. He has touches of the traditional in his clothing, but makes sure to offset that with a colorful tie or a three-to-four-button suit . . . just enough to set him apart from the ideal Mormon image, but never enough to estrange him in any significant way from the culture that he loves.

Finally, there is ABISH FIELDING, who is 15 years old. She is slightly offset from the rest of the family in the portrait. Her style also sets her apart. They may be subtle to a more secular eye, but they are enough to show noticeable signs of rebellion in her culture. A second set of ear rings. Maybe even a small nose stud. Net gloves. Very short hair, maybe spiky. A skirt that is a little too short. A top that doesn't have quite enough sleeve. And thus, in a glance, we see a family dynamic in the portrait, one that is fairly accurate to what the family actually experiences.

Enter MAXWELL and DAISY FIELDING.

MAXWELL. Half an hour late. Do you think we should be worried?

DAISY. We could call her—she did leave a cell number.

MAXWELL. I don't know. We don't want to seem overanxious, I suppose.

DAISY. You're nervous?

MAXWELL. Well, the money would help. Especially with Naomi wanting to serve a mission . . .

DAISY. She said she'd be willing to save up for it.

MAXWELL. We paid for Joel's.

DAISY. She knows things are tough right now.

MAXWELL. They're not that tough.

DAISY. Yes, they are. Max, I talked to Naomi last night—she said she'd be fine. She's not expecting . . .

MAXWELL. What we do for one child, we need to be willing to do for all the children.

DAISY. She knows you're willing. It's just . . .

MAXWELL. We've got to be fair to the kids, Daisy.

DAISY. Joel and Naomi aren't kids anymore . . .

MAXWELL. It's doable. If Daisy wants to save up money, she can put it to graduate school. That would be good. Joel is using student loans for his graduate studies, so it's even.

DAISY. (*With a smile*) Even. (*Beat.*) At your old job you could do these kind of things and we could make it work. But since the layoffs, well, you don't make the kind of salary you once did. You can't provide everything for them, Max. You don't have to prove yourself to us.

MAXWELL. It's not about proving anything. It's about being . . .

DAISY. . . . fair.

MAXWELL. (*Beat.*) Am I that predictable?

DAISY. After 23 years of marriage, I sure hope that I can predict you.

MAXWELL. While I can never seem to guess what you're thinking. You're stressed about this. Why?

DAISY. Oh, I'm fine. You know my nerves.

MAXWELL. What's wrong?

DAISY. I'm fine.

MAXWELL. Daisy . . .

DAISY. (*Imitating*) Max . . .

MAXWELL. Sweetheart, you know I don't let go of these things.

DAISY. You're going to let go of this one.

The doorbell rings.

DAISY (CONT'D). She's here.

For a moment MAXWELL and DAISY hesitate. They don't know why, they don't even notice enough to understand it, but they both flinch, as if they were ready to avoid a slap. The moment is brief, almost imperceptible, and then it is gone as fast as it came.

MAXWELL. Thank goodness.

MAXWELL and DAISY answer the door together, and the door opens to SAM FOREST. SAM is a woman of presence. She dresses in a put together, sophisticated style. She is attractive and stylish, but also gives off an intentional air of intellectualism and worldliness. When she speaks, it's with a crisp, East coast accent.

DAISY. Oh.

SAM. Mr. and Mrs. Fielding?

MAXWELL. Just call us Max and Daisy. We're plain people that way.

SAM. I'm Sam Forest. It's a pleasure to meet you.

DAISY. Come in, Sam. Is that short for Samantha?

SAM. No. It's just Sam.

DAISY. Well, it's lovely.

MAXWELL. Have a seat, Sam.

SAM. Thank you.

MAXWELL. Daisy?

DAISY. I'll be back in a moment.

DAISY exits into the kitchen.

MAXWELL. I'm guessing the East Coast?

SAM. The past several years, yes. Originally I'm from Georgia.

MAXWELL. Really?

SAM. I know . . .

Re-enter DAISY with a tray, on which are small plates with muffins and tall glasses of juice.

SAM (CONT'D). Oh, you really didn't have to . . .

DAISY. Please, Sam.

SAM. All right. (*Takes a juice amd muffin. Bites into the muffin:*) Oh. Yes, very, very good.

DAISY sits, pleased by the sincere reaction.

MAXWELL. You don't have a single trace of the accent.

SAM. Thank you.

DAISY. Which accent?

MAXWELL. Sam is from Georgia.

DAISY. Really?

SAM. I've been living in Boston for years until now.

DAISY. What brings you here?

SAM. Grad school.

MAXWELL. Oh, you're down at the University. Our son Joel is going to grad school there as well. He's going for a PhD in American History. Both he and our daughter Naomi have moved back in with us for a while to help them save money.

DAISY. Naomi is in a—transitional period. She's thinking about going to graduate school in anthropology.

MAXWELL. But she's also considering going on a mission, anyway, so grad school may be a ways off still.

SAM. Mission? A military thing? Or the peace corps?

MAXWELL. Oh, no—for our Church.

SAM. Of course. Sorry. So she'd be helping the poor in Zimbabwe or Brazil or something of that sort?

MAXWELL. Oh, they could send her anywhere. It'd most likely be a proselyting mission.

SAM. Oh, yes, uh, Mormons, right? Latter-day Saints? The boys with the white shirts and ties. I didn't know you let women do that, too.

DAISY. Yes, we "let" them . . .

SAM. Yes, uh, sorry. I must admit I don't know much about your Church except from things you read in the news and, well, *Angels in America.*

DAISY. What is that?

SAM. Er, a play. Well, two plays.

DAISY. Interesting. It involves the Church then? Do you think we'd like it?

SAM. Well, uhm . . .

DAISY. Oh, don't tell me it's like that dreadful *Big Love*?

SAM. Oh, I wouldn't say it's like *Big Love* at all. Well, not really . . .

DAISY. You know the Church doesn't practice polygamy anymore, right? Not since 1890. The things you see on TV about those people in Texas or Colorado City, that's really fringe, not a part of our Church . . .

SAM. Yeah, I knew that . . .

DAISY. We're more Mitt Romney than Warren Jeffs, if that makes sense.

SAM. Uhm, I'm sure if that really helps your . . .

DAISY. Or Harry Reid, if that's where you lean politically . . .

SAM. Really, I didn't mean to . . .

DAISY. Well, I guess this Angels play of yours couldn't be much worse than that *Book of Mormon* musical . . .

MAXWELL. Daisy. Ease off. Let the poor girl gather her wits, won't you?

DAISY. Oh. Yes. I'm sorry, Ms. Forest. Sometimes it's—well, when we lived in Utah, we didn't really have to worry about explaining ourselves all the time, you understand. I'm sure you understand, wanting to be understood on your own terms.

SAM. (*With a genuine smile.*) Certainly.

MAXWELL. Enough chit chat then. You're here to look at the basement apartment.

SAM. Yes. The apartment.

MAXWELL. Come on down.

> MAXWELL, DAISY, *and* SAM *head down the door to the basement. After they exit,* JOEL *enters the front door. He has grabbed the mail and, after throwing his school books, etc. onto the couch, he finds a Netflix envelope. ABISH comes down the stairs and grabs the Netflix out of his hands.*

ABISH. Oh, I got it!

JOEL. Hey!

> ABISH *rips open the envelope, takes out the* DVD.

ABISH. *Gettysburg*?

JOEL. Ever seen it?

ABISH. Another one of your history movies!

JOEL. Afraid so.

ABISH. I hate when it's your turn to pick.

JOEL. What would you prefer, an indy Ellen Page feature?

ABISH. Infinitely more!

JOEL. Come on, you know the Civil War's interesting . . .

ABISH. Okay, liked *Gone with the Wind* well enough. Just no more World War II films, please! Sure, *Schindler's List* or *The Great Escape*, I like those, but if there's one more movie about hiding Jewish refugees in the floorboards, or some opposition group trying to take down the entire Third Reich, or some swing dancers being cremated by the Hitler youth, I swear to you, I'm going to tear off my clothes and protest at the Chinese Theater!

JOEL. Okay, let's be a little more respectful, Abish.

ABISH. How could I forget? I'm talking to history's apostle . . .

JOEL *looks at his sister with more than a slight sense of exasperation.*

ABISH (CONT'D). Oh, come on, Joel, don't be so serious. See that is what's wrong with you! So serious! So sober! Our little Eeyore: "Thanks for noticing me."

JOEL. Look, you're being offensive, you know?

ABISH. Yeah.

JOEL. And that's where you like to be, in everyone's face, demanding attention . . .

ABISH. Ease off, Joel! Jeez, it's like every conversation I have with you turns into this big downer!

JOEL. There are certain things that deserve respect. Certain events . . .

ABISH. Yeah, yeah, you've told me all of this before. Heil History!

JOEL. Our worlds seem so big to us. But we're really small. In history's scope, we're just . . .

ABISH. You think I'm small?

JOEL. We're all small, and . . .

ABISH. I'm not small. I'm valuable.

JOEL. There are whole movements, whole revolutions—and we're, yes, we're small.

ABISH. Well, then "small" as I am, what does it matter if I listen to the establishment's versions of history?

Enter DAISY from the basement door.

DAISY. Okay, what's happening up here?

ABISH. Oh, were we bothering you, Mom? I didn't think anyone could over hear our *little* conversation.

DAISY. Look, your father and I are showing somebody the basement apartment. Could we not scare her into thinking that she'd be living below a family of cage fighters?

ABISH. Sure, Mom, sure, you got it. I was going out anyway. I was just going to crawl into a hole somewhere and brood upon the fact that I don't matter.

JOEL. Abish, really, that's not at all what I meant and you know it.

ABISH. You know, Joel, maybe you're right. Maybe these big battles and culture wars of yours are unstoppable forces that are just ready to swallow us whole. But, if that's the case, don't you think little people like us should just get out of the way and the let the storms, I don't know, pass us by? Otherwise, well, man, we're going to get crushed.

ABISH exits out the front door.

DAISY. What was that about, Joel?

JOEL. I think I just alienated Abish.

DAISY. Again?

JOEL. I'm sorry, Mama. I don't know why we don't get along. We were just talking about movies.

DAISY. She's young . . .

JOEL. No, that's what I usually say, but fifteen's not really that young. Not young at all really. And she's smart for her age. Really smart.

DAISY. Too smart?

JOEL. I don't think there's such a thing as too smart. Just not smart enough. And that's about how I feel right now.

DAISY. You're about as clever as they come, Joel.

JOEL. Clever? Yes, so clever. What an inadequate word that is . . .

DAISY. Oh, Joel, don't be hard on yourself. You can be so . . .

JOEL. . . . sober? Yeah. (*A sad, short laugh.*) "Thanks for noticing me . . ."

DAISY. That's not what I was going to say. Now, Joel . . .

JOEL. I have to look up some things at the library for a paper . . .

DAISY. That can wait, can't it? Hey, let's watch a movie tonight, the whole family. And, look, our new Netflix is here! When Naomi gets home we can make some popcorn and . . .

JOEL. You know, I'm not sure I'm in the mood. I've seen that movie before anyway.

Exit JOEL. MAXWELL and SAM enter from the basement.

MAXWELL. Everything all right up here?

DAISY. Sorry for that, Sam. I promise, you usually can't hear a peep from down there . . .

SAM. You should have heard the knock-out-drag-'em-outs that my family had. And the profanity! My family knew how to look the part of good Southern Baptists, but there were times when we made the Osbourne family look like the Cleavers. But, obviously, I've left all that behind.

DAISY. I'm not sure if I'm supposed to know who the Osbournes are but, really, we're usually such a tight knit . . .

SAM. You don't have to sell me anymore, Daisy. I've decided to take your offer, if that's still all right with you two.

MAXWELL. Well, yes—definitely, yes!

SAM. Good. I've been looking at a lot of places and—well, they've been kind of scary. I don't have a lot of money—living off student loans right now, you see, so I can go to school full time—and I don't know anybody in this city who would be my roommate. I was getting kind of scared until I came here and . . .

DAISY. Well, the Lord led you right to us then!

SAM. Uh, I'm not sure if—the Lord had much to do with it, but I'm glad I found you.

MAXWELL. Good. Very good! You want to drop by in the morning and we'll talk more in depth about the agreement and sign all the necessary papers.

SAM. Great. It's so great that it has its own bathroom, kitchen, but— you said the only entrance is from up here?

MAXWELL. Right.

An uncomfortable pause.

DAISY. I suppose we'll all just have to get nice and friendly.

SAM. Right. Friendly.

It is as if SAM is about to say something more, but she bites her tongue and smiles—not so genuinely this time. For a moment, DAISY and MAXWELL sense this.

DAISY. I hope that, well, that you can maybe join us for dinner every once in a while. We don't have to be strangers.

SAM. (*Pause.*) Well, you know, sure, why not? It will be so nice to have a roof over my head.

The tension releases, and everyone becomes more comfortable.

MAXWELL. Good, good! A roof overhead, huh? Well, I think you'll find that this place means a whole lot more to us than that!

MAXWELL opens the door for SAM.

MAXWELL (CONT'D). This is now your place, too, Sam.

SAM. (*She takes this graciously.*) Thank you, Max. Thank you, Daisy. I'll see you in the morning.

Exit SAM. MAXWELL and DAISY exchange happy grins.

MAXWELL. Well, sweetheart, there's our extra $400 a month!

Blackout.

SCENE 2

Enter NAOMI from the stairs, in her pajamas. She goes through the mail and sees a wedding invitation. She opens it and smiles warmly, but then becomes slightly depressed. She goes over to her purse and takes out a photo of her and her boyfriend Tyrell. She compares the pictures, trying to imagine her and Tyrell in a wedding dress and a Tux. This depresses her and she tears up and throws away the wedding invitation. She exits into the kitchen. Enter SAM, JOEL, DAISY, and ABISH from the front door, carrying moving boxes, etc.

SAM. Thanks again. I couldn't have done this by myself.

DAISY. If Max hadn't had work, he would have loved to help, too. And, of course, Abish has school.

JOEL. Where's Naomi?

DAISY. She was out late last night. I didn't have the heart to wake her.

JOEL. Out late? With whom?

DAISY. Uh, I don't think that's my business to tell . . .

JOEL. Wait. Does Naomi have a boyfriend?

DAISY. As I said, not my business to . . .

JOEL. Why hasn't she told me?

SAM. Are you two close?

DAISY. Naomi and Joel have been close since they were very small. Attending each other's birthday parties, hanging out with each other's friends . . .

SAM. That's nice. My brothers and I were constantly at each other.

Enter NAOMI with a bowl of cereal.

NAOMI. Oh.

DAISY. Naomi, put on some clothes . . .

NAOMI. What?

ABISH. Mom, chill. She's perfectly modest.

NAOMI sits on a couch and digs into her cereal.

DAISY. They're her PJs, honey.

ABISH. Mom, if Sam is going to live here, she may see sights much more revealing than Naomi's PJs.

SAM. (*Unconsciously looking at JOEL*). I sure hope so.

Everyone pauses, slightly shocked. ABISH lets out a muffled laugh.

SAM (CONT'D). Uhm, I said that out loud, didn't I? (*Pause.*) I—I'm going to take this one down stairs.

Bright red with embarrassment, SAM ducks her head behind a box and exits downstairs.

DAISY. I think it's time for you to move out again, Joel.

ABISH. As long as he doesn't move downstairs . . .

DAISY. Abish!

JOEL. I think I have a box to move.

DAISY. Not alone down there, you're not!

JOEL and NAOMI open the door downstairs to find that SAM has come back up. JOEL and SAM stop at each other awkwardly.

SAM. I didn't mean for what I said to come out like that.

JOEL. I know.

SAM. Not that there would be anything wrong with that! I'm sure you would look great if I caught you in a towel.

DAISY. Nobody will be catching anybody in towels!

SAM. No! Of course not. What I meant was . . . well, I'm surprised that slipped out. Usually I'm pretty guarded and—well, not that there is anything to guard! I mean I'll be living downstairs and you'll be living upstairs and we'll be so close we'll be practically family. It would be like incest!

DAISY. There will be no incest either!

NAOMI. I don't know, they might be a good couple, Mom. No offense, though, Sam, we'd have to convert your first.

SAM. Excuse me?

NAOMI. Oh, don't take me seriously, Sam. Just playing with you.

DAISY. But she's right. Mormons don't generally marry outside of the . . .

NAOMI. Mom, I said I was just playing.

DAISY. But it's true.

ABISH. Mom!

JOEL. I'm not marrying Sam, nor will I be prancing around downstairs in a bathrobe, so drop it. Nothing to worry about.

Tense pause.

SAM. Is that the last box? I'll take it down.

Exit SAM.

ABISH. Well, we made a great first impression.

NAOMI. I shouldn't have said that. That was stupid.

DAISY. It was true. She has to understand that although Joel and she are similar ages, there won't be any . . .

JOEL. Mom.

NAOMI. It wasn't kind.

DAISY. And what were all those comments about towels and incest? I told your father that bringing in a non-member wasn't a good idea . . .

ABISH. Mom, there's nothing wrong with her not being Mormon!

Pause.

DAISY. Of course there isn't. You're right.

Pause.

JOEL. Maybe one of us should talk to her.

NAOMI. I will.

DAISY. I think that would be best. Come on, you two, you've been a great help today. I'll treat you to some IHOP.

JOEL. Mom, you don't have to resort to pancakes . . .

DAISY. You've never said no to breakfast food in the afternoon.

JOEL. All right. Thanks. Some comfort food sounds great.

DAISY. And, Naomi . . . give Sam my apologies.

Exit DAISY, ABISH, and JOEL. Enter SAM.

SAM. I'm sorry, I . . . where'd your family go?

NAOMI. A ritualistic ceremony involving maple syrup.

SAM. What?

NAOMI. I'm Naomi. I didn't properly introduce myself.

SAM. Sam.

SAM and NAOMI shake hands. NAOMI stops short for a moment, a peculiar expression crossing her face. She looks at the handshake and then at SAM. She then drops SAM's hand, embarrassed.

SAM (CONT'D). Is everything all right?

NAOMI. Excuse me. Déjà vu.

SAM. What do you mean?

NAOMI. It's not important. Look, my Mom and Joel were so sorry about how that went. Me too. Sometimes awkward things get said that nobody means and . . .

SAM. What was the déjà vu?

NAOMI. No, really, it's nothing.

SAM. I can tell when people are lying to me to be polite. Spit it out.

NAOMI. No, it's—really, never mind, it's creepy.

SAM. Creepy?

NAOMI. People think it's creepy.

SAM. They think what is creepy?

NAOMI. I—I have dreams.

SAM. Well, what's wrong with that? We all have dreams, don't we? Me, I'm studying journalism and communications. I want to be a social and political writer.

NAOMI. No. Like night time dreams. *Dreams.* They're vivid and meaningful, with this spiritual, overpowering feeling and—and sometimes I dream something and—and it comes true.

SAM. I—hm. Sorry, but I think I'm going back downstairs.

NAOMI. I told you it was creepy. I usually don't tell people . . .

SAM. Then why are you telling me this?

NAOMI. To explain that moment.

SAM. Well, you didn't do a very good job. I'm still confused.

NAOMI. I've dreamed that moment before . . .

SAM. Handshakes are pretty common things . . .

NAOMI. I dreamed about you. I'm surprised that I didn't recognize you right away. I had a dream once, a very short, but very vivid dream where I was shaking some one's hand. She looked a lot like you, I guess. I had forgotten all about it until I was—I was even wearing pajamas. I know, I know, it sounds a little mystic . . .

SAM. Ya think?

NAOMI. It got weird there, and, really, it just got weird here, too, so—so sorry for all of it.

SAM. Okay. Thanks.

NAOMI. Good. Good.

SAM. But, just so you know, I don't believe it. The dream thing.

NAOMI. I understand.

SAM. I mean, not at all. Not that I think you're lying. But it was just a dream and maybe I reminded you of it, but it was just a dream. Prophecy and that sort of mystic whatever . . . Well, I'm sure that's great for you, but I'm an atheist.

NAOMI. Totally cool. I shouldn't have told you. I stopped myself, but then you just kind of pushed me into it.

SAM. Okay, all right. We'll just forget it then. And, okay, how can I say this right? No offense, but, well, I'm never going to join your Church, you understand that, right?

NAOMI. My church? Oh, yeah, really, I was just joking about that . . .

SAM. But you understand that? I'm never going to join your Church. I'm never going to join any Church. I just want that out in the open so there aren't any misunderstandings or hurt feelings.

NAOMI. Oh, yeah, sure. Uhm . . .

SAM. I left my faith for a reason. I had a friend—Tyler. He was a member of the congregation I attended. I loved him dearly. He was gay. Our minister said that God could cure him, that God had never intended him to be that way, so God would open a way for him to be free.

NAOMI. Sam, just so you know, I really don't consider myself homophobic . . .

SAM. (*Didn't really hear* NAOMI.) Tyler tried and tried, he believed so much—so much! I've never met anyone who loved Jesus like he did. Which made his failure to live up to these impossible odds all that much more devastating for him. After they found Tyler dead—I couldn't handle it. And then my parents—they had the gall to warn me about the hell they believed Tyler was in. Not just because he was a homosexual, but also because he had committed suicide. I couldn't forgive my parents for that. It was faith like theirs, words like theirs that killed Tyler.

NAOMI. Sam, I don't believe in that kind of hell your parents described—a lot of Mormons don't. God has a good place for all of his children, differing kingdoms of glory which are a more just compensation for the varying degrees of goodness in the world. Your friend Tyler, even if by chance he's not in the highest kingdom of glory, he's still qualified for . . .

SAM. Tyler deserved the highest. He deserved the best of heaven. That's why I decided then that if God wasn't as anxious to love Tyler as Tyler was enraptured in loving God then that must mean that God simply wasn't there, for Tyler was the most beautiful human being I ever encountered.

NAOMI. Okay. Understood.

SAM. All right. Then we're good?

NAOMI. Good. Perfectly good.

SAM. Then it's nice to meet you, Naomi.

> *They shake hands, look down at the shake, realizing the context of the conversation, and then drop their hands awkwardly.*

NAOMI. You'll have to come up for dinner sometime.

SAM. We'll see.

> SAM *exits upstairs and* NAOMI *exits downstairs. Lights dim.*

SCENE 3

It's late, perhaps 3 AM-ish. The house is quiet. Enter ABISH and her friend JENNY POND. They are doing their best to be as silent as possible. Before they get to the stairs going up to her room, however, SAM enters through the downstairs door. SAM, upon seeing ABISH and JENNY, gives out a shriek. ABISH covers SAM's mouth.

ABISH. Sh!

SAM. Abish?

ABISH. Don't blow my cover!

SAM. Coming in or going out?

ABISH. Are you kidding? Coming in.

SAM. Well, I'm going out.

ABISH. Really?

SAM. Yeah. Meeting someone.

ABISH. Well, yeah, we were just with a couple of guys.

SAM. Cute?

JENNY. Very. Hi, you must be Sam. I'm Jenny Pond.

SAM. Nice to meet you, Jenny. I hope you girls had fun with the boys. Good night.

ABISH. Really? So you're not going to tell my parents?

SAM. Of course not. I remember what it was like at your age. But I am surprised that they wouldn't wait up for you on a school night.

ABISH. Oh, they thought I went to bed at 10.

SAM. Gotcha. So . . . were you . . . ?

ABISH. Was I what?

SAM. Having sex?

ABISH. Me? No!

JENNY. (*Laughs.*) Oh, you don't know our little Abish very well, do you?

SAM. Oh, yeah, your family is a little puritanical that way.

ABISH. Well, it's not like we were just holding hands watching *Cinderella* or anything. Give me *some* credit.

JENNY. What? Hey, I missed that part . . .

ABISH. You missed a lot of things tonight, Jenny.

JENNY. Okay, what base?

ABISH. Oh, get your mind out of the gutter, Jenny. You and Gordon were having your own kind of fun, but you know that I have certain standards.

JENNY. Your standards, your standards, always talking about your standards . . .

ABISH. Not that, well, not that I wouldn't want to sometimes, you know. I . . . okay, look at me, I never get embarrassed . . .

SAM. Please. Look, I of all people am not going to judge you.

ABISH. Well, I think I need to be more careful sometimes. With how he and I are going, well, it would just take a little more, just a few more barriers jumped over and—boom, game over, man.

SAM. Game over? Or just the beginning?

JENNY. Ooo, this is going somewhere interesting. I'm liking this Sam lady. But I'd better get going, girl. Sometimes my parents have a sixth sense about this kind of thing. Take care, okay?

ABISH. Okay, Jenny.

JENNY. And I want a full report on what's happening between you and Wally, okay? Tomorrow?

ABISH. Tomorrow.

JENNY. Every detail!

ABISH. Whatever, Jenny.

JENNY. It'll be totes wicked, you'll see. Nice to meet you, Sam.

SAM. Right back at you, Jenny.

JENNY. Every juicy detail!

Exit JENNY out of the front door.

SAM. So what's so wrong with having a little fun with your boyfriend?

ABISH. Look, I really don't expect you to understand our Church, and that's okay, but I—I don't know why I'm talking about this with you.

SAM. Why not? I don't know who else under this roof you would talk about it with. Have your parents even tried to have the sex talk with you?

ABISH. My Mom tried once. She went off about Adam and Eve and something about fruit and pollen and flowers and bouncy, little clouds.

SAM. You're kidding me.

ABISH. Then she said, "I'm glad we did this," and that was it.

SAM. Wow.

ABISH. Yeah. I learned more from watching network television than I did during our entire "sex talk."

SAM. So what's holding you back?

ABISH. (*A "well, duh," tone.*) Uh, my *religion.*

SAM. Is it *your* religion?

ABISH. Of course it is.

SAM. I'm not so sure about that.

ABISH. Look . . .

SAM. Hear me out for just a second. I've been watching you, Abish. Sure, I'm not up here often, but it doesn't take long to size you up.

ABISH. You don't know me, Sam.

SAM. Sure I do. I was just like you. Black sheep of the family, but still trying to find a middle way between my independence and my parent's religion.

ABISH. Look, I don't know how it was for you, but I'm not reduced that easily.

SAM. Reduced? No, you're trying to expand! You've got all these passionate feelings and skyrocketing thoughts and then these well-meaning, religious nuts try to put on all these restrictions and boundaries and blinders on you, and all you're trying to do is stretch into yourself, but you can't even do that! And, believe me, Abish, there's nothing wrong with finding yourself at your age. It's what angsty teenagers are supposed to do.

ABISH. I'm not angsty.

SAM *laughs good naturedly.*

ABISH. I'm not!

SAM. I didn't think I was either. But I'm glad I was, because it's what helped me finally break away.

ABISH. I'm not trying to break away. I'm just trying to be myself.

SAM. Sorry to break it to you, hon, but if you ever want to be yourself, breaking away is exactly what you'll have to do.

ABISH. And how do you know that being religious isn't exactly who I am?

SAM. Your parents? Yeah, completely. Joel and Naomi? Religion fits them like a glove. You? No, not even a god could keep you bottled up, Abish. You like the wind on your face too much.

ABISH. That's not how others see me.

SAM. What do you mean?

ABISH. At school. I try to fit in, not make a fuss, but they know I'm Mormon. Most people are cool about it, but there's this one group of kids . . .

SAM. Are you being bullied?

ABISH. Not the way you're thinking about it. At least, well, not physically. They're actually the really smart kids. Honors and AP students, the real competitive sort, you know. The kind of kids I usually really get along with, but—well, there's this group of them that are pretty intense about what they believe. Always picking a verbal fight with those of us who are conspicuously religious, always making fun of us. Saying we're what's wrong with the world, that the world would be better off with religion—without us. That sort of thing.

SAM. Abish, I—I see you as something so much more than any belief or creed. I see—well, if I believed in angels, I could see you rise with your trumpet and bless the whole world. Don't let anyone, not even me, tell you what your limits are. Just fly, girl, fly.

ABISH. Sam, that's really nice. Thanks.

SAM. I mean every word.

ABISH. I—I'm pretty tired.

SAM. Sure.

> ABISH *is about to go upstairs, when she stops.*

ABISH. Sam?

SAM. Yeah?

ABISH. I'm not saying you're right. I guess I really don't know whether I'm, like, religious or not, you know . . . but it's nice hearing another perspective. Refreshing, you know what I mean?

SAM. I'm just downstairs. Come talk anytime.

ABISH. Thanks.

> ABISH *exits upstairs.* SAM *heads to the front door, but not before* JOEL *enters from the kitchen, a bowl of cereal in hand.*

JOEL. I'm glad that Abish has such an inspiring role model to look up to now.

SAM. Joel! What are you doing up?

JOEL. My family has the strange habit of craving cold cereal at odd times in the night. We've had many a family discussion this way, not to mention the fact that we've kept Kellogg's in business during the recession.

SAM. I'm just on my way out the door.

JOEL. Hold it. You're not getting away that easy.

SAM. Really, I've got someone waiting for me and I've really had a hard time making connections lately so I don't want to screw this up.

JOEL. Yeah, I heard that part. I heard the whole discussion, actually. I had to crunch my Corn Chex pretty softly.

SAM. Well, I hope you're not going to turn the poor girl in. She's a teenager, it's pretty normal.

JOEL. Oh, it's not her I'm thinking about turning in. It's you.

Pause.

SAM. I just told her how I experienced it myself.

JOEL. Abish isn't you. Get that through your head. Whatever choices you made, she's not just pre-destined to make the same ones, okay?

SAM. I think you're misunderstanding me . . .

JOEL. We've respected your privacy. Respect ours.

SAM. I'm just showing concern for Abish. That's all, Joel. She can do whatever she wants.

JOEL. Thanks for the concern, but you're not a part of our family.

SAM. You're completely misconstruing me, Joel. Really, I'm just . . .

JOEL. Just consider it a warning, okay? Abish—well, she and I don't always see eye to eye. But I'm her big brother. I'm going to watch out for her. And I'd try to be a little more grateful. This family is providing a roof over your head.

SAM. But, as you're setting out so clearly, you're not providing me a home. Your family is getting your money from me. So leave me the hell alone.

Exit SAM. JOEL *exits into the kitchen. Blackout.*

SCENE 4

Enter MAX, ABISH, *and* DAISY, *in the middle of an argument.*

MAXWELL. I think we've been more than patient with you, Abish. You've felt the need to express yourself, to be an individual, we understand that, but this is different, this is important . . .

ABISH. Look, I'm going. I'll see you guys later, okay?

DAISY. You're not going anywhere, young lady. Sit down.

ABISH. I'm not sitting down.

MAXWELL. Then stand up. Sit down, stand up, I don't care! But, please, sweetheart, listen . . .

ABISH. It doesn't matter—it just doesn't matter . . .

DAISY. It certainly does matter! If there's anything that matters, it's the Gospel.

ABISH. What that man teaches isn't the Gospel!

MAXWELL. No, maybe not, but seminary should be an important part of your life. And Brother Jensen has to wake up just as early to teach you kids before school and he deserves a little support . . .

ABISH. A little support? Let me tell you what he told us last week. The lesson was on the priesthood, right? Sure, I can go with that. But, totally off topic, he goes off about the . . . the subservience of women . . .

MAXWELL. Subservience? I'm sure he didn't say it like that.

ABISH. Subservience, or whatever word he said—but he said that women still carried the curse of Eve and that's why men had the authority to rule over women! He said that women were meant to be mothers and only mothers and that we would be barefoot and pregnant for the rest of eternity, a baby intelligences machine! A spirit making robot!

MAXWELL. Now I'm sure he didn't say that!

ABISH. He might as well have.

MAXWELL. Daisy—what can you tell her, Daisy?

DAISY. Sweetheart . . . sweetheart . . . I . . .

ABISH. Mom, really, I don't want to go. It—it really hurts me to go. I don't feel the Spirit. I just feel dead. Worthless.

Pause.

DAISY. Well don't go then.

ABISH AND MAXWELL. What?

DAISY. Don't go.

MAXWELL. Daisy, I know that neither of us condone that kind of sexist thinking—especially from someone who's teaching our kids—but she has to go to seminary.

DAISY. No. She doesn't. Her mother gives her permission not to.

MAXWELL. Daisy, I think we need to talk about this . . .

DAISY. I'll get up early with her and we'll study the scriptures together. What do you think, Abish? Deal?

ABISH. Deal!

ABISH nearly bowls DAISY over with a huge hug.

DAISY. But every morning. 6 am.

ABISH. Every morning, I promise.

MAXWELL. Abish, now let's . . .

ABISH. Thanks for your support, Dad.

ABISH kisses her father on the cheek and exits up the stairs.

DAISY. Now, Max . . .

MAXWELL. So that's it? A unilateral decision? Is that your answer to chauvinism? If the man's not the leader in the home, then it transfers automatically to the woman?

DAISY. I know, Max, I know . . .

MAXWELL. We need to support Church programs . . .

DAISY. Max, it's not like a seminary teacher is her Bishop or has any real priesthood authority over her . . .

MAXWELL. I've met my share of seminary whackos and their weird folk doctrines, but still, she'd be studying the scriptures every morning at least and . . .

DAISY. She will be studying the scriptures still. With me.

MAXWELL. We study the scriptures already as a family . . .

DAISY. We haven't had family scripture study since Naomi moved out the first time . . .

MAXWELL. Well, maybe we should start again then, but that doesn't replace seminary. Naomi and Joel loved seminary. They talked all the time about how that's where they really felt like they started independently growing a testimony . . .

DAISY. Abish is very different than Joel and Naomi.

MAXWELL. Yes, which is why she needs seminary even more!

DAISY. Maxwell, look, I agree with you. Kids should go to seminary. It exposes them to the scriptures. But I think it's vital that we know who is teaching our child and how. And Brother Jensen is harming Abish's already fragile testimony.

MAXWELL. We can—we can talk to her about that . . .

DAISY. Or we can take her from harm's way. Let her learn the Gospel under our own roof, in our own home, the way we want her taught. Consider it my version of religious home school.

Enter NAOMI *from the stairs.* MAXWELL *and* DAISY *let the conversation drop.* NAOMI *notes the tension.*

NAOMI. You're fighting, aren't you?

DAISY. Everything's fine, sweetheart.

NAOMI. It's really awkward to be around when you're fighting.

MAXWELL. Really, Naomi, we're done. You off?

NAOMI. Yeah, I have a Presidency meeting.

MAXWELL. Do you like your new Relief Society President?

NAOMI. Sure.

DAISY. Sure?

NAOMI. Yeah, sure.

MAXWELL. What do you think, Daisy?

DAISY. Not a good sign.

NAOMI. I said sure. I like her fine.

DAISY. "Sure."

MAXWELL. "I like her fine."

NAOMI. Do you want me to gush?

MAXWELL. You usually do.

DAISY. People are kind of your thing. You like to gush about them.

MAXWELL. Unless they're . . .

DAISY. . . . judgmental . . .

MAXWELL. . . . uncompassionate . . .

DAISY. . . . or hypocritical.

NAOMI. I've never said anything like that about anybody.

DAISY. No, you haven't. You just don't gush.

MAXWELL. You "like them fine."

NAOMI. I don't like it when you guys tag team.

MAXWELL. Why don't you like her?

NAOMI. I like her.

MAXWELL. Okay. Why do you "like her fine?"

NAOMI. I think I need an apartment again.

DAISY. I've been saying that for a while.

MAXWELL. She needs to save her money.

DAISY. For her mission?

MAXWELL. For graduate school. I'm taking care of her mission.

NAOMI. Papa, you really don't have to . . .

MAXWELL. It's decided.

DAISY. Is it? I still think things mean more when a person works for them.

MAXWELL. I thought this was decided.

DAISY. I thought we were still in negotiations.

NAOMI. Yeah, Mom and I were talking . . .

MAXWELL. I know. But we paid for Joel's and we'll pay for yours.

NAOMI. It was different for Joel.

MAXWELL. Why?

NAOMI. Well, it's expected for guys, but . . .

MAXWELL. You're a girl?

NAOMI. It's a choice for me . . .

MAXWELL. It was a choice for Joel.

NAOMI. That's nice to say, Papa, but . . .

MAXWELL. Do you want to go?

NAOMI. (*Beat.*) Yes. (*Beat.*) Very much. (*Beat.*) Which is why I'm willing to pay for it.

MAXWELL. We paid for Joel, we'll pay for you. It's only . . .

ALL. . . . fair.

MAXWELL. Look, Naomi, sweetheart, you know, well, I'm really proud of what you've done in your life. I want to . . .

NAOMI. I've met someone.

MAXWELL. What?

NAOMI. A boy. Well, a guy. A man.

MAXWELL. Are you two serious?

NAOMI. Yeah. Pretty serious. I'm not sure if you'd . . .

MAXWELL. Yes?

NAOMI. . . . approve.

DAISY. Why not? Is he a member of the Church?

NAOMI. Yes. A convert.

MAXWELL. My mother was a convert, too.

NAOMI. Oh, I know. I wasn't saying that—that's not why . . .

DAISY. Does he treat you well?

NAOMI. I've never been treated better.

MAXWELL. I'm not seeing the problem here then.

NAOMI. He's African-American.

A long pause.

MAXWELL. And why do you think we would care about that?

NAOMI. I don't know. We've never talked about that sort of thing much in the family . . .

MAXWELL. And you think that means we might be racist?

NAOMI. I know a long time ago certain leaders in the Church said things about marrying other, well, other—cultures.

MAXWELL. Absolutely ridiculous.

NAOMI. Well, they said that certain cultures sometimes didn't mix well and . . .

MAXWELL. They definitely don't say that now. You can get that out of your head. Why, President Hinckley gave that whole talk against racism in General Conference several years ago. And, if you haven't noticed, the Church has been broadcasting a clear message in the "I'm a Mormon" commercials . . .

NAOMI. I heard how grandpa Frank used to talk about—well, the words he would use . . .

MAXWELL. My father was a product of his generation. That doesn't mean I would ever condone . . .

NAOMI. I'm glad to hear it. (*A broad grin replaces her stress.*) Really, really glad.

> Pause. Then NAOMI *gives her father an impulsive hug.* MAX-WELL *reciprocates warmly.*

NAOMI (CONT'D). Dad, my bishop says that if I get an offer, I should marry him as soon as possible.

MAXWELL. Does he now?

NAOMI. But I—I still want to go on a mission. Maybe that's why I—I don't know, I feel kind of guilty about all of it . . .

MAXWELL. Guilty?

NAOMI. I mean why should I take your money when I can . . .

MAXWELL. (*Good humoredly:*) . . . take his?

NAOMI. No! I mean—you know as well as I do that women are encouraged in Church to . . . to . . .

DAISY. (*With the slightest bit of acid in her voice:*) Get married as soon as you can and have lots of babies.

NAOMI. Pretty much.

> Both DAISY *and* NAOMI *look to* MAXWELL. *He studies* NAOMI *thoughtfully.*

MAXWELL. Well, obviously you'll eventually want to start a family . . .

> Pause.

NAOMI. Eventually?

> Pause.

MAXWELL. Your Bishop isn't encouraging about your mission?

NAOMI. Well, he's—he's kind of a typical Singles Ward Bishop, you know. He sees it as his life's mission to get us all married off and into the moral safety of full-fledged family wards.

MAXWELL. Do you love Tyrell?

NAOMI. I think so.

DAISY. You've been dating for how long?

NAOMI. Three months—but they've been an exceptionally good three months.

MAXWELL. And if you didn't go on your mission you think you might marry him?

NAOMI. With a little more time, I think I would.

DAISY. There's a lot of "I thinks" in here.

NAOMI. But I've always wanted to go on a mission.

MAXWELL. I know you have.

Pause. MAXWELL *looks at his daughter searchingly and then closes his eyes and sighs.*

MAXWELL (CONT'D). Do you want me to tell you what you should do?

NAOMI. That would be nice.

MAXWELL. Some sound, sage, unerring advice?

NAOMI. Isn't that what you're for?

MAXWELL. Well, here it is then. First, ignore what your Bishop told you.

DAISY. Careful, Maxwell . . .

NAOMI. But I thought a Bishop had right to receive revelation for his . . .

MAXWELL. Yes, I believe that, in special circumstances, especially when it has to do with issues that involve your ward. But this is your personal life. The Brethren say the family trumps even the Church, and this is about your future family.

NAOMI. I know, but . . .

MAXWELL. Let me make this clear, sweetheart. Once you're out of his ward, your decisions have no consequence or bearing upon his life. You may never see him again. He does not have to live with this decision, a decision that could alter the course of the rest of your life. But you have to live with it.

NAOMI. So you're saying I should go on a mission?

MAXWELL. You want advice? Here's my advice. Don't let your Bishop, or me, or any man, or any woman, make this decision for you. It's your personal life, so it deserves personal revelation.

NAOMI. I'm not sure that's what I wanted to hear.

MAXWELL. Don't be lazy.

NAOMI. Lazy?

MAXWELL. A "slothful servant" needs to be "commanded in all things," right? You know how big this decision is and you don't want to mess it up. So you want to shift the responsibility to someone else, anyone else.

NAOMI. I'm scared, Papa.

MAXWELL. Darling, since you were a little child, you were special. It seems like you had such a strong connection to your Heavenly Father. I've felt the Spirit many, many times, but you—you experienced it in a way I've never seen. Of all times, why would you try to trust me or your Bishop or anyone else over the Voice of the Lord that has been with you since childhood?

NAOMI. Thank you, Papa. Thank you, Mama.

DAISY. I'm not sure how much I really contributed to this conversation.

NAOMI. No, no, you're both amazing. But I've really got to go to that meeting.

DAISY. Yes, I'm sure your Relief Society President doesn't like tardiness.

NAOMI. She certainly doesn't.

MAXWELL. Ah, tell her to suck a lemon!

DAISY. Max!

MAXWELL. As far as I'm concerned, the Bishop should have made you president.

DAISY. Maxwell Owen Fielding!

MAXWELL. Am I not right?

>   NAOMI *laughs and then kisses* MAXWELL *on the cheek.*

NAOMI. You're always right, Papa. It runs in the family.

MAXWELL. See, she agrees with me!

NAOMI. But, honestly, Papa, she can have it. Relief Society President is a tough job. I'm content being a counselor. She has my full support.

MAXWELL. Just speak up in those meetings, all right? The Lord put you in there for a reason.

NAOMI. Sure thing. Bye . . .

MAXWELL. My children aren't wilting violets, you hear me? Make your opinion known, don't be a "yes-man"—er, a "yes-woman!"

NAOMI. (*With another laugh:*) Bye!

>   Exit NAOMI. DAISY *looks* MAXWELL *over with the familiar*
>   *exasperation that can only be held between long time spouses.*

DAISY. And we wonder why our children sometimes have big heads . . .

MAXWELL. I wouldn't have it any other way.

DAISY. Honestly, Max, what just got into you?

MAXWELL. What do you mean?

DAISY. You just told that girl not to ignore her Bishop and made fun of her Relief Society President. What happened to Mr. "Follow the Brethren" and "support Church programs"?

MAXWELL. I still believe that. I always will. But her Bishop and Relief Society President are hardly prophets or apostles or . . .

DAISY. Just like a seminary teacher had no authority over Abish.

MAXWELL. True. I get your point now. And I agree with it, so why are you . . . ?

DAISY. Her Bishop, her Relief Society President, they are doing their best. It's a tough, thankless road they have to travel. They deserve her support. Her help.

MAXWELL. And, knowing Naomi, that's exactly what she'll give them.

DAISY. I just wish I had some consistency from you!

MAXWELL. Look who's talking!

Both their last lines come out much more aggressively than they intended. They become embarrassed and a little stunned. There is a pause.

MAXWELL (CONT'D). I—I've always thought I was consistent. I've always tried to be consistent . . .

DAISY. You have—you are. I am the one who's . . .

MAXWELL. Who's what? You're what? Something's bothering you.

DAISY. I—I'm grateful that you're not like them, Maxwell. That you're compassionate and understanding and treat me like an equal . . .

MAXWELL. You are my equal, not *like* an equal. And, well, *sometimes* you're my superior.

DAISY. I guess that I just don't know what I would have done if I had married someone like Brother Jensen. Hearing what he was teaching Abish in seminary—I don't think a marriage like that would have lasted for me.

MAXWELL. Oh, Brother Jensen wouldn't have been good for you on so many levels. I've been to Scout Camp with that man and his personal hygiene left a lot to be desired. And he snores.

DAISY. So do you.

MAXWELL. I do not.

DAISY. What are you talking about? You've always snored!

MAXWELL. I sleep like a baby.

DAISY. A snoring baby.

MAXWELL. Woman, my manhood is cheapened by thy unruly tongue and thus I shall stop thy incessant chattering!

MAXWELL kisses DAISY.

DAISY. Well, I suppose your rough, manly ways aren't *always* a detraction.

They kiss again. Lights dim.

SCENE 5

SAM enters from the front door, with her friend ASHERA GROVER. ASHERA, a Wiccan, has a warm, spirited way about her. She wears clothing that suggests unfettered freedom, connectedness with nature, and a kind of wind-swept spirituality. Given the moment, she could be anything from Mother Earth to Loreena McKennit to Morgan Le Fay.

ASHERA. . . . and so, well, yeah, one of my friends almost became a Mormon. In the end the Pentecostals got to her instead.

SAM. Similar fates as far as I can tell.

ASHERA. Not the way she tells it. She says it's as if she had escaped the gates of hell. When one of her sisters joined the Mormons she had a fit! Strange thing is, she didn't react nearly as harshly when I became a Wiccan. Better a pagan idol than a false Christ, I guess.

SAM. The Baptists weren't too fond of the Mormons either. Always calling them a cult—some of it got pretty ridiculous. I even met a preacher—a preacher!—who literally thought that the Mormons had horns on their heads. Of course, as far as I can tell, the Baptists pretty much hated everybody.

ASHERA. Sam!

SAM. Believe me, Ashera, you should have heard them rail against Mormons, homosexuals, Jehovah's Witnesses, pagans, evolutionists, oh, and when I declared that I was an atheist, my family had a fit! In their minds, we were all pretty much lumped together as heathens and heretics.

ASHERA. That's not fair, Sam. You're just doing the same thing, putting all Baptists together like that.

SAM. Look, I know what I'm talking about. I lived with them most of my life . . .

ASHERA. Which makes it even harder for you to see them objectively.

SAM. I know what I saw.

ASHERA. And now you're living with the Mormons. How's that going for you?

SAM. We've had our strained moments, but we're getting along for the most part . . . they're really nice people. But mainly we stay out of each other's way.

ASHERA. So what happens when you get in each other's way?

> NAOMI enters the front door in a rush, with groceries. She accidentally runs into ASHERA and the groceries scatter.

NAOMI. Oh!

ASHERA. I'm so sorry, let me help you . . .

NAOMI. It's all right, I'm . . .

SAM. Sorry, Naomi, we shouldn't have been standing in the door way like that . . .

NAOMI. No, it's okay, it's just—are the eggs okay?

SAM. The eggs are fine.

NAOMI. Good. We're having Tyrell over again. Mom and I are making Lasagna—but we realized when we layering it that we forgot the eggs.

SAM. Eggs?

NAOMI. We use cottage cheese with eggs, instead of that weird spongy cheese people use—what's it called?

ASHERA. Ricotta?

NAOMI. That's it! Disgusting stuff.

SAM. Oh, I love Ricotta . . .

NAOMI. Then you haven't tried our lasagna yet! Do you and your friend want to have dinner with us? We're having plenty!

SAM. Well, no, I don't think . . .

ASHERA. That would be lovely.

SAM darts ASHERA a dark look.

NAOMI. (*Calling out to the kitchen:*) Mom! Sam and Ashera are eating with us!

DAISY. (*Off stage, in the kitchen:*) That sounds lovely!

NAOMI. You two can just wait up here, if you want. We just have to put it together and thrust it into the oven now. Can you answer the door, if Tyrell rings? (*Pause. To ASHERA:*) What was your name again?

ASHERA. Ashera.

NAOMI. Cool. Like the Semitic Mother Goddess.

ASHERA. (*Pleased:*) I'm impressed. Most people think I'm named after He-Man's twin sister.

NAOMI. I love reading about different religions and mythologies.

ASHERA. Mormons don't frown on that?

NAOMI. Brigham Young said that Mormons should accept all truth, no matter what source it comes from.

ASHERA. Well, color me surprised.

DAISY. (*Off stage:*) Naomi? You coming?

NAOMI. Coming, Mama! Sorry. But I'd like to talk later.

ASHERA. Sure thing.

Exit NAOMI.

SAM. I thought we were going out for dinner?

ASHERA. What are you complaining about? Free food! Don't you ever eat with them?

SAM. What would we talk about?

ASHERA. Well, you could talk comparative religion with Naomi, for one thing.

SAM. I don't talk about religion.

ASHERA. What have we been doing then?

SAM. I don't talk about it with religious people.

ASHERA. I am religious.

SAM. You don't count. You're a . . .

ASHERA. A pagan? A witch? Careful, Sam . . .

SAM. I'm sorry. Well, it's not like Wicca is an organized religion . . .

ASHERA. Sure, a lot of us are. I belong to the British Tradition Wicca. A high priest and priestess are in charge of my coven . . .

SAM. I mean like catechisms or articles of faith . . .

ASHERA. "An it harm none, do what you will . . . "

SAM. Or a firm theology . . .

ASHERA. The Law of Threefold Return, the Five Elements, reincarnation, the Summerland, The Charge of the Goddess . . .

SAM. Look, all I'm saying is you're different and that's a good thing! You're not like them!

ASHERA. And what are "they" like, Sam?

There is a knock. ASHERA and SAM look at each other.

ASHERA (CONT'D). Well, she did say that we should answer it.

ASHERA goes to the door and answers it. In the doorway is TYRELL HOWARD, a handsome, African-American man. He dresses sharply, and has a significant presence and bearing.

TYRELL. Oh. Uh—am I in the right place?

ASHERA. You're Tyrell?

TYRELL. Yeah.

ASHERA. Then you're in the right place. Come in, come in, welcome to their humble abode! Look at me, don't I play the gracious proxy hostess!

TYRELL. How do you know the Fieldings?

ASHERA. I'm friends with the monster in the basement. My name's Ashera.

TYRELL. Interesting. Like the consort of Yahweh.

ASHERA. Man, I like you people!

TYRELL. Naomi's introduced me to all sorts of new myths.

ASHERA. How do you know it's just a myth?

TYRELL. Oh, I think very few things are *just* myths. I'm getting a PhD in anthropology. Mythology and ritual have held a long impact on the human species. I don't dismiss it lightly. (*Noting SAM.*) Sam, right?

SAM. That's me.

TYRELL. Nice to meet you again. Naomi has a very high opinion of you.

SAM. She hardly knows me.

TYRELL. Then you must have left an impression.

ASHERA. She certainly does that. Have a seat, won't you? Can I get you something to drink? I know these Mormons don't go for hard liquor, but I'm sure I can find something tantalizing . . .

SAM. Ashera . . .

ASHERA. What about proxy hostess didn't you understand, Sam?

TYRELL. (*With a smile.*) I think I'm okay, thanks.

ASHERA. Are you sure? I'm sure I could dig out some appetizers out of the freezer.

TYRELL. You should own a hotel.

ASHERA. Oh, no, indoors usually make me feel cramped. I own a small house, but it has an even bigger yard.

SAM. She likes being close to the trees.

ASHERA. No roof for me! I try to sleep outside as often as is practical. Even sometimes during a light rain. There are lots of fun things you can do in the rain.

SAM. Now you're just flirting with him! She doesn't sleep in the rain.

ASHERA. I do so. And when Sam turns into a mermaid she sleeps underwater. That is until she is woken by passing sailors and then she drags them underwater with her melancholy melodies.

TYRELL *laughs. He gives a shrewd look at the two women.*

TYRELL. Somehow I feel that you two tend to enjoy yourselves.

ASHERA. Oh, I do! Sam, on the other hand, tends to brood.

SAM. I do not.

ASHERA. It's even worse when she drinks. Right now she's just giving you a bit of tame melancholy and pessimism.

TYRELL. So you two off set each other. Yin and Yang?

SAM. She's a pain up the yang is more like it.

TYRELL. What do you do for a living?

ASHERA. I'm a computer programmer.

TYRELL. I wouldn't have guessed that.

ASHERA. Most people don't. Especially when they find out that I'm a witch.

TYRELL. Literally?

ASHERA. Well, a Wiccan. Does that scare you?

TYRELL. Hardly. I'm a Mormon. We have to file the horns on our heads.

ASHERA. So, it's true!

ASHERA and TYRELL laugh, with SAM a little disturbed.

SAM. You're a Mormon?

TYRELL. Does that surprise you?

SAM. Well, I guess I should have known that. Naomi wouldn't date anybody but a Mormon, but . . .

TYRELL. (*Nonplussed:*) You didn't expect a Mormon to be black.

NAOMI and DAISY enter.

NAOMI. I'd know that laugh anywhere!

TYRELL. The love of my life!

NAOMI and TYRELL kiss.

DAISY. (*Playfully:*) Some people are self conscious to display affection in front of their parents.

NAOMI. Never been a problem for me. Mama, this is Tyrell.

DAISY. Such a pleasure, Tyrell. Naomi has positively gushed about you—well, more than usual. The lasagna's in the oven. Max, Joel and Abish should be home soon.

NAOMI. Oh, I just thought they were upstairs.

DAISY. There was a bit of a blow up between Joel and Abish. Your father took them on a drive to do some damage control. I wish you had been here, sweetheart.

ASHERA. Would have that helped?

DAISY. Oh, hi. Your name is?

ASHERA. Ashera.

DAISY. Oh, like the Jewish goddess.

ASHERA. Wow, you guys are three for three!

DAISY. Kind of a common interest in this family. Ever read any Margaret Barker? She writes some very interesting stuff about the early Hebrew worship of a female deity who was the wife of Yahweh . . .

ASHERA. No, I don't think I have . . .

DAISY. She talks about the Deuteronomists and King Josiah taking away plain and precious truths out of the Bible about our Heavenly Mother . . .

ASHERA. Heavenly Mother? Do Mormons believe in . . . ?

NAOMI. Oh, Mama, you're totally Mormonizing her. (*To* ASHERA:) Barker's a Methodist.

DAISY. She might as well be a Mormon. In fact, maybe she will be. Do you know if the missionaries have ever tried . . . ?

NAOMI. Mother!

ASHERA. Yeah, well, my reading list tends towards the pagan rather than the Judeo-Christian.

DAISY. Oh.

A tense pause.

TYRELL. (*Changing the topic:*) To answer your first question, Ashera, it would have helped.

ASHERA. What's that?

TYRELL. Having Naomi here would have helped with the blow up between Joel and Abish. From what she tells me, she's kind of the peacekeeper around here. I call her the bomb squad.

DAISY. She's always had a special relationship with her older brother since they were very little. And Abish really respects her.

NAOMI. Oh, they'll be fine. Joel and Abish really do love each other.

DAISY. Well, they have a funny way of showing it.

NAOMI. Love often does.

Enter MAXWELL, JOEL, *and* ABISH.

MAXWELL. Well, we all made it back alive. These two have now promised to behave themselves.

JOEL. Sorry it made us late, Mom.

ABISH. Yeah, sorry, Mom.

DAISY. Oh, it doesn't affect me. Dinner's still in the oven.

MAXWELL. And this is Tyrell. Good to meet you!

> TYRELL *and* MAXWELL *shake hands.*

TYRELL. Thank you, sir.

MAXWELL. Sir, nothing! Call me Max. Tell me, Daisy, what do you think of this lad? Is he what you would call handsome?

DAISY. Very.

MAXWELL. That's what I thought. Good taste, Naomi. (*Beat.*) That's my indication that you can relax, Tyrell.

TYRELL. Oh, uh, sorry, sir, uh, Max. Of course.

MAXWELL. Don't stand on pretense here. This is our home. As long as you are friends with my daughter, you are a more than a welcome guest. You are a part of us.

SAM. Hm.

MAXWELL. Oh, Sam! Have you finally decided to take up our invitation?

DAISY. And we've invited her friend Ashera to dinner as well.

JOEL. Ashera? Like He-Man's sister!

> DAISY *and* NAOMI *roll their eyes, groan, etc.*

JOEL (CONT'D). What? I loved those shows as a kid.

MAXWELL. A pleasure to meet you, Ashera.

ASHERA. Likewise.

MAXWELL. Looks like you've met most everyone else, but this is my daughter Abish and my son Joel.

ABISH. Hi.

JOEL. Hello, Ashera.

ASHERA. Nice to meet all of you.

NAOMI. This turned into quite the party!

DAISY. Not too overwhelming is it, Tyrell?

TYRELL. Not at all. I come from a much larger family than this. I feel right at home.

MAXWELL. How many kids?

TYRELL. 11.

ABISH. 11! Wow, did your parents not have a television?

NAOMI. Abish!

TYRELL. (*Laughs.*) No, it's perfectly all right. My Mom, well, she read this book called Cheaper By The Dozen when she was a kid—not the Steve Martin film, obviously, but the original—so ever since then she wanted to have a dozen kids. Thankfully, my Dad had the kind of job where he was in a position to support that many kids and, well, here we are.

ASHERA. You said she wanted a dozen. She missed one.

TYRELL. Well, it's better to aim for the stars and miss, I guess.

ABISH. Wow, that's like 99 months of pregnancy! That's over 8 years!

TYRELL. Yep, she's a pretty impressive lady.

SAM. Well, don't you think . . . ? (*Beat.*) Sorry.

TYRELL. What? What were you going to say?

SAM. Well, I was just—well, don't you think that's a little irresponsible? We've got enough people in the world as it is.

TYRELL. Well, I was number 10, so I guess the then question is: was it a mistake to have me?

SAM. No, that's not what I'm saying at all . . .

TYRELL. Then what are you saying?

ASHERA. I think what Sam is saying that . . .

SAM. Look, I have my opinions, that's all. It's not personal.

TYRELL. No, you already crossed the personal line with that black Mormon comment.

MAXWELL. What?

NAOMI. Tyrell, let's not get . . .

TYRELL. Thanks for trying to defuse me, Naomi, but let me say this. Sam, right?

SAM. Really, I shouldn't have said anything.

TYRELL. But you did. You said it and now you have to own it. So tell me what is your idea of the religion a black man should have?

ASHERA. Sam, maybe an apology will let us all . . .

SAM. Like I said, it was nothing personal—but, okay, sure, it is especially surprising for me to see an African-American join a religion that is historically racist.

TYRELL. You're treading on thin ice . . .

SAM. Knowing that the Mormon Church denied their priesthood to black people until nearly 1980, well, I don't think I'm being the offensive one. I think that's just being aware of history and dismaying at the sad irony.

JOEL. History?

ABISH. Oh crap. She just let the genie out of his bottle.

JOEL. Let's talk about history for a second. Joseph Smith and most of the early Mormons had a very broad view of race for their time. Part of the reason the Saints were driven from Missouri was because of their abolitionist tendencies. Joseph Smith ran for president on a platform that included the eradication of slavery. He himself ordained a black man, Elijah Abel, to the priesthood office of a seventy, which is just below an apostle. So don't tell me that he was a racist, especially in his historical context.

ABISH. Really? Well, then what happened? Why did we change?

TYRELL. It happened under Brigham Young . . .

SAM. Surprise, surprise.

MAXWELL. I'm not comfortable with where this conversation is going. Let's not have contention . . .

TYRELL. Look, Sam, you don't know anything about it, all right? Don't you think I get grief all the time about this? Sure, somewhere down the line something got screwed up. The leaders of the Church have tried to change things for the better, and most members of the Church have let all that go and are kind and open minded—but you still hear some of the old justifications.

SAM. And you want to subject yourself to that? The "mark of Cain," that's what they called it, right? You were supposedly descended from this mythological figure—you were cursed! Even before you were born, you were wicked, unclean! Isn't that what they used to say? See, I've done my reading, too.

DAISY. Sam, you're our guest, please have some . . .

SAM. Tyrell, the sad irony is that you've traded one curse for another. People give you grief? Well, maybe they should. For you've marked yourself, all right. You've justified all that racism and have given the Mormons a free pass.

TYRELL. And where do you think the Mormons got the tendency from? It wasn't until Mormons started gaining converts from the Southern Churches when these ideas started creeping into the Church. A lot of other religious people try to peg this on the Mormons, to discredit them, but the thing is that their Churches were the ones who taught the Mormons the idiotic mess! Unless you're a Quaker, if you go back far enough, every group is dirty, nobody's hands are clean.

ASHERA. Well, then maybe we should all become Quakers.

NAOMI. Ashera, I don't think that's helping.

SAM. I don't want anybody to become a Quaker! I don't want anyone to become a Mormon, or a Baptist, or a Muslim, or, yes, even a Wiccan, Ashera.

ASHERA. All right, Sam, calm down, you're not being yourself...

SAM. All these religions and creeds, what have they done, but create division and prejudice? Religion takes people like all of you—who are basically good, basically decent—but then fills your heads with all these little thoughts, these limiting attitudes, this divisive silliness! You think you're noble, you think you're being moral, but you're just hanging all your little hatreds upon the cross of Jesus Christ!

MAXWELL. That is enough!

This last statement from MAXWELL *comes out ferociously. Everyone looks at him, a little shocked.*

SAM. Mr. Fielding...

MAXWELL. I've tried to be patient, Sam, I've tried to be open minded, but when you blaspheme my Lord and Savior, I will have no tolerance for that!

NAOMI. Papa, let's—let's just let it go.

MAXWELL. Let it go—after what she just said about your boyfriend, and your religion, and your family?

NAOMI. Yes.

MAXWELL *looks at his daughter searchingly.*

MAXWELL. (*To* TYRELL:) I hope you know how lucky you are, young man.

TYRELL. I sure do.

SAM. Thanks, Naomi. I—look, this went badly, we all need to cool down. Sometimes when I get worked up I say things I regret. We can make this work. I think we're really helping each other out here, you know?

NAOMI. Then let's just forget it all and have some dinner.

SAM. Well, maybe dinner's not such a good idea right now. You know, maybe we all need some space and time. Come on, Ashera, let's go.

ASHERA. I was invited to dinner.

SAM. Let's go.

ASHERA. If it's all right with the Fieldings, I would like to stay.

DAISY. If that's what you want, you're more than welcome.

SAM. Ashera?

ASHERA. The Mormons weren't the only ones you were attacking.

SAM. I—I got carried away.

ASHERA. You still haven't said you were sorry.

SAM. (*Beat.*) It's what I believe, Ashera. I can't help that.

ASHERA. I know. But I still think I'd prefer to eat with the Fieldings tonight. And I think you should, too.

SAM. Maybe another time. Really, although I'm not sorry for what I believe, I am sorry how it came across. Have a nice dinner.

Exit SAM, out the front door.

ABISH. Well, that was fun.

Blackout.

SCENE 6

That same night. There are voices from the kitchen, where everyone is finishing eating. There is laughter and animated discussion. ABISH enters from the kitchen. She sits glumly. After a moment, NAOMI enters.

NAOMI. Abish?

ABISH. Hey.

NAOMI. Hey.

ABISH. What are you doing out here? Aren't you supposed to be in there with Tyrell? That's sort of the point, isn't it?

NAOMI. Didn't you say you had homework to do?

ABISH. Well, obviously, you saw my angsty, teenaged attempt to get attention for what it was. Sorry, I actually do have homework, so I'll go upstairs . . .

NAOMI. What's wrong, Abish?

ABISH. I—well, everyone was getting along so well in there . . .

NAOMI. That's a bad thing?

ABISH. Well, everyone was getting along—except me.

NAOMI. Did we say something wrong?

ABISH. No, no, everyone's just great. I, uhm, never mind.

NAOMI. No, go ahead.

ABISH. Is this what everyone goes trough at my age? This—I don't know—this oppressive loneliness?

NAOMI. Sorry to break it to you, sweetie, for some people, it's not just your age. For some people it doesn't ever go away.

ABISH. Is that how you feel?

NAOMI. Sometimes.

ABISH. Even with Tyrell?

NAOMI. Sometimes.

ABISH. How do you feel the other times?

NAOMI. Well, sometimes it's just, well, placid. No extreme emotion either way and then . . .

ABISH. Then?

NAOMI. Then all of that goes away when I feel God close.

ABISH. You talk like that a lot, but—I never know what you mean. I mean, is it like some manic phase?

NAOMI. Is that what you think I am? Manic-depressive? Bi-polar disorder?

ABISH. How am I supposed to know?

NAOMI. I know this sounds all mystical and whatever—and I don't really expect most people to understand it, not really—but *you've* got to understand. It's like—it's like I hear this distant voice—not with my ears, but like my spirit is hearing this distant call. I absolutely tremble sometimes. It comes upon me and I feel connected to everything, to everybody. Everything else burns away and I'm . . . happy is an inadequate word for it. I'm—it's sometimes fleeting, you understand, but for at least a moment, a brief moment, I'm—complete.

ABISH. I've never felt complete.

NAOMI. I know.

ABISH. (*Pause.*) Does Tyrell make you feel complete?

NAOMI. Tyrell is one of the best men I have ever met.

ABISH. But?

NAOMI. Abish, if you're waiting for some guy to make you complete, then it's not going to happen. That's not how it works. Love is beautiful, it's wonderful, but . . .

ABISH. Love?

NAOMI. Yeah, I love him. I've known that for a while now.

ABISH. Are you going to marry him?

NAOMI. I hope to—someday.

ABISH. But not now.

NAOMI. I hear the voice calling.

Enter TYRELL.

TYRELL. Everything all right?

ABISH. Sorry to take Naomi from you, Tyrell. I'm just going up. Thanks, sis.

NAOMI. Let's talk about this later, okay?

ABISH. Okay.

Exit ABISH, up the stairs.

TYRELL. I have a sister like you. She connects together all of the separate parts.

NAOMI. I worry about her.

TYRELL. It's that age.

NAOMI. It's more than that. Tyrell, I'm really scared sometimes. I feel like there's something big that's about to happen in my family . . .

TYRELL. When you say "you feel," you mean one of your . . .

NAOMI. Yes. I've been having all these impressions and dreams—so many of them lately—am I completely crazy?

TYRELL. If that's crazy, then I don't want to be sane.

NAOMI. But, if I'm right, it's not good. Or at least not pleasant. Whatever's on the horizon, it could give a blow to my family that we may not recover from.

TYRELL. But they'll have you. They have always had you to help heal the wounds.

NAOMI. Not this time.

TYRELL. What do you mean?

NAOMI. I'm—I'm going to be gone.

TYRELL. I don't understand.

NAOMI. Tyrell, I've decided to go on a mission.

TYRELL. A mission? For the Church?

NAOMI. Yeah.

TYRELL. But—but I thought things were going so well between us.

NAOMI. They are.

TYRELL. I don't get it. Naomi, not now, obviously, but if things kept on the way they were, well, I was planning on . . . on . . .

NAOMI. Proposing? Yeah, I know.

TYRELL. So is that why you're going, to get away from me?

NAOMI. Of course not! Tyrell, I—I love you.

TYRELL. You do?

NAOMI. Yes.

TYRELL. Then why would you want to leave?

NAOMI. Because it's not just a mission. It's *my* mission.

TYRELL. And then what?

NAOMI. Then, if you haven't fallen in love with some other smart, beautiful girl, we can think of getting back to that proposing part.

TYRELL. But you said that you believe your family is going to be in some sort of trouble. Why would you leave now?

NAOMI. I guess maybe that's the way God's planned it. (*Pause.*) Are you upset?

TYRELL. Disappointed.

NAOMI. I—I understand if you want to end everything now.

TYRELL. Naomi, you're forgetting something.

NAOMI. What's that?

TYRELL. I love you, too.

NAOMI. Then we're still . . . ?

TYRELL kisses NAOMI. Enter JOEL.

JOEL. Oh, uh, sorry. When you're ready, Dad's making some banana shakes for us . . .

NAOMI. Awesome. Come on, it's a bit of a tradition . . .

Enter ASHERA.

ASHERA. Hey, these banana shakes are looking pretty good. Get in here before I drag you in! As much as all of us would enjoy that, you know that I'd win.

TYRELL. Shakes sound great to me.

Exit TYRELL and NAOMI.

ASHERA. You too, hot stuff.

JOEL. You talking to me?

ASHERA. I don't see anyone else in here.

JOEL. Thanks for the charity, but no one's ever mistaken me for Hugh Jackman.

ASHERA. Don't get me wrong, Hugh could have fun with me anytime, but he's not my type.

JOEL. And who's your type?

ASHERA. I thought I already made that clear, hot stuff.

JOEL. Uh . . .

ASHERA. Get in here, will you?

JOEL. Yes, ma'am.

Exit JOEL and ASHERA.

SCENE 7

Late that same night. JOEL, NAOMI, TYRELL, and ASHERA are talking, thoroughly enjoying each other.

ASHERA. You can't be serious!

JOEL. I swear, I'm knocking out at this man's door, and then he comes out with a Book of Mormon ready to pounce me about "the principle." I had heard of Bible bashing before, but never Book of Mormon bashing.

ASHERA. He was a full out polygamist?

JOEL. And was intent on showing me where the Church had been led astray in giving it up.

TYRELL. Well, what happened?

JOEL. We were invited in and his three wives were very gracious and we all had a very thorough debate.

ASHERA. So did he convince you?

JOEL. What?

ASHERA. The multiple wives thing. Come on, it must have been tempting to a young, celibate missionary.

NAOMI. Look, Ashera, you've made him blush!

TYRELL. Classic!

JOEL. No—I wasn't interested at all!

ASHERA. Mm-hm.

JOEL. I'm a one girl kind of guy. Dedicated monogamous.

ASHERA. Good.

> ASHERA *winks and smiles flirtatiously at* JOEL.

TYRELL. He's getting even more red!

JOEL. Look, really, I wasn't interested! In polygamy, I mean. I mean— well, especially with what ended up happening to the guy . . .

NAOMI. What happened?

JOEL. He got struck by lightning.

ASHERA. He did not!

TYRELL. Now *that's* Mormon folk lore!

JOEL. Honest truth. I heard it from one of the members.

TYRELL. Then it's definitely folk lore!

ASHERA. All his poor widows . . .

NAOMI. Ashera!

> *They all laugh. Enter* SAM. *The laughter dies and there's an awkward moment.*

ASHERA. Hey, guys, can you give me a moment alone with Sam?

SAM. No need, Ashera, I'm just going to go to bed.

ASHERA. Sam, look, we're going to talk. Guys?

NAOMI. Sure. We'll just be in the kitchen, okay? Feel free to join us, too, Sam.

SAM. No, no, please, I'm going to bed soon.

NAOMI. You're always welcome.

JOEL. Hey, Naomi, let her be. She wants to feel sorry for herself, let her feel sorry for herself.

NAOMI. Joel . . .

JOEL. Don't get into lecture mode on me, Naomi. She's the one who needs to be turned around.

NAOMI. Joel!

Exit JOEL.

NAOMI (CONT'D). I'm so sorry about that.

ASHERA. Let me talk with Sam, Naomi. I'll be right there.

NAOMI. Okay. See ya later, Sam.

SAM. I appreciate it, Naomi. You, at least, make me feel welcome.

Exit NAOMI, TYRELL, and JOEL.

SAM. You wanted to talk. Talk.

ASHERA. That ended badly tonight.

SAM. Doesn't look like it ended so badly with you.

ASHERA. They're good people.

SAM. Yeah, I know. But they're deluded.

ASHERA. And you think I'm deluded, too?

SAM. I think you're gullible.

ASHERA. Well, then you won't like what I'm going to say next.

SAM. All right.

ASHERA. After Mr. and Mrs. Fielding went to bed, I got talking to Joel, Naomi and Tyrell. They were telling me a little about their faith . . .

SAM. You're right, I'm not going to like it.

ASHERA. You know, I'm a little interested in it . . .

SAM. Oh, Ashera!

ASHERA. The way they talk about it—they're very spiritual. And, as downplayed in their religion as she's become, they believe in a Mother God like I do, and these, well, I call it magic, but they call it priesthood and spiritual gifts, but they're just the different words we come up for God's power, aren't they? Now there's huge differences, I know that, but I'm open. To Jesus Christ, to prophets, to—well, I—I've agreed to let their missionaries talk to me.

SAM. Well, Mormon or Pagan, what does it matter to me? It's all ridiculous.

SAM is about to go to her door downstairs, but ASHERA stops her.

ASHERA. Sam, wait . . .

SAM. You abandoned me tonight.

ASHERA. I've never seen you behave like that. You may be moody sometimes, but I've never seen you be cruel.

SAM. I can't help believing what I believe, and is it doing anybody any favors by bottling it in, by constantly editing myself?

ASHERA. Then tell me about it. I'm your friend.

SAM. I think you chose your real friends tonight.

ASHERA. I'm your friend. That hasn't changed!

SAM. I love you more than a sister, Ashera. But I'm wondering how much dissonance it brings into my life to be constantly around people who believe so differently than me, where everything is bound to turn into division. Friends, they're supposed to make us feel safe, aren't they? And it seems like you felt safe with the Fieldings, right from the beginning. Maybe you were right to stay with them tonight.

ASHERA. No, Sam, really there's got to be . . .

SAM. Maybe we all just need to keep to our own communities, to those who will affirm our values. (*Pause.*) But I keep thinking about Abish.

ASHERA. What about Abish?

SAM. I don't want people like her swallowed up into this, you know. She just sat there, drinking up all of Joel's justifications, straining for any reason to stay. I don't want to see her lost in this cult. There's got to be something I can do . . .

ASHERA. They're not a cult.

SAM. Says the Wiccan.

ASHERA. Sam!

SAM. Sorry. That was uncalled for. But, really, see what this does? If you're going to join the Mormons—well, that creates an even bigger chasm. Being around each other like this puts us in such tension, such constant disagreement. Do you think that's healthy for either of us?

ASHERA. Yes. I think our friendship is very healthy.

Suddenly SAM *gives* ASHERA *an impulsive hug.*

SAM. Thank you for saying that. I'll miss you.

ASHERA. Sam . . .

SAM. No, really, you've been so good to me. Until tonight. And tonight I really needed you. I thought you were my community here, but I was wrong. They're becoming your community, I already see it in your eyes. You're wanting to be a part of them, yearning for it. So this is where we part ways.

ASHERA. (*Hurt.*) If that's how you want it, Sam. But you didn't have to do this. You really didn't have to do this.

Exit ASHERA *into the kitchen.* SAM *is about to go downstairs when she stops. She goes to the upstairs entrance and calls up.*

SAM. Abish?

ABISH *comes down.*

ABISH. Hey. What's up?

SAM. I was wondering if you wanted to come down with me. I thought we might discuss some of the things Joel and Tyrell were saying tonight.

ABISH. Oh, sure. That sounds interesting.

SAM. Cool.

SAM and ABISH exit downstairs.

SCENE 8

It is very early in the morning. ABISH and DAISY are reading the scriptures together, as they read them every morning since their deal. They are currently reading from the Book of Mormon.

ABISH. ". . . and he inviteth them all to come unto him and partake of his goodness; and denieth none that come unto him, black and white, bond and free, male and female; and he remembereth the heathen; and all are alike unto God, both Jew and Gentile."

This strikes ABISH as significant. She pauses to read it over again to herself silently.

DAISY. Abish?

ABISH. That's really cool. Does he mean it?

DAISY. Nephi?

ABISH. No. God.

DAISY. Of course. You're precious to our Heavenly Parents, Abish. We all are.

ABISH. Mom—I'm ready to go back to seminary.

DAISY. Are you sure? Because I've liked this . . .

ABISH. So have I. Let's keep doing it. But I'm not going to let what Brother Jensen believes determine what I believe or how I feel about myself. What he says doesn't determine whether I have a seat at the table.

Enter SAM from her room. She seems distraught.

ABISH (CONT'D). You okay, Sam?

SAM. I . . . I'm . . .

DAISY. Do you want to sit down and read with us?

SAM. No, uh, not my thing.

ABISH. But sit down. Okay? We've got some chocolate milk. Chocolate milk always makes me feel better.

SAM. Really, I just needed some air.

ABISH. Sit down. I'll get us all some chocolate milk. In fact, I'll bring the whole jug.

Exit ABISH.

SAM. Chocolate milk?

DAISY. Sorry we don't have any hard liquor to offer.

SAM. I'm going to drown my sorrows in chocolate milk?

DAISY. It's the Fielding way. And anyway, the point is not to drown your sorrows, dear. It's to deal with them.

Enter ABISH with a tray of glasses and chocolate milk.

DAISY (CONT'D). I can pour.

ABISH. Are you all right?

SAM. No, really, I'm not into this kind of thing . . .

ABISH. What kind of thing?

SAM. I'm a private person.

DAISY. Then you moved into the wrong house.

SAM. Look, I appreciate it, but I'm just the tenant who lives in the basement.

DAISY. You're so much more than that.

DAISY hands SAM the chocolate milk.

SAM. Really, I'm not . . .

DAISY. You do like chocolate milk, don't you?

SAM. Well, yes. I do.

DAISY. Then drink up.

SAM looks at her chocolate milk, baffled, but then starts to drink. She drinks nearly the whole glass.

SAM. That's good.

SAM looks up at ABISH and DAISY and then bursts into tears.

DAISY. Oh, Sam, dear, it's okay. Let me pour you another. (*With a pleasant smile.*) On the house.

SAM. This isn't real.

ABISH. Well, she's not June Cleaver, but she sure tries sometimes. Really, though, she's a closet feminist.

DAISY. Hush.

ABISH. I didn't see you deny it, Mom.

This elicits a smile from SAM.

SAM. Y'all are really odd.

DAISY. Y'all? Why, that almost sounded down-right Southern of you, Sam. Did we suddenly get the Georgia Peach back?

SAM. It was—just a slip. I . . .

SAM struggles with her tears again.

DAISY. What is it, Sam?

SAM. My Mama—they just—I just got woken up by a call . . .

DAISY. Is she all right?

SAM. No, she—she's struggled with diabetes for a long time and her heart finally . . .

> *SAM breaks down. DAISY sweeps SAM up in her arms and SAM, for once, welcomes her warmth and grips her tightly.*

DAISY. Oh, Sam . . .

SAM. (*For a moment, just a moment, SAM's Southern accent returns:*) I broke her heart when I left. It wasn't just their religion, it was—I left it all behind. Couldn't handle that sort of dissonance in my life. I left them behind. It's been five years since I talked to Mama, except for a few awkward Christmas calls. My parents are good—good— they were good folks. It's just—it's been so long since I've seen them and now with Mama gone . . .

> *SAM's sobs no longer allow her to say anything more.*

DAISY. Darling, she's not gone.

SAM. You know I don't believe any of that.

DAISY. In the end, it doesn't matter what any of us believe. God doesn't label us with those terms. God calls us "daughter" or "son." Someday, Sam, this whole world's darkness and despair will just burn away and will be replaced with something smooth, something bright. All our imperfections and littleness will burn away.

ABISH. Mom, that's not going to help. Sam, don't worry about all that. That's all gone, those are all just memories. We don't have to bring religion into this right now. Right now this is about you losing your Mom—it's about your pain. I know things have sometimes been strained, but you can have a home here. We can be a home for you.

SAM. (*Pause.*) No. My home died tonight. My family were the only home I ever had, and now with Mama dead—it's gone. Gone forever. Thank you for the chocolate milk, but I think I'm going to need something a little stronger tonight.

> *Exit SAM down the stairs. ABISH stands to go after her, but DAISY grabs her hand.*

DAISY. Let her go, Abish.

ABISH. If we let her go, what does that say about us?

DAISY. It says that we trust our Heavenly Father and Mother to look after their own children.

ABISH. I'm their child, too. So she's my sister.

> DAISY *is about to object again, but then simply nods.* ABISH *exits, after Sam.* DAISY *looks after her, as lights fade to black.*

SCENE 9

> *Lights raise to reveal* JOEL *reading a thick history book.* NAOMI *and* ABISH *peek out of the kitchen door.* JOEL *looks back and they duck back into the kitchen.* JOEL *shrugs it off. Slowly, stealthily* NAOMI *and* ABISH *enter the living room. They each have a jar of peanut butter, which they both quietly dip their hands into, pulling out globs of it onto their palms and fingers. They then approach Joel. As* JOEL *in engrossed in his book, they are able to pounce on him and smear it all over his face, etc.*

JOEL. Agh! (*Beat.*) Oh-ho, you two are dead-*dead* meat.

> *In a swift motion,* JOEL *steals one of the peanut butter jars, as the girls shriek and retreat, exiting into the kitchen, as* JOEL *follows them in earnest, applying the peanut butter to his own hands. The living room is empty for a short moment before SAM enters from her room, in exercise attire. As she makes her way towards the front door,* JOEL, ABISH, *and* NAOMI *burst back into the room, chasing each other with the peanut butter. There is a great deal of shrieking, threatening, taunting, etc.*

SAM. What the hell are all of you doing?!

> *They all look to* SAM.

SAM (CONT'D). Wait. No. Just no. I'm about to go to the gym.

JOEL. You can choose, Sam. Smooth?

NAOMI. Or chunky?

SAM. Noooo!

They all chase and then pounce on SAM, smearing her with the peanut butter. SAM retreats into the kitchen with the three of them following. DAISY enters from upstairs.

DAISY. What's going on down here?

There is a knock at the door. DAISY answers it and reveals JENNY.

JENNY. Hi, Mrs. Fielding. Abish and I are supposed to study tonight . . .

SAM re-enters, followed by the FIELDING SIBLINGS, all of them yelling and shrieking. SAM has armed herself with Jam and Nutella. They are all covered with the various gooey substances.

JENNY (CONT'D). Oh, it's one of *those* days.

SAM. Jenny! Help me! Here!

SAM tosses JENNY the Nutella.

JENNY. (*With a wicked smile:*) Totes awesome.

JENNY jumps into the fray, helping SAM. DAISY seems a little shocked, as MAXWELL enters, making his way from down the stairs.

MAXWELL. What is going on down here? Are you all children?

DAISY. Yes, you all should be ashamed of yourselves, at your age! Abish, give that to me, right now.

ABISH hands DAISY the peanut butter. Cooly, calmly, DAISY goes over to MAXWELL and smears it on his face.

MAXWELL. I knew I shouldn't have come down.

MAXWELL merely goes back up stairs without another word.

DAISY. Have fun, kids.

DAISY hands ABISH the peanut butter and goes back upstairs. There is a tense moment where they all eye each other.

ABISH. Now if only the culture wars were this fun.

JENNY. I say every man for himself.

A pause and then they all attack each other indiscriminately. Eventually they all collapse to the floor, laughing.

JOEL. Sam, remind me never to get into a real fight with you. You get vicious.

SAM. I'm a whole hog kind of gal.

JOEL. Whole hog? Well, ain't that the Southern belle in you!

SAM. Mock me at your own risk, Joel. I still am armed and dangerous.

JOEL. Bring it, Kentucky fried!

JOEL and SAM have their own private battle for a moment, struggling on the floor.

JENNY. My money's on Sam.

NAOMI. No argument there.

JOEL and SAM finally stop, having tangled themselves in a much more intimate position than they had expected. There is a breathless moment. There is a knock and they both scramble to their feet.

SAM. I'll get it.

NAOMI. (*With a smile:*) Well, now look who feels right at home.

SAM opens the door to reveal ASHERA.

SAM. Ashera?

JOEL. Oh! Oh, you're early!

ASHERA. No, actually, I'm right on time.

SAM. What's happening?

ASHERA. Uhm, Joel and I, we sort have a . . .

JOEL. A date. We have a date.

SAM. Oh. I wasn't aware that you two . . .

JOEL. Uhm, it's just a date. That's all it is for now.

SAM. For now?

JOEL. I mean . . .

TYRELL enters from the front door.

TYRELL. It's actually a double date. But it looks like we may be a little delayed.

ASHERA. We'll wait and let you clean up.

Exit JOEL and NAOMI.

ABISH. You can come up to the bathroom to clean up, too, if you want to, Jenny.

JENNY. Actually, I'm kind of digging this look.

ABISH. You can be so weird sometimes.

JENNY. I'll be up in a second.

Exit ABISH.

JENNY (CONT'D). Yowsas, I wish my family did things like that!

TYRELL. Oh, mine did. Remind me some time and I'll tell you about the great jelly bean war.

ASHERA. Hey, Sam. How are you doing?

SAM. Hey, Ashera.

ABISH. I heard about your Mom.

SAM pauses, looking at ASHERA and biting her lip a bit, before suddenly exiting down the stairs.

ASHERA. Hey, Sam . . . Sam!

ASHERA exits down the stairs, following SAM.

JENNY. Whoa, things suddenly got tense.

TYRELL. It's been like that around here lately.

JENNY. Really, I just wish people would just learn to chillax.

TYRELL. It's kind of a complicated situation.

JENNY. Yeah, that's always the big excuse, isn't it? "It's complicated." But, you know what, look at me and Abish, we've been best friends forever and we believe totally different things!

TYRELL. Where do you fall on the spectrum?

JENNY. Somewhere between agnostic and "love one another." Or, if you believe my Mom, I worship myself. Which is kind of true.

TYRELL. It sounds like you've been a good friend to Abish.

JENNY. Well, I mean like, look at her. She's totes spectacular!

TYRELL. Do you ever argue?

JENNY. About religion? Hell no. I mean we talk about what we believe, sure. But what she believes has nothing to do with who she really is.

TYRELL. Hm. I'm not sure if I really believe that or not. Belief is a powerful thing.

JENNY. So is the human personality. Anyway, Abish is right, this gooey stuff is starting to really stick. I'd better clean up. Nice to finally meet you, Tyrell!

TYRELL. Right back at you, kid.

Exit JENNY, up the stairs. JOEL enters, cleaned up.

JOEL. Where's Ashera?

ASHERA burst in from downstairs, followed by SAM.

SAM. That's not what I meant, Ashera, and you know it!

ASHERA. I'll be outside when you're ready, Joel.

Exit ASHERA, out the front door.

SAM. Damn.

JOEL. Still burning bridges, Sam?

SAM. Well, my mouth just opens sometimes and it actually communicates what's in my brain.

TYRELL. No surer way to get in trouble. Let's take my car, Joel. I'll let Ashera into the back and we'll be waiting for you guys, okay?

JOEL. Thanks, Tyrell.

Exit TYRELL out the front door.

SAM. Joel . . .

JOEL. I'm sorry things have been kind of rough here for you, Sam . . .

SAM. Well, I guess I haven't made it easy on myself . . .

JOEL. . . . but I hope you know someday how right we are.

SAM. Excuse me?

JOEL. It's important to find yourself on the right side of eternity.

Exit JOEL out of the front door. NAOMI comes back down the stairs, carrying a wrapped package.

NAOMI. Where did everyone go?

SAM. They're out in the car.

SAM is about to go back downstairs, but NAOMI's voice stops her:

NAOMI. Hey, Sam, that was fun.

SAM. (*With an appreciative smile:*) Yeah, it was, wasn't it?

NAOMI. It can be like that, you know.

SAM. Like what?

NAOMI. Happy.

SAM. Sure. Zipedeedooda.

NAOMI. No. Really. I haven't seen you happy for a while.

SAM. And you're always happy?

NAOMI. No. Not really. You got me there. But that moment we all just had—that was happy.

SAM. That a gift for Tyrell?

NAOMI. Actually, it's for you.

SAM. For me?

NAOMI. I know how you feel about certain things—but this makes me happy. I thought maybe you could give it a chance.

NAOMI hands SAM the gift and then exits out the front door. As SAM opens it she becomes more and more visibly upset. It is a Book of Mormon.

SAM. Damn it, Naomi. You just spoiled the moment.

Exit SAM.

SCENE 10

JOEL enters, in a suit, huffing and puffing down the stairs with a suitcase.

JOEL. (*Calling out to NAOMI.*) Whatever happened to no purse or scrip?

Enter NAOMI with another suitcase.

NAOMI. Oh, shut up.

JOEL. Tsk, tsk, tsk. Really, Sister Fielding, is that language befitting a representative of the Church?

NAOMI. How about the laying on of hands?

JOEL. I thought they didn't let you take this much stuff.

NAOMI. That suitcase isn't for me.

JOEL. Then why am I lugging it around then?

NAOMI. Tyrell is coming to pick it up.

JOEL. This whole suitcase is for Tyrell?

NAOMI. He said he has some extra storage space. I thought it would free up some room for Mama and Papa, especially with Sam living downstairs.

JOEL. Well, what if he "Dear Janes" you?

NAOMI. Then he's been instructed to bring it back here.

JOEL. Wowsers, you talked about it?

NAOMI. Look, can we drop it?

JOEL. Why are you so irritable?

NAOMI. I'm about to leave my family and comforts and trek around Russia . . .

JOEL. Isn't this what you wanted?

NAOMI. It's what I need.

JOEL. I bet it's not too late to back out.

NAOMI. Joel Michael Fielding, are you suggesting . . . ?

JOEL. Look, you know it's not as necessary for . . .

NAOMI. Just because I'm a girl, doesn't mean this isn't just as much of a personal calling for me, okay?

JOEL. I'm just still a little surprised. When you brought Tyrell in three months ago, I was sure . . .

NAOMI. Joel, I need your support in this.

JOEL. But are you sure you're not just trying to prove something? That you're not throwing away something beautiful for a statement?

NAOMI. This—this is my coming of age. It's different for different people, but I need this. Please, tell me you understand.

JOEL gazes at his sister for a moment.

JOEL. Of course I do. My mission, it changed me in ways which only other missionaries understand. We've shared so much. I'll be excited to share that with you, too.

NAOMI. Thank you.

There is a knock.

NAOMI (CONT'D). That's Tyrell . . .

NAOMI goes to answer the door, but instead of finding Tyrell, ASHERA is standing in the doorway.

NAOMI (CONT'D). Oh, Ashera! I'm guessing you want to see Joel . . .

ASHERA. Joel? No way, sweetheart! Today's your day! (*ASHERA warmly embraces NAOMI.*)

ASHERA (CONT'D). Anyway, I don't want to give Hot Stuff a bigger head than he already has.

JOEL. Don't I even get a kiss?

ASHERA. Oh, I'm always ready for one of those.

ASHERA and JOEL kiss.

JOEL. I invited Ashera to the setting apart. I hope you don't mind.

NAOMI. Mind? It's perfect! She is, after all, my first convert.

JOEL. *Your* first convert? I think I was the major influence there . . .

Enter TYRELL through the open door.

TYRELL. I thought that the honor belonged to me!

NAOMI. Hey, sexy.

NAOMI kisses TYRELL.

JOEL. Well, you're not going to be able to do that for much longer.

NAOMI. I haven't been set apart yet.

An even more passionate kiss.

JOEL. You think we should leave them alone?

ASHERA. I was actually hoping we'd follow suit.

Enter MAXWELL, DAISY, and ABISH from upstairs dressed ready for the setting apart.

ABISH. Gross. I thought they couldn't do that anymore.

JOEL and NAOMI separate.

JOEL. Oh, you don't fool any of us, Abish. What's your boyfriend's name again? Wally, wasn't it?

DAISY. Boyfriend?

ABISH. Et tu, Joel?

NAOMI. Well, she is sixteen now, Mama.

DAISY. Yes, that means she can date, but it doesn't mean she can snog the first boy who takes interest.

JOEL. Mom, did you just say "snog"?

DAISY. Look, I've read *Harry Potter*, I know what you kids get up to these days.

ABISH. Mom, you're embarrassing yourself.

DAISY. We'll talk about this later, Abish.

ABISH. I'm gonna get you, Joel.

JOEL. Just watching out for you, Sis.

ABISH. Getting your twisted kicks is more like it.

JOEL. Why not do both?

MAXWELL. Everyone ready? The Stake President won't wait forever.

Enter SAM, with a packaged gift.

SAM. Hey, wait. Naomi gave me a going away gift last night. I just wanted to return the favor. Tit for tat, you know.

NAOMI. Oh, thank you, Sam. That's very gracious.

SAM. Don't thank me.

SAM hands NAOMI the gift and then exits back downstairs.

JOEL. What is it, Naomi?

NAOMI. It feels like a book.

NAOMI opens the gift. NAOMI's face falls upon reading the title. She hands it to TYRELL.

TYRELL. *The God Delusion* by Richard Dawkins.

ASHERA. Oh, Sam.

MAXWELL. How dare she?

NAOMI. No, Dad, it's okay. I left her a Book of Mormon last night. I guess it didn't go over well.

DAISY. But to give you something like this—right when you're about to leave on your mission . . .

NAOMI. Like she said: tit for tat.

MAXWELL. I'm going to go talk to that girl.

ABISH. Dad, no . . .

MAXWELL. It's highly offensive . . .

NAOMI. Just like I offended her.

MAXWELL. I won't have it.

NAOMI. We've got to get everyone to the Stake President's—don't let this spoil things, Dad.

MAXWELL. If she's going to live under our roof, she has to understand that there are lines we don't cross.

ABISH. Let me talk to her.

MAXWELL. What?

ABISH. She might listen to me.

DAISY. She's right, Max.

ABISH. Leave me the keys to the little Honda and I'll be over in just a moment. President Harkins likes to give a speech before everything anyway—usually long ones.

MAXWELL. All right. But keep us in the loop, okay?

ABISH. Okay, Dad.

MAXWELL *hands* ABISH *the key to the Honda.*

NAOMI. Be kind, Abish. We'll wait for you.

ABISH. I'm proud of you, you know.

NAOMI. Thanks, Abby.

MAXWELL. All right, everyone, let's go.

Exit NAOMI, TYRELL, JOEL, MAXWELL, DAISY, and ASH-ERA. ABISH goes to the door to the basement and shouts down.

ABISH. Sam, get your cowardly butt up here!

ABISH goes and sits, waiting. Enter SAM.

SAM. They left, huh?

ABISH. It was a mean thing to do—it was small.

SAM. I told Naomi months ago that I wasn't going to join your Church. If she wanted to expel some sort of Mormon missionary guilt or something, fine. But when you push your beliefs on someone like that, then the other person is going to push back.

ABISH. She just gave you a book.

SAM. And I just gave her one back. Neither of us is going to read them, so what does it matter?

ABISH. I thought you were getting along with the family better.

SAM. Abish, you're so lucky to have such a loving, wonderful family. I'm serious about that. But they're all gullible. You, though, Abish, you're—I have such high hopes for you.

ABISH. Hopes?

SAM. Look, out of your whole family—well, you know what they're like.

ABISH. Not from your point of view. Enlighten me.

SAM. Everyone in your family has their good points—I really admire them—but come on. I see your frustration with them.

ABISH. That's my business, not yours.

SAM. You know, I've said enough. I'll just go back downstairs.

ABISH. Wait. You can't just leave it hanging like that.

SAM. I shouldn't have said anything.

ABISH. Look, you can do that to Naomi or Mom, they care about being kind and nice and whatever. Well, I'm not nice. And I don't care whether you're nice. So if you have something to whine about, well, just get it over with.

SAM. There's no reason to get offensive.

ABISH. Offensive? Oh, is the shy, little Molly Mormon offending the modern, sophisticated . . . erm . . .

SAM. Secularist?

ABISH. Sure, secularist! Modern, sophisticated secularist!

SAM. Oh, Abish, stop being so melodramatic. You know as well as I do that you don't believe a word of the crap you've been fed.

ABISH. No, you just can't understand why I believe it.

SAM. Every little way you present yourself, every little rebellion, it's all proof that you're just straining to break out of the oppressive . . .

ABISH. Whatever problems I have with some of the stupid things Mormons do, it doesn't mean that I have troubles with the religion. I completely believe . . .

SAM. Do you? Really?

ABISH. Yes!

SAM. So it's this whole Holy Spirit thing, this Holy Ghost, Pentecostal flame that's just burning through you to testify! Testify!

ABISH. Sam, for as long as you've been with us, you still don't understand us at all. Jeez, you're just . . .

SAM. That's how you know! Oh, you know! Suddenly the doubts and contradictions and hypocrisies . . . they're just blown out of the water! All due to a happy feeling! A happy, naive, blissful-state-of-ignorance, feeling!

ABISH. Feeling? Feeling! You think it just boils down to emotionalism, to, well, like, a kumbaya pep rally? Is that what you think we're talking about?

SAM. I come from the South, young lady, I know better. Oh, I saw the clapping and the singing and the yelling and the pitch fevered, erratic tongued celebration of . . .

ABISH. Whoa, if you think a Mormon meeting is anything like those, well, wow, then you haven't slept through some of the boring talks I have.

SAM. You don't fool me. Isn't that how all of you talk? Dreams, promptings, burnings, "spiritual" experiences! How is that supposed to show any sort of solid . . . ?

ABISH. It's not supposed to show any solid anything! That's the point! It's a completely personal experience!

SAM. And so it doesn't prove a single thing to anybody, but you . . .

ABISH. Exactly! There's no one pushing you, no one forcing you—that's what Joseph Smith's First Vision is all about! Away from the revivals and the yelling and the movements and arguments and—well, away from the whole world and all the people telling you to join this church or that group or this political party or that club or this gang— and away from that, you just step into that grove of trees by yourself. Except you're not by yourself, because you realize God is there with you, can see you, hear you, small as you are, despite the big backdrop of this big world's mess—and even though you're whispering that little prayer—yet that is when God manifests to you!

SAM. Oh, and so you're a visionary, too, then? You've finally inherited that fire that your sister spouts off all the time? A little Joseph Smith, a miniature Joan of Arc?

ABISH. No.

SAM. Oh, come on, Abish. You don't go for that visionary insanity— lime disease, bi-polar, mass hallucination, sleep paralysis stuff! There is a rational explanation for each and every mental disease or physical hiccup passed off as a religious experience! Your sister may dip into those extremes, but I'd be hard pressed to expect it from you!

ABISH. Oh, you're talking to the wrong person! I never said I've had an experience like that!

SAM. Then why have you been spouting off . . .

ABISH. Because I believe her. I believe those who have said they had those experiences. For I've discovered that is my gift of the Spirit. I have the gift of faith. I believe.

SAM. Oh, you *believe*! Just take it on faith? Without any evidence? Even without the "personal" evidence you've just been running on about?

ABISH. Oh, it's plenty personal.

SAM. Come on! Abish, you're a smart girl, don't go for that kind of cop out . . .

ABISH. You believed once, didn't you? In your Baptist days?

SAM. I accepted once. Unthinking acceptance.

ABISH. That's not the same. There's plenty of Mormons like that. Just going with the religion because it's easier to follow the crowd—never asking themselves the hard questions because they don't even want to know the answers. The real Mormons haven't zoned out, and they haven't, like, fallen away or jumped ship. They are the ones asking the hard questions and are willing to take it when God gives them the hard answers—and then live by those answers!

SAM. Abish, I'm your friend . . .

ABISH. Cool. Then leave my religion alone.

SAM. I'm trying to help you!

ABISH. Why do you think I would need you?

SAM. What if I need you, Abish? We're connected, you and I. We've both felt that.

ABISH. Connected? Since when did you believe in any sort of connection? What do words like friend or family mean to those who see absolutely no meaning in life!

SAM. Now that's not fair. They mean all the more to me because I don't believe in all of that. When it's gone, it's gone! And I've already pushed too many away, Abish. I didn't mean to push you away, too.

ABISH. Just leave us alone. Why don't you find somewhere else?

SAM. (*Hurt.*) You don't mean that.

ABISH. Maybe I do.

SAM. In either case, I'm afraid that's not your decision. I have an agreement with your parents.

ABISH. That's going to change.

SAM. Abish, really. Let's just calm down. Out of everyone, you and I have been able to . . .

ABISH. Me and God, well, I think we can figure out a way to force your hand.

SAM. I thought you said that God doesn't talk to you.

ABISH. Oh, I never said that. He and I, well, we use a kind of sign language. He makes things very clear to me.

SAM. Well, good luck with that, because I'm not planning on going anywhere.

ABISH. You know, Sam, no matter what I may lack which is so evident in the rest of my family, I've got an ability that they don't.

SAM. And what's that?

ABISH. I'm not afraid to get my hands dirty.

SAM. (*Laughs.*) Abish, I love you, but, well, I'm supposed to be afraid of a 15 year old girl?

ABISH. 16. Remember, I'm 16 now. And, lady, believe me when I say that I'm having a coming of age.

SAM. Abish, I think we took a wrong turn here.

ABISH. Really? Because I think you may have just propelled me forward, Sam. Thanks for that, at least.

ABISH exits out the front door. SAM, confused and hurt, looks after ABISH, until she, too, takes on a steely resolve. She goes to the door and yells after ABISH:

SAM. Well, Supergirl, I'm still here! Bare your teeth all you want—I'm still here!

SAM exits down the stairs. Lights dim.

SCENE 11

Enter JOEL with ASHERA. JOEL is flipping through the mail as he enters.

ASHERA. So what's the Netflix?

JOEL. It was Abish's turn, so I'll bet you it's a quirky, independent flick. (*He opens the Netflix envelope.*) What did I tell you? *Lars and the Real Girl.*

ASHERA. Good taste! Love that movie.

JOEL. Okay—I suppose it was pretty good.

ASHERA. Pretty good? It was one of the best films that year.

JOEL. Yeah, I guess so.

ASHERA. Oh, come on, not everything has to be as epic as *Amistad*— or *Hotel Rwanda*!

JOEL. Now that's choice cinema.

ASHERA. I know. You've made me watch *Amistad* with you three times!

JOEL finds a letter from NAOMI in the mail.

JOEL. Oh, look! Naomi's first letter.

ASHERA. Doesn't she e-mail?

JOEL. Oh, sure, Mom makes her. But she likes the romantic element of letter writing. Paper and ink and all that. She said that she's going to save the juiciest stuff for the letters.

ASHERA. That's one way to perk an audience. (*JOEL starts to open the letter, but ASHERA stops him.*) Do you really want to open that without your parents?

JOEL. You're right. Mom would kill me. Be right back.

JOEL exits upstairs.

ASHERA. Wait. Did you see that there's one here for Sam, too?

Enter SAM.

ASHERA. Speak of the devil.

SAM. Practicing your hyperbole again, Ashera?

ASHERA. You got a letter.

SAM. For me?

ASHERA. Haven't you ever got a letter here before?

SAM. I get my magazines and bills, but who gets letters anymore?

ASHERA. Naomi's old fashioned like that. And you can't blame her—the personal touch of an actual signature—gotta love it.

SAM. Naomi wrote it? Why?

SAM takes the letter.

ASHERA. Maybe to see how you're doing.

SAM. More like taking the chance to preach me a sermon.

SAM puts the letter in her pocket.

ASHERA. You two didn't exactly end on the best of notes.

SAM. Seems to be happening a lot lately. Speaking of, why are you talking to me?

ASHERA. Is that so strange?

SAM. You don't have to.

ASHERA. Have to what?

SAM. Try to be nice.

ASHERA. We were close once.

SAM. And I wish as much as you do that we still were, but . . .

ASHERA. I didn't want to kill our friendship.

SAM. You didn't kill it. I did.

ASHERA. Sam . . .

SAM. Really, it's not personal. Lines get drawn in the sand. People choose sides. I chose mine, you chose yours. Let's leave it at that.

ASHERA. We're not playing Risk, Sam. There doesn't have to be some sort designation between Axis and Allies.

SAM. There are movements beyond our control, Ashera. Sure, they crush some special, intimate things—marriages, families, personal friendships—but if we're really honest with each other, we all have to follow in the shadows of the monoliths.

ASHERA. No matter the cost?

SAM. If there's to be any progress in the world, if it's ever going to get better, if right is ever going to get the upper hand, we've got to crush the myths of the enemy.

ASHERA. We? Not we.

SAM. Me and mine. My people.

ASHERA. Who's become the prophet now?

SAM. It's how religion got the upper hand. They weren't afraid to fight for what they believe in. But our weapons won't be armies or bombs—we'll take the higher road. We'll conquer through education. Through ideas. Through democracy. Through the arts and media. It's an equal playing field now and both sides have the same tools at their disposal. Now we just have to rush and see who's able to gather up the most on their side. And I aim to be a good recruiter.

ASHERA. This doesn't sound like you.

SAM. You never knew me, Ashera. You never knew my heart.

ASHERA. I suppose not.

SAM. You think it sounds paranoid? So did I once. But you get a taste of the opposite side's fire, their hypocrisy and their tyranny, then you realize it's one way or the other. The table is already set, Ashera. Now you just have to decide what side you want to play for.

Enter JOEL, MAXWELL, and DAISY from upstairs.

JOEL. Sorry that took so long.

DAISY. Maxwell's a very heavy sleeper—it's hard to coax him from his naps.

MAXWELL. I could have read it later.

DAISY. It's her first letter from the field.

MAXWELL. I've been reading the e-mails . . .

DAISY. It's her first letter!

There is a knock at the front door.

JOEL. I'll get it.

JOEL answers the door to reveal TYRELL. He has a magazine in his hand.

DAISY. Tyrell, you're in luck! Naomi's first letter.

JOEL. Hey, come in.

TYRELL brushes past JOEL and confronts SAM. He hands her the magazine.

TYRELL. Explain this.

SAM. I didn't know you read *The Freethinker*, Tyrell.

TYRELL. Explain it. To them.

SAM. I don't have to explain myself to anyone.

MAXWELL. What's going on?

TYRELL. If you won't tell them, I will.

SAM. Go ahead. It hardly matters anymore.

DAISY. Tyrell? What's wrong?

TYRELL. I have a friend at work—well, he's more like a verbal sparring partner, but we have fun. Well, he Facebooks me this article in a magazine he reads and, lo and behold, guess which family features prominently in it?

JOEL. What?

TYRELL. Oh, it only gets better. Listen to the title: "Living Under the Mormons: Observations On Religious Oppression" by Sam Forrest. It's twisted, Sam.

JOEL. Tyrell, let me see that.

TYRELL. Go ahead. I certainly don't want to read it ever again.

DAISY. Sam, we took you in our home . . .

SAM. And I paid for the right to be here. Paid every cent.

MAXWELL. And you think—you think money excuses this? This is our home. This is our family!

SAM. I'm certainly no family of yours. You made it pretty clear how alien I am to you and your beliefs.

JOEL. (*Reading from the article:*) "The Fieldings are what any observant person would call 'good people.' They have their flaws and their faults, but generally they're not bigots, they're not in any sense bad—except for one glaring exception. Their adherence to the Mormon creeds makes them prey to the inherent weakness of organized religion. They are caught up in a system of intolerance and exclusion while not ever truly being aware of it, which evidences the greatest tragedy of the whole scenario. No matter how much they try to struggle with their inheritance, or justify it, or explain away its deficiencies, they will always carry the mark that will distinguish them as part of the monstrous shadow that is much bigger than any of them."

DAISY. You really believe that about us?

MAXWELL. I want you out of this house.

SAM. I'm still paid through the rest of the month, Mr. Fielding.

MAXWELL. Get out of our house!

SAM. Your house? For this month at least I have bought the right to that basement, to this walkway, to that door! For this month this is my house, too!

JOEL. It all starts with the rhetoric.

SAM. You're good people—I said that!

TYRELL. And then called us marked!

SAM. And to how many people, how many groups has your Church done that exact same thing to? You of all people, Tyrell, should know that!

TYRELL. I'm not justifying prejudice on any side, and you know as well as I do that is exactly what you're doing, Sam—stoking prejudice!

SAM. You want to talk about the sins of the fathers? Then let's take a look at the imposters and charlatans which brought all of you into bondage—slaves of ignorance and superstition! Yes, I call it a mark, not given by an uncaring God who would curse an innocent person's skin, but instead a power grasping demagogue who would manipulate . . .

MAXWELL. Enough!

SAM. I want to break these chains, Mr. Fielding. If I can't break them off you, then I'm going to reveal them for what they are to the rest of the world!

JOEL. Even if we have to be the sacrificial lambs to do it?

SAM. Religions are all just complex systems of psychological and emotional manipulation . . .

MAXWELL. I said enough!

SAM. No, I'm not going to shut up until I've had my say. I won't be silent any more.

MAXWELL. And you think $500 a month gives you the right to lecture us, to upend our lives and . . .

SAM. I think the truth gives me the right to do it!

DAISY. Please, everybody, let's just calm down and . . .

JOEL. Truth? You think you know the truth about us? About any of us?

DAISY's cell phone rings. She ignores it.

DAISY. Please . . .

JOEL. Has it ever occurred to you that we may be basing our belief on something much more powerful than special interest groups or conniving ministers?

DAISY's cell phone continues to ring.

SAM. So you keep telling me, but I've never seen the evidence!

JOEL. You've never cared to see it! You've never had the right intent!

DAISY's cell phone rings again, she turns it off.

SAM. Intent!

MAXWELL. We allowed you into our home—we trusted you.

There is a knock at the door.

DAISY. Oh, for heaven's sake, can't we get any privacy?

MAXWELL. I trusted you!

SAM. You never trusted me! You just ignored me. Left me to my own devices in the basement!

The door knocks again, more urgently.

DAISY. Can we all keep this down while I take care of this?

DAISY goes to the door and answers it. JENNY is at the door. Her distress is immediately apparent.

MAXWELL. You come here, mock our beliefs, tell your tales, and expose our family to the hate and ignorance of those who are just looking for an excuse to . . . !

DAISY. Jenny? What's wrong, sweetheart?

JENNY. I—I should have called you immediately. I didn't have your number, but I finally realized Mrs. Johnson did. Something really bad has happened . . .

DAISY. What do you mean? What happened?

SAM. Prejudice? You all keep talking talk to me about prejudice! You're not your Mormon pioneer ancestors! You're not being pushed from state to state anymore or mobbed or killed anymore. What do any of you actually know about prejudice? Mormons always have this martyr complex . . .

JENNY. I—I don't know what to say. Mrs. Fielding, I'm so sorry—it all happened really fast . . .

DAISY. Will all of you be quiet? Something's happened at the Johnsons down the street . . .

SAM. You dare set yourself up as the victims after what your Church did with Proposition 8, for the every day heart break and hardship your Church makes for . . .

MAXWELL. We're protecting our values! Our homes! We're protecting them from people like you!

DAISY. Wait, Abish was with you. Where's Abish?

SAM. And that's what we say about you! How is your life, your life-style any more sacred than what my side experiences? You think my condemnation is harsh? I've been told I'm going to hell by my own family!

MAXWELL. This is where we are meant to be safe. You invaded it!

JENNY. Mrs. Fielding . . . Oh, Mrs. Fielding . . .

SAM. I'm trying to show you the truth!

DAISY. No. No, no, no . . .

MAXWELL. You have desecrated our home!

The conflict stops instantaneously as everyone looks to DAISY *as she lets out a strangled cry of grief.* MAXWELL *is immediately by her side, embracing* DAISY *as she breaks down in unintelligible tears and cries.*

MAXWELL (CONT'D). Jenny, what's going on?

JENNY. I . . . I . . .

MAXWELL. For Heaven's sake, what is it?!

JENNY. We already called 911, but once the ambulance got there . . .

MAXWELL. What happened?

JENNY. Me and Abish were at the party at John's house—but there were some kids there who have always teased her about being a member of your Church. They . . .

MAXWELL. Just tell me what happened!

JENNY. I—I don't know how to say this, Mr. Fielding.

MAXWELL. Tell me, please, tell me.

JENNY. (*Emotional, having a difficult time telling this:*) I'm sorry, Sam, but somebody posted your article on Abish's wall, and then started spreading it around. Some people at the party had read the posts and the group was laughing and taunting—and Abish got mad and there was a serious argument. Abish got in their face about it and started attacking their beliefs, too. Apparently they pretended to be sorry about it later and they had these cookies—they were hash cookies, but it was laced with something, I don't know what kind of drug it was, but it was really strong—they thought it was some kind of twisted joke to keep feeding them to Abish all night. Nobody knows who originally brought the cookies, and I don't think they really knew what was in them . . .

MAXWELL. No, no, no, please, Heavenly Father, no . . .

JENNY. I'm so sorry, by the time we realized what happened and the ambulance got there—I'm so, so, so sorry. Abish is dead.

DAISY clings even tighter to MAXWELL, *her sobs increasing.* MAXWELL *cries out and clings back.* TYRELL *stands in the back quietly stunned.* JOEL *sits where he is and buries his face into his hands.* SAM *looks about, at a loss.* ASHERA *looks at her with a confused anger.*

ASHERA. Sam . . .

SAM, looking once more on the wreckage, runs her hands through her hair and tries to say something—anything—anything that will somehow fix this. She grasps for the letter in her pocket, the letter from NAOMI.

SAM. I—Ashera, I don't want to know what the letter says. Is it possible . . . ?

ASHERA. Sam, you need to get out of here . . .

MAXWELL. What is she still doing here?!

SAM, frightened, exits. MAXWELL *and* DAISY *come unglued with grief,* ASHERA *comforts* JOEL *and* TYRELL *sits, still rocked with both grief and realization. As the cries ascend to heaven, the lights, and the cries, dim to blackness and silence.*

SCENE 12

Enter NAOMI, *dressed in her missionary clothing and tag. She looks around, as one does when one has been away from home for some time. Soberly, she goes over to the family portrait, looking specifically at* ABISH. *Enter* JOEL, ASHERA, MAXWELL, *and* DAISY. MAXWELL *is carrying in* NAOMI's *luggage. They all look at* NAOMI *and stop soberly.* MAXWELL *goes over to her, putting his arm silently around her.*

NAOMI. I figured I was probably going to miss Joel and Ashera's wedding. But I didn't expect a funeral.

MAXWELL. The letter you wrote for the service was beautiful. Joel delivered it beautifully. That's when I—finally broke down.

JOEL. Today is a happy day. Let's not . . .

NAOMI. Please, Joel, it's like we've been avoiding her ever since I got off the plane. I don't want to ignore my little sister.

The doorbell.

DAISY. I'll get that.

DAISY opens the door to reveal TYRELL, with NAOMI's other suitcase in tow.

TYRELL. Looks like I've got good timing. I saw you pull up into the driveway just as I turned the corner.

NAOMI. Tyrell!

NAOMI rushes to TYRELL and hugs him.

DAISY. Naomi, you haven't been released by the Stake President yet.

MAXWELL. Let it go, sweetheart. It's not like they're making out.

ASHERA. Yet.

DAISY. Ashera! Honestly, the things you say sometimes.

TYRELL. Your bag, as promised.

JOEL. Maybe it's best we let these two talk a bit.

DAISY. But no making out!

NAOMI. Gotcha, Mom.

Exit DAISY, MAXWELL, ASHERA, and JOEL. There is an almost bashful pause between the NAOMI and TYRELL.

NAOMI (CONT'D). I honestly didn't expect you here when I came back—at least not without a ring on your finger.

TYRELL. What about "I love you" didn't you catch?

NAOMI. So we're still there?

TYRELL. We're still there. That is if—well, you've been gone for a year and a half. If you want to date other people at first . . .

NAOMI. Is that what you want?

TYRELL. I already tried that when you were gone, but I couldn't think of anybody but you. Nobody measured up.

NAOMI. At least you didn't keep yourself in cold storage.

TYRELL. Well, there was this one hot chick . . . (*NAOMI punches TYRELL in the shoulder.*) Kidding! Kidding! (*Beat.*) Well, kind of . . .

NAOMI. Really?

TYRELL. I didn't want to write about it in the letters. I thought it would only distract you. But she was the closest I came to being really serious with someone, but . . .

NAOMI. But?

TYRELL. I'm only going to say this because I know you'd appreciate it . . .

NAOMI. Intriguing . . .

TYRELL. Promise to think I'm not weird or psycho . . .

NAOMI. Maybe disturbing . . .

TYRELL. I—I had this really vivid dream.

NAOMI. Okay, now you're talking my language.

TYRELL. You must have rubbed off on me, because I never dream like that—but in the dream I was in this desert of clear, brilliant sand, like it was made of glass. Then I saw you standing there and I saw you take off a veil. Well, you actually kind of ripped it off your face, and there was this big tearing sound and I felt like I saw you, the real you for the first time. And then you came to me and . . .

NAOMI. And?

TYRELL. Well . . .

NAOMI. Come on.

TYRELL. You kissed me. A simple, affectionate kiss. And I was really, really happy. That's it. The dream was over. Should I not have told you that?

NAOMI. Who are you talking to?

TYRELL. Yeah.

NAOMI. But Tyrell . . .

TYRELL. Yeah?

NAOMI. Let's not rush, okay? I need to get settled back into myself. A mission—it puts you in a different place, God 24/7, you know? I loved that, but—I want you to look at *me* when we kneel across that altar.

TYRELL. *When* we kneel?

NAOMI. Too presumptuous?

TYRELL. Today, lady, you could say anything and I'd cry out, "Amen!"

NAOMI. Butterscotch.

TYRELL. Amen!

NAOMI. Harry Potter.

TYRELL. Amen!

NAOMI. Einstein Bagels!

TYRELL. Amen! Amen! Amen!

NAOMI. I love you.

TYRELL. Amen.

They kiss. NAOMI *pulls back coyly.*

NAOMI. Mom's right. I haven't been released yet.

TYRELL. Then let's get that Stake President over here.

Doorbell.

TYRELL (CONT'D). I suppose you're going to be pretty popular today. All sorts of people will want to see you.

NAOMI goes to answer it.

NAOMI. I've got it!

NAOMI opens the door to reveal SAM. NAOMI just stands there in shocked silence for a moment.

SAM. Hi, Naomi.

Enter MAXWELL.

MAXWELL. Naomi, who's at the . . . (*Sees SAM.*) No. No, you're not welcome here, Sam.

SAM. Please, Mr. Fielding, I've come to . . .

MAXWELL. I don't care why you've come.

SAM. I've been carrying this for over a year. Please, just hear me out.

MAXWELL. There's no hearing it out!

Enter DAISY, JOEL, and ASHERA.

DAISY. Darling, what's going . . . ?

They all stop.

ASHERA. Sam, this is not a good idea.

SAM. I need this . . .

JOEL. You talk about what *you* need? You dare come here and think that we care at all about what you need?

SAM. Please, Mr. and Mrs. Fielding, I know what I did was . . .

NAOMI. You killed my little sister!

NAOMI slaps SAM. This shocks everyone, most especially NAOMI herself.

TYRELL. Sam, really, I think it's time you left.

SAM. Naomi, what was in the letter?

NAOMI. What letter?

SAM. The letter you sent me. You sent me a letter before we found out about Abish's death. I—I never read it.

NAOMI. I had totally forgotten about writing that.

SAM. What was in the letter?

NAOMI. An apology.

SAM. What?

NAOMI. I apologized for being pushy with the Book of Mormon before I left. You had already told me that you weren't interested so—so I apologized.

SAM. Oh.

NAOMI. What did you think I wrote?

SAM. I—I don't know what I was thinking.

MAXWELL. What is she still doing here?

SAM. Mr. Fielding, I just want to say my peace, I want to make . . .

MAXWELL. Not today, not with us. If you want to make peace with God, that's what you should do, but you can't expect us to . . .

SAM. I can't make peace with God! I don't believe in God!

MAXWELL. Then without God, Sam, you've got nothing to hold onto, because we're not going to . . .

> DAISY *who has been sitting silently this whole time, stands. Everyone is silent as she approaches* SAM *and places her hand on* SAM's *cheek and looks* SAM *deeply in the eyes, really connecting to all of the pain, loss, guilt, striving and desperate hope that* SAM *is going through. After this moment of real connection,* DAISY *speaks for the first time. Everyone looks to her.*

DAISY. We have to change. We can't do this anymore.

MAXWELL. Daisy, this is asking too much . . .

DAISY. Seven times seventy, Max.

MAXWELL. I know, but she—she was . . .

SAM. She was your little girl.

> MAX *looks at* SAM, *at a complete loss.*

SAM (CONT'D). Max, you must believe me—I loved her. She was the last person I would have ever wanted to . . .

MAXWELL. No, no, please, don't . . .

DAISY. (*To MAX:*) Max, I looked at Abish and what I saw was the future of the Church—the future of this family. She was everything I had so often wanted to be, but felt like I couldn't be, because of our culture, because of my habits, because of my upbringing. She was a little wild, a little emotional, a little impulsive, true, but she also so often was right. Saw things clearly, saw things honestly—she was authentic. And then when people came along to try and tear down her faith, tear down our hope, I was very resentful, but I understood a little. They did so to keep their own beliefs intact, because they're trying to make sense of it all, too. And because they love her, too. Sam did what she did defensively, like we so often do. We're often as cruel to them as they are cruel to us.

MAXWELL. I need time, Daisy.

DAISY. (*Giving MAX some space, DAISY switches to SAM.*) Sam, when you try and take our future, our children, and when I know your words are affecting them—that's when it hits me the hardest. Because you're taking away our progress. Joel, Naomi—Abish. They have so much more potential in them than I ever hoped for myself. They fly so high and I—sometimes I just marvel. But, if they're shot down, if you don't allow them to lift the rest of us up, to push us towards progress—then we're left behind.

SAM. I don't want to get left behind either, Daisy. I know, I really know what it feels like to be alone. But I'm not you, I'm not any of you, I can't believe what you do. With my experiences, with my hard fought beliefs, all I am, as I am, I'm simply not capable of accepting that.

DAISY. You're going to eat dinner with us tonight.

MAX. Now, Daisy . . .

SAM. I don't know if that's a good . . .

DAISY. Please. Eat with us.

SAM *hesitates, but then simply nods.*

JOEL. Mom, we've already had dinner.

DAISY. Then dessert. Maxwell, can you make some banana shakes?

MAXWELL. I . . .

DAISY. Please, Max, all of us need this.

JOEL. Mom, really, no, we can't do this. She comes here with a little emotional manipulation, an atheistic hail Mary, and—and that's it? She gets fast and free absolution for killing your daughter?

ASHERA. Joel . . .

JOEL. No! I—I had my own things to make up to Abish. Bridges I had yet to build, apologies I wanted to make and—and I was robbed of that chance. The guilt I hold is not so easily erased, so why should hers be?

NAOMI. I'm in as much pain as you are, Joel, but Mom is right. It wasn't her fault.

JOEL. Yes, it was!

TYRELL. Abish was killed by a bunch of stupid kids . . .

JOEL. . . . who were spurred on by her words. *Her* words! Yes, free speech is a right, but it's also a privilege. When words are purposely constructed to hurt, to make another person or group into a hiss, a curse, when words are used to shame without love, to break down without offering healing in its aftermath—then those words have been abused, they have been turned into a weapon.

SAM. Tyrell, you mentioned love. Is this love?

JOEL. No, no! You don't get to dictate when I feel what. You don't get to manipulate me like that.

SAM. I'm not trying to manipulate. But I'm not the monster you make me out to be either. You don't get to use words without consequence either.

JOEL. Every movement has its leaders, and the fierce anti-Mormonism that exists today is led by the banners of ardent atheists and impassioned evangelicals alike, from the right and the left, from every side. You all may not see the big picture, but I do, and I see the side that Sam chose and what that movement is trying to do to us.

SAM. Maybe you're right. Or maybe I was. Maybe we're as divided as we both thought, with no way of reconciliation, no common ground. But I hope we were both wrong. That's why I'm here. Despite all that has happened, I hope that—that there can still be a kinship between us.

JOEL. Kinship? No, in this life and in the next, our kingdoms are going to be divided, Sam. God may be able to forgive you, I hope he does, but unless you change in more major ways than you've shown, we'll need to be put in different rooms, because I'm not going to accept what you did to our family in the name of your cause.

NAOMI. Joel, how can you say that? Christ's grace and atonement—isn't that what the Gospel is all about?

JOEL. If a person repents. If a person accepts that grace and chooses to change. Sam hasn't really changed, she just feels bad and she just wants us to tell her it's okay to feel better.

SAM. I have changed, Joel. I have changed so much. The world will never be the same for me, it can't be. But what I'm telling you is that even before all of this, I was still a good person even then. I didn't mean for any of this to happen.

JOEL. Your article persuaded me otherwise.

SAM. I was only stating my beliefs . . .

JOEL. But you were under our roof, living with our family. You dragged us into it!

SAM. No, no, it wasn't personal!

JOEL. Faith is always personal.

NAOMI. Joel, Sam was Abish's friend. She more than any of us would have welcomed Sam back.

JOEL. We can't know that because Abish is dead. And I won't so easily forget that. When Sam's gone from the house, just give me a call and I'll be right back.

NAOMI. Joel, you can't mean that . . .

JOEL. Back off, Naomi.

Exit JOEL. NAOMI is about to go after him when ASHERA stops her.

ASHERA. Give him a little space, Naomi. We can talk to him later.

SAM. Is that how you feel about me, too, Mr. Fielding? Beyond hope?

MAXWELL. What I feel right now is very different than what I believe.

SAM. And what do you believe?

MAXWELL. That God loves you just as much as my little girl.

NAOMI. Can—can we pray, Papa? Maybe that will help.

MAXWELL. I—I don't really feel like praying . . .

DAISY. Which means we probably should. Does anybody mind if I say it?

No one objects.

SAM. I—I don't know if I can do this with you.

ASHERA. Don't make it a sign of belief then, Sam. Just a sign of love.

They all look to SAM and she nods. They gather in a circle and kneel. ASHERA initiates hand holding until they have linked themselves together.

DAISY. Dearest Father, we are grateful for thee; for our Mother; for our blessed Savior, thy precious son Jesus; and for the Holy Spirit. We have failed thee so often, but these words amongst the writings of thy prophets comfort us, these words that have haunted my memory ever since I heard them uttered by my littlest child . . . (*It is evident that she has painstakingly committed this scripture to memory:*)

". . . and he inviteth them all to come unto him and partake of his goodness; and denieth none that come unto him, black and white, bond and free, male and female; and he remembereth the heathen; and all are alike unto God, both Jew and Gentile." Our Abba, our— our Papa—let us remember. In the name of thy Child, Jesus Christ, Amen.

They all say "Amen," except for SAM. *Wordlessly, they all kneel there for a moment. Then* SAM *stands.*

SAM. On rare occasions I wish I could still believe. But I just can't. With what I've experienced, with what I feel like I know to be true, I just can't believe.

NAOMI. Just as our experiences can't lead us to anywhere but belief.

TYRELL. Even when it would be easier not to believe.

DAISY. Especially then.

SAM. Then where on earth does that leave us?

MAXWELL. (*Beat.*) Banana shakes?

SAM. (*Beat.*) Banana shakes.

Quietly, they all exit into the kitchen.

THE END

Note: This section was supposed to be a part of Scene Six of Act One, but was deleted due to a number of issues. It made an already lengthy scene even longer; was particularly "talky"—even preachy—in an already dialogue driven, overt play; dwelled awkwardly on the race issues that were addressed elsewhere; and derailed the main plot. There are still elements of this scene that I like, though, especially as it incorporates a dream I once had, and relates the conversion story of a friend of mine, Danor Gerald. Thus I have included it here for the curious, but with the instruction that it not be included in any productions of the play, unless a director feels particularly compelled. Like many deleted scenes, it was cut for very good reasons.

DELETED SCENE

TYRELL kisses NAOMI. Enter JOEL.

JOEL. Oh, uh, sorry. When you're ready, Dad's making some banana shakes for us . . .

NAOMI. Awesome. Come on, it's a bit of a tradition . . .

JOEL. Actually, can I talk to Tyrell for a moment?

NAOMI. Now, Joel, if this is some sort of brother's interview to grill Tyrell, then . . .

JOEL. Don't worry, Naomi, I was just curious about something.

TYRELL. It's okay, love. I want to get to know Joel better anyway.

NAOMI. Okay. But no stupid questions, Joel.

JOEL. Are any of my questions ever stupid?

NAOMI punches JOEL in the arm.

NAOMI. No stupid questions.

JOEL. I stand by my previous . . . (*NAOMI hits him in the arm again.*) Okay, no stupid questions!

NAOMI. He can be an intellectual bully sometimes.

TYRELL. Oh, I think I can hold my own.

NAOMI. I know you can. *(NAOMI kisses TYRELL on the cheek and then does the same to JOEL.)* Play nice, boys.

   Exit NAOMI.

JOEL. Sorry. I'll make this quick.

TYRELL. No problem.

JOEL. First off, I wanted to apologize for Sam's behavior tonight. She's living with us, and I think Mom and Dad need the money and . . .

TYRELL. Her problem, not yours, Joel.

JOEL. I know, but—it's obvious that Naomi cares a lot about you and, well, I want to make sure you know how welcome you are here.

TYRELL. Thanks, Joel.

JOEL. I mean—I mean really welcome. Especially with me—I'm usually protective of Naomi—her and I, we have a special connection.

TYRELL. She's told me.

JOEL. Yeah, and, well, it's not just me overcompensating or anything, but I'm really cheering you two on.

TYRELL. Why's that?

JOEL. Well, I better not say . . .

TYRELL. No, go ahead.

JOEL. Uh, has Naomi mentioned our—our gifts? Spiritually, I mean.

TYRELL. Uh, yeah. Is that okay?

JOEL. Yeah, Naomi and I are a little open sometimes. Dangerously open.

TYRELL. Yeah, believe me, dating your sister—I know.

JOEL. Obviously, you've got to be careful with who you share things with—ironically, visionaries are sometimes kind of underground in the Church . . .

TYRELL. Is that how you see yourself? A visionary?

JOEL. Sounds presumptuous, I know.

TYRELL. Yeah.

JOEL. And that's what they told Lehi—Joan of Arc—that's what they told Joseph Smith—not that I'm comparing myself to them—there's no comparison. But they were too presumptuous—they were too open—and they were punished for it. All that pearls before swine talk, it's true. The swine are ready to trample and rend you.

TYRELL. I hear a "but" in there.

JOEL. But sometimes when you become so secretive, so closed off—it gets lonely. You have all these beautiful things to tell only to discover that you're gagged. Look, I'm being stupid. Let's go in and get those shakes.

TYRELL. No, go ahead, Joel. You think you're connected to me. I want to hear why.

JOEL. I—I had this dream once. I was walking with this beautiful black woman. And by beautiful, it was inside and out, it was almost as if she radiated. We were having this wonderful, intimate talk and I felt just so—so connected to her. Then we came upon this—it was a dream, so obviously not everything is logical—I saw this kind of wall or mirror or portal. I saw this, well, this panorama of African Americans. Some were modern, some were wearing period clothing, some of them were happy, some were very sober, while others—others had this seething—anger. I was startled. Why was I being shown such anger? I've thought a lot about it since then, the injustice we humans put on each other. Sometimes the anger shouldn't be resented or defended against—sometimes the anger is deserved.

TYRELL. I hope you're not cheering for me and Naomi just because I'm black, Joel.

JOEL. No, of course not. I want the best for you and Naomi, no matter where that leads. And you seem about as good as they come.

TYRELL. Good. Because I'm so much more than my race: positive and negative.

JOEL. And that's my point. Sam, she had some good points. The Church's history with race—it's not always pretty.

TYRELL. Nor is it without it's miracles. Have you read about the experiences in Africa before the priesthood revelation?

JOEL. Oh, yeah, a real Pentecost. Love that stuff. Dreams, miracles, visions. Africans all over their continent being miraculously drawn to the Church without having any previous connection to it. It shows me who's Church this really is, no matter what we stupid human beings do to screw it up.

TYRELL. I'm not like you and your sister, Joel, as much as I yearn for it. Nothing dramatic like that. But that doesn't mean it wasn't any less real. I had been searching, you know. My family had always been religious, but we had all gone different paths—Jehovah's Witnesses, Pentecostals, Catholics—we all scattered to the four winds denominationally. I hadn't decided. Then a Mormon commercial came on the television one day. One of those "Family, Isn't It About Time?" commercials. There wasn't anything special about it, it was pretty generic, even corny, but I had this—well, I felt the Spirit. All these words then tumbled into my head and I wrote them all out. Several months later I was invited to take the discussions by a classmate's roommate. Even though they told me things that were new to me, well, none of it seemed wrong. I kept waiting for them to say something wrong. If they had, I would have moved on. All I felt was the Spirit, that—that warmth and peaceful clarity. It wasn't long before I was baptized.

JOEL. But people have said plenty of wrong things since then, haven't they?

TYRELL. Oh, yeah. Mormons can say some pretty stupid things sometimes. But that wasn't the point anymore. The point was that God had touched me. I was in His hands now.

Enter ASHERA.

ASHERA. Hey, boys, these banana shakes are looking pretty good. Get in here before I drag you in! As much as all of us would enjoy that, you know that I would win.

TYRELL. Shakes sound great to me.

Exit TYRELL.

ASHERA. You, too, hot stuff.

JOEL. You talking to me?

ASHERA. I don't see anyone else in here.

JOEL. Thanks for the charity, but no one's ever mistaken me for Hugh Jackman.

ASHERA. Don't get me wrong, Hugh could have fun with me anytime, but he's not my type.

JOEL. And who's your type?

ASHERA. I thought I already made that clear, hot stuff.

JOEL. Uh . . .

ASHERA. Get in here, will you?

JOEL. Yes, ma'am.

Exit JOEL and ASHERA.

Noel Miller Nichols as Sam Forest, Ivy Worsham-Gambier as Daisy Fielding, and Peyton Geery as Maxwell Fielding. Photo by Natalie Watson Nelson.

Seth Ephraim Scott as Joel Fielding, Sarah D'Agastino as Abish Fielding. Photo by Natalie Watson Nelson.

Sarah D'Agastino as Abish Fielding, Noel Miller Nichols as Sam Forest. Photo by Natalie Watson Nelson.

Kendra Schroeder as Naomi Fielding, Ivy Worsham-Gambier as Daisy Fielding, and Peyton Geery as Maxwell Fielding, Sarah D'Agastino as Abish Fielding, Victoria Murray as Ashera, and Seth Ephraim Scott as Joel Fielding. Photo by Natalie Watson Nelson.

Zachary Figures as Tyrell Howard, Kendra Schroeder as Naomi Fielding, Ivy Worsham-Gambier as Daisy Fielding, and Peyton Geery as Maxwell Fielding, Sarah D'Agastino as Abish Fielding, Victoria Murray as Ashera, Noel Miller Nichols as Sam Forest, and Seth Ephraim Scott as Joel Fielding. Photo by Natalie Watson Nelson.

Seth Ephraim Scott as Joel Fielding and Victoria Murray as Ashera. Photo by Natalie Watson Nelson.

Kendra Schroeder as Naomi Fielding, Seth Ephraim Scott as Joel Fielding, and Zachary Figures as Tyrell Howard. Photo by Natalie Watson Nelson.

Seth Ephraim Scott as Joel Fielding, Victoria Murray as Ashera, Kendra Schroeder as Naomi Fielding, and Zachary Figures as Tyrell Howard. Photo by Natalie Watson Nelson.

Ivy Worsham-Gambier as Daisy Fielding, and Sarah D'Agastino as Abish Fielding. Photo by Natalie Watson Nelson.

Sarah D'Agastino as Abish Fielding, Ivy Worsham-Gambier as Daisy Fielding, and Noel Miller Nichols as Sam Forest. Photo by Natalie Watson Nelson.

Sarah D'Agastino as Abish Fielding, Noel Miller Nichols as Sam Forest, Seth Ephraim Scott as Joel Fielding, and Kendra Schroeder as Naomi Fielding. Photo by Natalie Watson Nelson.

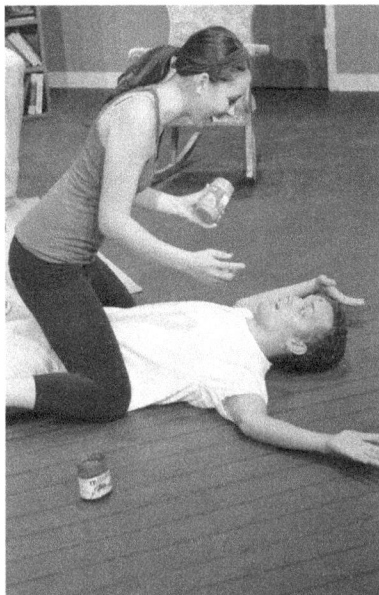

Noel Miller Nichols as Sam Forest and Seth Ephraim Scott as Joel Fielding. Photo by Natalie Watson Nelson.

Seth Epraim Scott as Joel Fielding. Photo by Natalie Watson Nelson.

Alana Gordon as Jenny Pond and Sarah D'Agastino as Abish Fielding. Photo by Natalie Watson Nelson.

Kendra Schroeder as Naomi Fielding and Ivy Worsham-Gambier as Daisy Fielding. Photo by Natalie Watson Nelson.

Sarah D'Agastino as Abish Fielding and Seth Ephraim Scott as Joel Fielding. Photo by Natalie Watson Nelson.

Zachary Figures as Tyrell Howard, Kendra Schroeder as Naomi Fielding, Victoria Murray as Ashera, and Seth Ephraim Scott as Joel Fielding. Photo by Natalie Watson Nelson.

Sarah D'Agastino as Abish Fielding and Noel Miller Nichols as Sam Forrest. Photo by Natalie Watson Nelson.

Ivy Worsham-Gambier as Daisy Fielding. Photo by Natalie Watson Nelson.

Ivy Worsham-Gambier as Daisy Fielding and Alana Gordon as Jenny Pond. Photo by Natalie Watson Nelson.

263

Noel Miller Nichols as Sam Forest and Ivy Worsham-Gambier as Daisy Fielding. Photo by Natalie Watson Nelson.

Noel Miller Nichols as Sam Forest, Zachary Figures as Tyrell Howard, Seth Ephraim Scott as Joel Fielding, and Kendra Schroeder as Naomi Fielding. Photo by Natalie Watson Nelson.

Noel Miller Nichols as Sam Forest, Victoria Murray as Ashera, Peyton Geery as Maxwell Fielding, Ivy Worsham-Gambier as Daisy Fielding, and Kendra Schroeder as Naomi Fielding. Photo by Natalie Watson Nelson.

Zachary Figures as Tyrell Howard. Photo by Natalie Watson Nelson.

Noel Miller Nichols as Sam Forest, Zachary Figures as Tyrell Howard, Seth Ephraim Scott as Joel Fielding, and Kendra Schroeder as Naomi Fielding. Photo by Natalie Watson Nelson.

Yeshua

A Gospel Play in Two Acts

For my children, that they may always know that their father believes in the Son of God and for my wife Anne, whose spiritual journey has been so aligned with mine: Spiritually, we understand each other.

"What we choose to embrace, to be responsive to, is the purest reflection of who we are and what we love."

— Terryl and Fiona Givens, *The God Who Weeps*

Yeshua

Act One

SCENE 1

YESHUA *lays still, almost as if he were dead, on a slab of stone that is used as a bed, tomb, and table throughout the play. The lights are dim. There is a low, vibrating, humming sound. It is not manmade, nor is it overpowering. Subtle, yet unmistakably present, the sound has the sense of an ancient energy rather than a modern creation. As if it came from a source that has existed long before the earth was even formed, an energy that perhaps has always existed. Before too long the humming is accompanied by whispers. They are not sinister, but are certainly mysterious. We cannot yet quite make out what the whispers are saying at first, but then certain words are distinctly heard, among the indiscernible ones:*

WHISPERS. Word . . . Beginning . . . God . . . Made . . . Life . . . Life . . . Light . . . Light!

On the last "Light!" a bright light appears above Yeshua and shines down upon his body. More whispers are then discerned among the indistinguishable words:

WHISPERS (CONT'D). Witness . . . Believe . . . World . . . Knew Him Not . . . Receive . . . Power . . . Sons of God . . . Believe . . . Blood . . . Flesh . . . Of God . . . Dwelt Among Us . . . Glory . . . Grace . . . Truth . . . Witness!

The lights fade down to their previous dimness. A door opens and light then floods in from that source, silhouetting the figure

*within the door frame. The bright light behind the figures fades
to reveal* MOTHER MIRIAM, *the mother of Yeshua. She walks
to* YESHUA *and shakes him gently.*

MOTHER MIRIAM. Wake up—Yeshua. Yeshua, wake up.

YESHUA *awakes, rising strongly, taking in a deep breath. The
whispers and the deep humming are suddenly cut off.*

YESHUA. Mother?

MOTHER MIRIAM. I didn't mean to startle you.

YESHUA. I was dreaming. The same dream as last night. There's still
parts of it I am trying to . . .

MOTHER MIRIAM. I need you.

YESHUA. Mother, can you wait a moment? I'm trying to understand
what is being said . . .

MOTHER MIRIAM. Your brother's wedding . . .

YESHUA. Has that already started? Why didn't anyone wake me?

MOTHER MIRIAM. We couldn't find you—like usual. What are you
doing down here?

YESHUA. I was tired.

MOTHER MIRIAM. Well, you've missed the wine then. It's all gone.
That's why I need your help . . .

YESHUA. Well, if it's gone, I don't see how I can . . .

MOTHER MIRIAM. Yes, you can.

YESHUA *understands what she is asking him.*

YESHUA. Mother, this is not just something I can call on for every
unimportant . . .

MOTHER MIRIAM. This is important.

YESHUA. I know that you're stressed, but my Abba has intended it for . . .

MOTHER MIRIAM. It's your brother's wedding and there is no more
wine.

YESHUA *looks at his mother searchingly. A soft smile breaks on his face.*

YESHUA. Mother if you always pray like this, my Father will give you any righteous desire—if only because you weary him so much!

MOTHER MIRIAM. There's got to be some advantage to being a stubborn, old widow.

YESHUA *softly, affectionately touches his mother's face and then kisses her on the top of her head.*

YESHUA. Tell them to bring the jars in here. I'll take care of it.

MOTHER MIRIAM *embraces her son tightly and kisses him on the cheek.*

MOTHER MIRIAM. Thank you, Yeshua.

MOTHER MIRIAM *exits.* YESHUA *looks after her and then seems weighed down by the heaviness of some intense thought. He then laughs ironically. He looks up to God, his Father.*

YESHUA. I often wondered how it would start. But wine at a wedding? Not exactly what I would call dignified. (*The lightness of the joke fades as the heaviness comes back.*) Abba, I don't think I'm ready yet.

A few SERVANTS *start bringing in jars of water (the* SER-VANT'*s lines can be divided amongst them).*

SERVANT. Master Yeshua . . .

YESHUA. Do not call me Master. There is only one Master, our Abba.

SERVANT. Yes, Yeshua. But this water—surely it's not appropriate for such an occasion. It's meant for cleaning.

YESHUA. Then it's perfect. It will be how they remember me.

YESHUA *comes over the water, whose clear, bright, moving light reflects upon his face. As he changes it, the light turns to a red, moving light shining upon his face.* YESHUA *closes his eyes for a moment, exhaling, as if energy has passed away from him. The* SERVANTS *are stunned.*

SERVANT. As red as blood . . .

YESHUA dips a cup into it and hands it to one of the SERVANTS.

YESHUA. Drink.

Each SERVANT drinks.

SERVANT. That's the good stuff!

The SERVANTS laugh, but then YESHUA looks at each of them searchingly.

YESHUA. This is not a mere trick.

SERVANT. Of course not.

YESHUA. Remember me.

The SERVANTS nod and then, still in awe, pick up the jars and bring them out. YESHUA looks up to his Abba.

YESHUA (CONT'D). Please, Abba, prepare me for this.

SCENE 2

A group of men and women have surrounded THE BAPTIST, among them are YOCHANAN ZEBADYAH, YA'AQOV ZEBA-DYAH, and ANDREAS, as well as members of the Pharisees, the Sadducees, and other members of the Jewish community. On the outskirts is a woman, MIRIAM. She is nervous to be there. THE BAPTIST is standing in water (whether literal water, or portrayed through some other way such as lighting, etc.). He is a wild looking man, with camel hair and leather clothing, austere and stoic.

THE BAPTIST. Come, be immersed and cleansed! Confess your sins and be clean!

PHARISEE #1 makes his way through the crowd towards PHARISEE #2. MIRIAM, unaware of him, almost bumps into him and the PHARISEE recoils from her. She falls to the ground.

PHARISEE #1. Get away from me!

MIRIAM. I am sorry, sir.

PHARISEE #1. Don't talk to me! If you touched me—well, can you imagine? Go—go!

MIRIAM retreats to a group of other women. THE BAPTIST notes this, disapprovingly, but then continues.

THE BAPTIST. Prepare the way of Adonai and make his paths straight! Show your commitment to Adonai with a clean heart and clean hands!

PHARISEE #1. I will submit to this, Yochanan. It is prudently done. The Law tells us to be clean vessels. As a Pharisee, I see the wisdom in this.

THE BAPTIST. What I offer can't clean you.

PHARISEE #1. I keep the law, I purify myself in all things. I do not eat any unclean thing, I do not touch the impure person, nor the dead. I am clean!

THE BAPTIST. You are not clean. What I offer is so much more than washing your hands, reading off a list, or a ritual bath!

There is murmuring among the group.

PHARISEE #2. Do you dispute the law?

THE BAPTIST. No.

PHARISEE #1. Then baptize me—I'm clean! I follow the Law of Moses. The Law has said, "You shall be holy: for I the Lord your God am holy." It is so with me. I tithe, I sacrifice, I should not be denied anything.

Enter YESHUA, unnoticed by everyone. He watches quietly.

THE BAPTIST. The Law also says, "You shall not hate your brother in your heart . . . You shall not avenge, nor bear any grudge against the children of your people, but you shall love your neighbor as yourself." (*Indicating MIRIAM.*) From what I have seen, you have not kept the Law after all.

PHARISEE #1. Then I don't believe you understand it.

THE BAPTIST. Bring forth fruits of repentance—apologize to this woman, and I will baptize you.

PHARISEE #1. To a woman? Who do you think you are?

THE BAPTIST. I immerse people in water, to help them repent. But there comes a man after me who is mightier. I am not worthy to bear his shoes. I can baptize you with water. He can baptize you with fire. (*PHARISEE #1 is about to turn away until the BAPTIST says:*) The next question then is: who do you think you are?

PHARISEE #1. I am a son of Abraham, he is my father. I don't have to answer to you.

THE BAPTIST. God is able of these stones to raise up children to Abraham. The day will come when people of all nations will be able to adopt Abraham as their father.

PHARISEE #2. Blasphemy!

THE BAPTIST. You're a generation of vipers! Who has warned you to flee the wrath to come? The axe is laid against the root of the trees, those who don't grow good fruit will be cut down and thrown in the fire.

> *PHARISEE #1 seems rattled for a moment, as if he is considering it. He looks towards* MIRIAM, *but then shakes it off and angrily exits, followed by other* PHARISEES. YOCHANAN ZEBEDYAH *and* YA'AQOV ZEBEDYAH *step forward.*

YOCHANAN. May I be baptized, Yochanan?

YA'AQOV. Me as well?

THE BAPTIST. Yochanan, Ya'aqov, good to see the sons of Zebedyah back again. Have you brought forth the fruit of repentance?

YOCHANAN. We are—imperfect. But we want to love like you love.

THE BAPTIST. No. Not like me. Like God loves.

YA'AQOV. Yes. I want to be truly clean.

THE BAPTIST. Good answer.

ANDREAS also stands forth.

ANDREAS. So do I.

THE BAPTIST. And what is your name, sir?

ANDREAS. Andreas. I desire to follow Adonai with all my heart.

THE BAPTIST. Then come, my brothers. Come and bury the man of sin and be reborn.

As the BAPTIST baptizes YA'AQOV, ANDREAS, and YOCHANAN, MIRIAM makes her way to the front of the group. When the two brothers are baptized, she seems enamored with the process and is full of desire to follow them. But something in her makes her hesitate. She almost frantically leaves, before she runs into YESHUA and tumbles to the floor.

MIRIAM. Oh, I am so sorry, so sorry.

YESHUA doesn't recoil from her touch, but rather gently takes her hand and lifts her back to her feet. He doesn't let go of her hand. MIRIAM looks down at the touch, confused.

MIRIAM (CONT'D). Don't you know who I am?

YESHUA. Tell me who you believe you are.

MIRIAM. I am Mad Miriam.

YESHUA. I know you by another name.

MIRIAM. I am Mad Miriam! The woman with seven devils. They don't touch me. I am unclean.

Suddenly DARK VOICES are heard, whispering and hissing. MIRIAM reacts to them. We see dark shadows play on MIRIAM, which she also reacts to. No one else, except YESHUA hears or sees them. There are those that discretely distance themselves from MIRIAM.

DARK VOICES. Unclean! Like an issue of black blood—flow, flow like a river—unclean! Your spirit like a river, flowing out of you—never to return—Mad Miriam—Mad, Mad Miriam—unclean!

MIRIAM. No—no!

YESHUA touches her cheek and the DARK VOICES are suddenly gone. MIRIAM looks up at YESHUA with surprise. His gentleness eases her nerves.

YESHUA. Go. Be baptized by him.

MIRIAM turns towards the BAPTIST, yearning. The BAPTIST, finished with the other two, reaches his hand to MIRIAM.

MIRIAM. I—I am unclean!

MIRIAM exits in a frightened rush.

YESHUA. Miriam!

THE BAPTIST. Yeshua.

The BAPTIST scrambles out of the water and embraces YESHUA, as they both laugh and exclaim in joy.

YESHUA. You were missed at Ya'aqov's wedding. Not very becoming of a cousin.

THE BAPTIST. Well, you know how I live now—we're very strict not to—imbibe in riotous living.

YESHUA. I also hear that you are dabbling in politics.

THE BAPTIST. My comments about Herod—those are nothing.

YESHUA. That's not what I've heard. Are you being careful? Your Essenes aren't supposed to express anger. Agree with your adversaries quickly or they'll think you are their enemy.

THE BAPTIST. I do not mind if he thinks I am his enemy.

YESHUA. He is a powerful man. He could put you in prison—or worse.

THE BAPTIST. Don't worry yourself about me.

YESHUA. I have a foreboding about this . . .

THE BAPTIST. I will not hide and mince in the face of evil, Yeshua. Antipas Herod is no better than his butcher father!

The crowd picks up on this. Some nod and voice assent, while others whisper disapprovingly to each other. Some even leave as the BAPTIST turns to them and addresses his views publicly after noting their eavesdropping.

THE BAPTIST (CONT'D). The Herods pretend to follow the law, to convert to our religion, and want to be called orthodox—but despite how they clamor about their marriage ties to the Maccabee line, they are not children of God—only their actions can make them children of God! Herod's marriage to his brother's wife is not lawful, and so he has truly shown where his allegiance lies: in his passions!

This stirs more intense reactions from those gathered. YESHUA takes the BAPTIST aside.

YESHUA. Don't give that which is holy to dogs, Yochanan. If you give your pearls to swine, they will turn and rend you.

THE BAPTIST. Then let them rend me. I am not afraid of the consequences of speaking my heart.

YESHUA. I'm worried about you.

THE BAPTIST. The day will come when you, too, will have to stand before the powerful and tell them the simple, insulting truth.

YESHUA. In the right time, in the right place.

THE BAPTIST. Well then, maybe this is my time and my place. But why are you really here, Yeshua? I doubt an intense desire to discuss the current political climate brought you all the way out here.

YESHUA. I have come to be baptized.

THE BAPTIST. But—I need to be baptized by you, not the other way around.

YESHUA. Allow it to happen this way for now. I need to fulfill all righteousness.

The BAPTIST *nods. They go into the water together. The group gathers around to witness it, and* YOCHANAN, ANDREAS, *and* YA'AQOV *seem especially drawn to the ordinance. The* BAPTIST *immerses* YESHUA, *and when he arises, we either see some kind of representation of a dove, or at least hear it cooing and flying. A* VOICE *is also heard:*

VOICE. This is my beloved Son, in whom I am well pleased.

The voice is neither loud, nor dramatic. Yet, although it is quiet, it is piercing. Most of the crowd seems not to hear it, except for YESHUA, *the* BAPTIST, YA'AQOV, ANDREAS, *and* YOCHANAN.

THE BELOVED. Did you hear that?

YA'AQOV THE JUST. Yes. I thought I was crazy for a moment . . .

ANDREAS. He—he can't be . . .

YESHUA *hugs his cousin and then walks out of the water and exits.*

THE BELOVED. Follow him.

YOCHANAN, YA'AQOV, *and* ANDREAS *try to follow* YESHUA, *but are cut off by the people who are crowding around the* BAPTIST.

YA'AQOV. We're losing him!

THE BELOVED. I can't see him. Where did he go?

YA'AQOV. He's gone.

SCENE 3

The crowd around the BAPTIST *freezes in place.* SATAN'EL *enters. He does not look traditionally demonic or sinister. His appearance isn't modern, nor contemporary to* YESHUA'*s era. Instead he has a simple otherworldliness. He looks over the crowd, looking for* YESHUA.

SATAN'EL. He's gone.

SATAN'EL snaps and the lights turn out, making the crowd disappear, except for a single light on SATAN'EL.

SATAN'EL (CONT'D). Again.

A multitude of stars appear. SATAN'EL climbs some stairs. At the top of the stairs suddenly appears one of the MALACHIM (angels) with a flaming sword. This MALACH is a truly intimidating, awe inspiring being, a knight, guardian, or sentinel of the universe.

SATAN'EL (CONT'D). I need access to him.

The MALACH is silent.

SATAN'EL (CONT'D). Yeshua. I need access to Yeshua. Or Yahweh. Or whatever you want me to call him now.

More MALACHIM (of both genders) gather around the bottom of the stairs, similar in appearance to the first. SATAN'EL goes back down the stairs to confront the ones at the bottom.

SATAN'EL (CONT'D). Look, I understand that you're protective, but this is necessary.

The MALACHIM raise their swords a bit, in warning positions.

SATAN'EL (CONT'D). Oh, please! Look, really, I understand that we've had a rough history, but it's my right. I am Ha-Satan, "The Accuser." I am Satan-El, the god to obstruct and oppose!

MALACH. You may be the god of that earth, but you are no true god.

SATAN'EL. This is my title, this is my priesthood, this is my responsibility. You may not like it, but I have my role, just as you have yours. And he is not exempt! Especially him!

SATAN'EL tries to move past the angels, but they encroach upon him.

SATAN'EL (CONT'D). What, are you afraid? That he'll fail? Don't you Malachim have faith in this god of yours?

The MALACHIM *hesitate.*

SATAN'EL (CONT'D). You try to hide him from me, don't think that I haven't noticed. You're not supposed to do that.

The MALACHIM *become defensive again.*

SATAN'EL (CONT'D). Where is he?

YESHUA *suddenly appears praying.*

SATAN'EL (CONT'D). Talking to Father. Fasting even. For quite some time, by the looks of it. It looks hot, too. Where is he, the desert? He'll be weak with hunger, exhaustion, and heat. Perfect. (SATAN'EL *advances towards* YESHUA, *but the* MALACHIM *stop him.*) Don't you get it? (SATAN'EL *goes back up to the stairs and confronts the* MAL-ACH *on top of them.*) Do I need to bring this to the Ophanim or the Cherubim or the Seraphim? Perhaps the Sons of El? Get me Micha'el or Gabri'el or Rapha'el—get me Metatron!

MALACH. Lucifer, Son of the Morning . . .

SATAN'EL. Why does everyone still insist on calling me that? One person interprets a Hebrew's reference to a defeated Babylonian King to be me and suddenly it's all the rage!

MALACH. It fits your fallen nature . . .

SATAN'EL. (*Suddenly hostile.*) You don't know my nature, nor my wrath.

MALACH. You are not worthy. You are the Dragon who drew away one third of the stars of heaven . . .

SATAN'EL. I have a job to do. Every court needs a prosecuting attorney.

MALACH *hesitates and then motions to the other* MALACHIM. *They exit.*

MALACH. You have bounds.

SATAN'EL. I know my boundaries. Now leave me to my work.

Exit MALACH. SATAN'EL *descends the stairs, now finally alone with* YESHUA. *The lights become harshly bright and there is sound of* BUZZING, *desert insects.*

YESHUA. Abba! Please, don't leave me yet!

YESHUA becomes aware of SATAN'EL.

SATAN'EL. Hello, Yeshua. Sorry to break up the conversation, I know it's been a while. I had to clear up a bureaucratic nightmare up top, but you'll be seeing more of me from here on out.

YESHUA doesn't answer and goes over and sits away from him.

SATAN'EL (CONT'D). They're already spreading rumors now—speculating. They thought the Baptist was impressive, but after he deferred to you—well, the tongues are flapping now! They think you're someone pretty great.

YESHUA. No one is great, except our Father.

SATAN'EL. Oh, you deign to answer me this time! That's progress. Yes, get those fools talking about you. Oh, but what would they say if they heard who you really think you are? (*YESHUA doesn't answer.*) Tell me, you little man from Galilee, how do you expect anyone to believe you when you tell them that you're the literal Son of God?

YESHUA. You know who I Am.

SATAN'EL. I know who you are, son of man. But do you know who you are? Yes, I know about all those visions, visitations you think you've been receiving—you think that they've told you that you're something special. Tell me, you insignificant carpenter's son, how do you know you're not delusional? Yes, your mother tells you that she had a miraculous conception—and she had your step father believing that story, certainly. But perhaps it's much more simple than that. Perhaps it was merely the story made up by a young woman who was desperate not to become outcast as a single mother. (*This makes YESHUA visibly angry. He stands and walks to SATAN'EL. YESHUA then calms himself and sits back down, again facing away from SATAN'EL.*) I have seen it so many times. These little actors, these little liars, using other people's good faith to manipulate their own place in the world. But you—yes, I know that you're different. I see that, an honest face like yours. You believe. Why, you're self-deceived! And your broken little mind has made you mad with it, with hallucinations, day dreams, and voices. Sadly pathetic.

YESHUA. I know who I Am.

SATAN'EL. Well then! You know, you know! Just keep telling them that you know! Not much of a logical argument, but perhaps you can convince them with sheer earnestness. I'm sorry, my simple, small, Galilean carpenter, these worldly Sadducees, learned Pharisees, and entrenched sinners aren't going to buy that. No, they'll want proof. Evidence. Can you give them that? (*YESHUA doesn't answer.*) You're looking pretty hungry there, Yeshua. Do you religious types think that such waste does anybody any good? The Romans sacrifice their food, too, burn it like your Jews. They think the smoke ascends to their gods and then the gods eat it. Pretty preposterous. (*YESHUA doesn't answer.*) Well, you'll certainly need to be more Cosmopolitan in your approach, that's certain. That trick with the wine was nice. Why, that's it—you saw how those servants looked at you afterwards. Now that's a statement, that's showmanship! You'll need some of that, if you want to get anywhere with this self-proclaimed god-ship of yours. In fact, let's go with that, shall we? Let's kill two birds with one—stone. (*SATAN'EL picks up a stone and places it before YESHUA.*) We'll give you something to eat, hungry as you are, and prove your divinity in the process. If you are truly the Son of God, make this stone into bread.

YESHUA *finally stands and faces* SATAN'EL, *speaking calmly:*

YESHUA. "Man shall not live by bread alone, but by every word that proceeds out of the mouth of God."

SATAN'EL *pauses, but then continues as if nothing had happened.*

SATAN'EL. Yes, this Son of God business is going to be tricky, that's certain. Especially with these Jews. Let's face it, after King Josiah they became pretty entrenched with this one god idea. Stubborn Deuteronomists. Yes, putting a second god on their roster is going to be a hard sell, believe me, I've tried. They tend to stone people who try and do that. It's all rather—precarious. (*SATAN'EL snaps his fingers and the lights change. YESHUA suddenly finds himself on the ledge of a tall temple. We hear the sounds of a brisk wind, which makes YESHUA's situation all the more precarious.*). Herod's temple. An impressive piece of workmanship. The man was a scoundrel, but at least he understood the religious devotion of the people.

YESHUA. Why have you brought me here?

SATAN'EL. Look, they're gathering. Look at all these devout pilgrims. Going through the ache and agony of their oppressed lives, being punished by the Caesars and the Herods and the Sanhedrins and the tax collectors—they cry to God, but does their God listen? These poor Israelites, driven and enslaved and misused by one nation after another, one leader after another. Do they receive any reward for their faith? Please, show them a God who loves them, who recognizes their sacrifices. If you are the Son of God, cast yourself down off this temple, for it is written, "He shall give his angels charge concerning thee: and in their hands they shall bear thee up, lest at any time thou dash thy foot against a stone." Prove yourself to them. Prove yourself to yourself. Show them their God.

YESHUA. It is written again, "Thou shalt not tempt the Lord thy God."

> *SATAN'EL pauses again, for the first time seeming to crack his collected exterior. It's only momentary, as he smiles gently and snaps his fingers. There is a light change again, as they hear the sound of birds and a light breeze. The stars appear again.*

SATAN'EL. Who wants a man-made heaven of stone, when you can have what our Abba already created for us? This mountain is a greater temple than any man has made. From here we can see the entire world. Every nation, every kingdom. This is my sanctuary, where I go to find—solace. From my loneliness, to my loneliness. A person like me has a lot to ponder on. But it's beautiful, and mankind just wants to destroy it all. They're ungrateful creatures. They mock every sacrifice we give them, they squander every chance of progress that we offer. You'll discover that very soon, if you keep on the course you're on. You may not remember this, but you and I used to have long discussions about those people down there. About what they were capable of—for good and evil. I had an idea once, can I share it with you? (*YESHUA doesn't answer.*) People talk about power as if it were a bad thing. I don't believe that. In the right hands, it's the only good thing. In your hands, for example, you would make that world good. Give you enough armies, enough leverage, enough force, why you could crusade through that world down there and create Zion, a new Jerusalem! They don't know what they need. They need a strong hand, a good hand to force them into their happiness, into their peace. I'm the Prince of that World now, and I haven't always had the best of help. But you, Yeshua, both you and I know that you're special. With your help, and the resources at your command, we can finally give that world peace. Everything you see down there—I'll give it to you. All these people and places and civilizations, I will give all of it to you, if you but recognize me as your ruler. Fall down and worship me, and then they will fall down and worship you.

There is a tense silence, where SATAN'EL is hopeful that he may have finally gotten through to YESHUA. But YESHUA disappoints him:

YESHUA. Get away, Satan; for it is written, "Thou shalt worship the Lord thy God, and him only shalt thou serve."

SATAN'EL. (*Pause.*) Good work, Yeshua. But we're not done.

The MALACHIM appear.

MALACH. You most certainly are.

SATAN'EL. Yes, the "boundaries."

SATAN'EL disappears. The MALACHIM bring YESHUA bread and drink.

MALACH. Adonai, Father is pleased. Your fast is over.

Blackout.

SCENE 4

The BAPTIST is sitting at the edge of the water. He looks within it, lost in thought, as if the water possibly held the answers to some deep seated questions of his. Enter YOCHANAN, YA'AQOV, and ANDREAS.

YA'AQOV THE JUST. You should hear them! Truly, you have caught the heart of this people!

The BAPTIST looks at these disciples of his, somewhat forlornly.

YOCHANAN. What is wrong, Rabbi?

THE BAPTIST. Wrong? Nothing is wrong.

YA'AQOV THE JUST. You should be happy. You have fulfilled your duty.

THE BAPTIST. Yes. I am fulfilled.

The disciples glance at each other uneasily.

ANDREAS. The man from Galilee that came those weeks ago . . .

THE BAPTIST. Yeshua.

ANDREAS. Yeshua. You seemed to—revere him.

THE BAPTIST. He is the one to truly cleanse us from sin. He is the one I often spoke of.

ANDREAS. How do you know this?

THE BAPTIST. I saw an angel once.

YOCHANAN. An angel?

THE BAPTIST. The angel told me of my mission to baptize with water. And he told that whoever I would see the Spirit descend upon, he was the one who would baptize with the Holy Spirit. When I baptized Yeshua, I saw . . .

YOCHANAN. The Holy Spirit in the shape of a bird. A dove.

THE BAPTIST. You saw this?

YOCHANAN. Yes, all three of us did.

THE BAPTIST. Then you must follow him.

Enter YESHUA. *They are all stunned to see him there, just as they were discussing him. The* BAPTIST *stands and acknowledges him in reverence.* YESHUA *returns the respectful attention.*

THE BAPTIST. Behold the Lamb of God.

YESHUA *turns to the disciples.*

YESHUA. What are you looking for?

YOCHANAN. Rabbi, where do you live?

YESHUA. Why does that matter?

YOCHANAN. Because where you go, that is where I want to be.

YESHUA. Then come and see.

YESHUA *exits and* YOCHANAN *and* ANDREAS *immediately follow, exiting with him.* YA'AQOV *hesitates. He turns to the* BAPTIST.

YA'AQOV THE JUST. What is to happen to you?

THE BAPTIST. That doesn't matter.

YA'AQOV THE JUST. Of course it matters. You have built up this tremendous following, you have influence now. That shouldn't go to waste. God built you up, and now you're just going to let this man take that away from you?

THE BAPTIST. A man can receive nothing, unless heaven gives it to him. Yeshua is preferred before me.

YA'AQOV THE JUST. You are a great man.

THE BAPTIST. Do not mistake this, Ya'aqov. I am not the Mashiach, but I have prepared you for him. The one at the marriage who is to marry the bride is the Bridegroom. I am the Bridegroom's friend who rejoices to see the wedding. Do you understand?

YA'AQOV THE JUST. I think so.

THE BAPTIST. He is going to increase, I am going to decrease.

YA'AQOV THE JUST. Where are you going to go? What are you going to do?

THE BAPTIST. Don't worry about me. Ya'aqov, believe him. Believe in him.

> YA'AQOV *nods. He then turns away from the* BAPTIST *and exits. The lights fade on the* BAPTIST. *In the darkness, vibrant music is heard. We are revealed chambers in the palace of* HEROD. *Among a group of Herod's admirers and grovelers, there is merriment, wine, and raucous laughter.* HERODIAS', *the wife of Herod, approaches her husband.* SATAN'EL *hovers in the background.*

HERODIAS. Herod—Antipas, my dear, I'm still not satisfied with our earlier conversation.

HEROD. Blast it, woman, can't you see that I'm trying to enjoy myself here? I absolutely refuse to mix pleasure and politics!

HERODIAS. No, this needs to be addressed now. He has insulted both of us!

HEROD. Do you think I like the man? The Baptist is no friend of mine.

HERODIAS. Then show your displeasure. Let him know who he's dealing with!

HEROD. Lower your voice, Herodias. You will not speak to me like that.

HERODIAS. I—I am sorry, my lord. But, truly, who really cares about the traditions of these little religionists? So what, you are divorced and I was married to your brother. Why should they care if I was married to your father! Why, that nice, little play we saw in Rome—er—*Oedipus the King!* We're not so bad as that, are we? Compared to that, the The Romans wouldn't even bat an eye at our relationship.

> SATAN'EL *soothes* HEROD *slightly.*

HEROD. It's not Romans I worry about. What does a woman know about these things? Referencing Sophocles as if she understood him.

SATAN'EL places his hand on HERODIAS's shoulder, encouraging her boldness.

HERODIAS. He undercuts your power. If you let him go unpunished, others will follow his example.

HEROD. The more I oppress their leaders, the more I defy their traditions, the more I silence their voices, the more they will resent me. I went against my good sense in marrying you!

The merriment is dying down, as the party goers are subtly riveted on this domestic drama unfolding before them.

HERODIAS. So you think I am your mistake? Your blunder?

HEROD. What I think is that if I push them anymore, I shall have a revolt on my hands. The Baptist has a following!

HERODIAS. Then you have no power. You are no ruler. You are no man! Everyone laughs at you as soon as they know you're not in earshot.

HEROD ferociously slaps HERODIAS. HERODIAS falls to the floor, then raises her hands to deflect any further blows.

HEROD. Do you want me to show you how much power I have? You want me to show all of these people how I have power in my own household?

SATAN'EL soothes both HEROD and HERODIAS.

HERODIAS. I'm sorry. Of course, you're right.

Grudgingly, HEROD accepts this. He then sits, as his guests stand around in shocked silence.

HEROD. Well, laugh! Get drunk, joke, flirt, grovel. That's why all of you sycophants are here, isn't it?

Nervously, the party resumes. SATAN'EL whispers in HERODIAS's ear. HERODIAS smiles.

HERODIAS. My lord, I have prepared a gift for your birthday.

HEROD. A gift?

HERODIAS. To show my devotion to you.

Sensual music begins to play. HERODIAS*'s daughter* SALOME *enters, dressed in dancer's clothing.*

HEROD. Herodias, what on earth is your daughter wearing?

HERODIAS. Just watch, Antipas. I think you will enjoy this.

SALOME *begins to dance.*

HERODIAS (CONT'D). All for you, my dear. (HERODIAS *begins to massage* HEROD*'s shoulders, he visibly relaxes.*) Yes, that's right, relax . . .

SALOME *continues to dance. When she finishes,* HEROD *beckons to her.*

HEROD. My dear, come here.

SALOME *approaches* HEROD.

HEROD (CONT'D). You're a true artist. Now just as I can punish those who displease me, I can also reward those who please me. Now think, think of me, my dear. Think of how powerful I am, and how far I can reach. Think of my influence and my strength. Now, as you think of all of that, think of something that I, and only I, can give you. Ask for it, and I vow to you that it will be yours. I am a man of my word and I can fulfill that word with the strength of my arm.

SALOMES *dashes to her mother to consult with her.*

SALOME. Mother, I don't know what to ask for.

HERODIAS. Do you love me?

SALOME. You know I do.

HERODIAS. Then ask him this for me, and my love will reward you for the rest of your life.

HERODIAS *whispers into* SALOME*'s ear. The daughter nods and walks over to* HEROD.

HEROD. What riches have you decided upon, my love?

HERODIAS'S DAUGHTER. Uncle—I mean Father. Father, I would like . . .

HERODIAS'S DAUGHTER looks back to her mother, nervously.
HERODIAS encourages her.

HERODIAS'S DAUGHTER (CONT'D). Since you have promised me with an oath that whatever I want, I can have, there is nothing more sweet to me than this: I want the head of the Baptist in a charger.

HEROD pales and looks over at HERODIAS. HERODIAS looks at him with resolve and indicates all the people watching this exchange.

HEROD. (*His gaze still on HERODIAS.*) Call in my executioner.

Blackout.

SCENE 5

We hear the sounds of the sea, including gentle waves lapping, seagulls, etc. SHIMON (who is later called CEPHAS) is there with ANDREAS, YA'AQOV THE JUST, and the YOCHANAN, all of them helping SHIMON mend his fishing nets.

YOCHANAN. It's true, Shimon. Every word of it.

SHIMON CEPHAS. You must think I'm the most gullible man alive.

ANDREAS. Brother, we have seen this man do uncanny things. He has healed the blind, cured diseases, accurately prophesied . . .

SHIMON CEPHAS. This is a joke.

YA'AQOV. He said he'd meet us back here. You can see for yourself.

SHIMON CEPHAS. Look, we're fishermen. What do prophets have to do with us?

ANDREAS. Shimon, don't you ever just feel like we're living so little of the life Father and Mother intended for us?

SHIMON CEPHAS. Andreas, what I feel is that I have a family to feed. Can this prophet of yours be like Moses and give my wife and children bread to eat from heaven? For, if he can't, then I still need to go back to these nets every day.

Enter YESHUA.

YESHUA. Moses didn't give the bread from heaven. It was from Adonai.

SHIMON CEPHAS looks over at YESHUA and gives him a scrutinizing stare.

SHIMON CEPHAS. You must be the man my brother is talking about. Tell me, Yeshua, have you even worked a day in your life?

YESHUA. I was a carpenter.

SHIMON goes to YESHUA and inspects YESHUA's hands.

SHIMON CEPHAS. (*Searching pause.*) Good. Come fishing with us, Yeshua. Let's see if those arms of yours still know how to strain.

YESHUA. I would love to.

Lights fade on YESHUA and the fishermen and then rise again to show the passage of time. It is now night and the stars are out. They all draw in an empty net.

SHIMON CEPHAS. Well, Yeshua, some of that manna from God would be awfully nice about now.

ANDREAS. Shimon . . .

SHIMON CEPHAS. Don't worry, Andreas, I hold him no more responsible than I do anyone else. I am the one who is responsible for my family, and only me. But that's the thing, Yeshua, people will start blaming you if you start claiming to be God's mouthpiece. And no one can live up to those kinds of expectations, even a nice man like you.

YESHUA smiles at SHIMON and then looks up at the stars above them.

YESHUA. It's a beautiful night, isn't it?

SHIMON looks up. He also smiles.

SHIMON CEPHAS. You know, I hadn't noticed.

YESHUA looks at him knowingly and then hands his part of the net to SHIMON.

YESHUA. Cast the net on the other side.

SHIMON CEPHAS. Yeshua, we've been trying all night. We're tired.

YESHUA. One more time.

SHIMON CEPHAS. Yeshua . . .

YESHUA. Trust me.

SHIMON CEPHAS. (*Laughs.*) Well, I'll keep you to your word then.

YESHUA. Do.

SHIMON is taken aback by this. The fishermen glance at each other and then they all anxiously throw their net onto the other side of the boat and are immediately startled.

SHIMON CEPHAS. What! What!

YOCHANNAN. Pull, men! Pull!

YESHUA then joins them and pulls on the net also. They're all laughing with joy as they pull in a huge net of fish.

SHIMON CEPHAS. We're sinking! We need to throw some over!

ANDREAS. Amazing!

Once they've stabilized the boat, the fishermen look at each other in amazement and then all look at YESHUA. SIMON immediately kneels before YESHUA.

SHIMON CEPHAS. Leave me, Rabbi, I didn't believe.

YESHUA pulls SHIMON to his feet.

YESHUA. I will draw close to you, if you draw close to me, Shimon. You worried about your family. As you now can see, you're all better off with me, than without me. But I'm going to ask you to become fishers of men.

Lights fade on YESHUA and the fishermen.

SCENE 6

Enter YEHUDAH SICARRI, SHIMON KANAI, and TADDAI.

YEHUDAH SICARRI. This had better be worth our time, Taddai.

TADDAI. Believe me, Yehudah, this could be the most important meeting you ever attend.

SHIMON KANAI. Where is Barabba? You told us that Barabba had agreed to be here.

Enter BARABBA.

BARABBA. And so I did.

They gather around BARABBA, who carries himself with authority.

TADDAI. Barabba, this is Shimon and this is . . .

BARABBA. Yehudah.

YEHUDAH SICARRI. Barabba and I are well known to each other, Taddai.

TADDAI. Excuse me, I didn't know.

BARABBA. Well met, brethren. Kanai.

YEHUDAH, TADDAI, AND SHIMON. Kanai.

BARABBA. And what does kanai mean, Taddai?

TADDAI. One who is zealous on behalf of God.

BARABBA. Good, my friend. Zealous—that is the new name the Romans are giving us. Zealots. I like it, don't you? It's a name they have come to respect—even fear.

SHIMON KANAI. But that fear is turning into anger, Barabba. Is what we're doing having any effect?

BARABBA. Don't despair, Shimon. Our cause is just, our rebellion deserving. The Great Master of the Universe wants his covenant people free from oppression. He wants us free from this Roman yoke! And he will qualify all of us for the task at hand.

YEHUDAH SICARRI. Speaking of the task at hand, let's get into it. Why have you brought us here?

SHIMON KANAI. Tell him, Taddai.

TADDAI. I—I have a brother. He has become very prominent of late. He is a kind of rabbi, or teacher. Like Yochannan the Baptist . . .

YEHUDAH SICARRI. You are brothers with the Nazarene? Yeshua?

Enter SATAN'EL, *unseen and unnoticed the entire scene.*

SHIMON KANAI. So you've heard of him!

BARABBA. He is beginning to create a following.

TADDAI. Growing up, Mother and Father always treated him differently, had these strange stories about him and his—mission. Many of my brothers and sisters didn't take any of it seriously—until recently. Some of us were even—resentful—some of them still are. But the more I watch him, the more I am impressed. He is becoming a great man—a great man!

SHIMON KANAI. His doctrines are impressive and—and he has done miraculous things. Unexplainable things. Like Moses! Some are even calling him—they are calling him the anointed one.

YEHUDAH SICARRI. (*Genuine interest:*) The Mashiach? (*Then glancing at* BARRABA.) And what bearing has this upon us?

TADDAI. Don't you see? He has an audience! He has the people's attention! He can lead our people to revolt! He can lead us to freedom!

YEHUDAH SICARRI. Barabba is our leader.

BARABBA. Yehudah, it doesn't matter who the leader is. What matters is the liberty of the Covenant People. And if this Yeshua can better further that end than I can, then who am I to stand in the way? I want you two to keep following this Yeshua of Nazareth. If he has the influence, and if he is one with our cause, I want you to tell me.

Now, if you'll excuse Yehudah and I, we have some other matters to discuss. Kanai.

TADDAI AND SHIMON. Kanai.

Exit TADDAI and SHIMON KANAI.

YEHUDAH SICARRI. You're not serious about stepping aside for this man, are you? I mean, really, can any good thing come out of Nazareth?

BARABBA. I need you to be more careful with what you say, Yehudah. You are too impulsive. Especially for what I want you to do.

YEHUDAH SICARRI. You have an assignment for me then?

BARABBA. Pull out your dagger.

YEHUDAH SICARRI pulls out his dagger, which has been hidden beneath his robes, and kneels before BARABBA, raising his dagger in front of him.

YEHUDAH SICARRI. In the name of Adonai, I have covenanted to be a Sicarri, one of the dagger men. I am like a blade in the hand of the Holy One, to cut off the wicked from the righteous, like diseased flesh from the bone. I am willing to die, to burn as fire, if that fire will bring down the enemies of Adonai. Amen.

BARABBA. Amen. Now with that holy oath, I give you your sacred mission.

YEHUDAH SICARRI. Thank you for your trust in me.

BARABBA. Yehudah, I want you to become a follower of this Yeshua. Become his friend, gain his trust, become part of his inner circle. If he can be of any use to us, I want you to sway him to our cause.

YEHUDAH SICARRI. I understand.

BARABBA. But, Yehudah, if this Yeshua stands in our way, you are to find a way to sweep him from our path—with whatever method that's necessary.

YEHUDAH SICARRI. Barabba . . .

BARABBA. Is this not part of your oath?

YEHUDAH SICARRI. Yes, but . . .

BARABBA. Are you with me or against me?

YEHUDAH SICARRI. I am with you.

BARABBA. Then go, Yehudah Sicarri, and bring our people closer to freedom. Kanai.

YEHUDAH SICARRI. Kanai.

SATAN'EL whispers something in BARRABA's ear.

BARABBA. And Yehudah?

YEHUDAH SICARRI. Yes?

BARABBA. You're right. I wouldn't willingly give up my power. But I am willing to share it for the good of our people. I would share it with Yeshua of Nazareth. If you serve me well, you also would rise high in our great nation to come.

YEHUDAH SICARRI. You honor me.

Exit YEHUDAH. Exit BARRABA.

SCENE 7

It has become very dark. SATAN'EL is about to exit as well, until he sees MIRIAM enter. MIRIAM can see him and tries to retreat from him, but is unable to.

MIRIAM. Get away from me!

SATAN'EL. You resist too much, Miriam. How many of my friends have taken up within you now? Only seven? Why, I know mortals who have a whole Legion and they live completely normal lives. If you don't resist their presence, your guests can make life sensational for you. If you make room for me in there, there's no limit to what we can do for you. I'll even crowd out the others for you, if you'd like.

Make your mind more focused. I have some authority with them, you know.

MIRIAM. I don't want anything to do with you, any of you!

SATAN'EL. That's a shame. Then I'm afraid it's not going to get any better for you. We know human psychology backwards and forwards. We know which chords of the brain to pluck and strike to get just the right amount of dissonance . . .

MIRIAM. Please . . .

SATAN'EL. Please? Oh, well since you said please!

Entertained, SATAN'EL *laughs but then voices are heard.*

YESHUA. (*Voice Over:*) Do you believe that I can . . . ?

MARTA. (*Voice Over:*) Please, I know you can help my sister!

ELEAZAR. (*Voice Over:*) We both believe!

SATAN'EL. No—dig in, you idiots! He's here! Fight for her!

A change happens in MIRIAM *as the devils within her take over. Suddenly* YESHUA *appears.*

MIRIAM. Let us alone! What do we have to do with you, Yeshua of Nazareth?

YESHUA. Let her go.

SATAN'EL. Leave them alone! Haven't you done enough to our kind, you tyrant?

MIRIAM. Have you come to destroy us? Holy One of God! Please, don't torment us! Don't send us into the deep!

YESHUA. Hold your peace! Get out of her!

MIRIAM screams, as does SATAN'EL, *but suddenly* SATAN'EL *is gone and there is a great deal of light that gradually appears, with a group of people surrounding* MIRIAM *and* YESHUA, *including* MIRIAM's *sister* MARTA *and her brother* ELEAZAR; *Yeshua's disciples, male and female; and curious onlookers, both believing and hostile. MIRIAM, whose devils are finally gone, looks around in wonder.*

MARTA. Miriam? Are you all right?

ELEAZAR. How do you feel, sister?

MIRIAM. (*Pause.*) I can hear birds. (*Pause.*) Marta. Eleazar.

YESHUA. Miriam, stand.

MIRIAM. How is this possible?

YESHUA. Your sister Marta and your brother Eleazar have great faith. Your family is happy to see you.

MIRIAM embraces ELEAZAR and MARTA. There is some fervent debate among those gathered, until one confronts YESHUA.

PHARISEE #1. You cast out devils by the power of the devil. You cast them out by the chief of devils Beezlebub!

YESHUA. (*Laughs.*) Well, that would be rather foolish of Beezlebub! If Satan is divided against himself, how can his house stand? A house divided, falls.

MIRIAM. Then what does this mean?

YESHUA. The kingdom of God has come upon you. It is within you.

MIRIAM. Adonai, if you will have me, I will follow you.

YESHUA. Miriam—with you I didn't even have to ask.

Enter BROTHER YA'AQOV, MOTHER MIRIAM, RUTH, TAD-DAI, SHIMON KANAI, and YEHUDAH SICARRI. They approach ELEAZAR.

BROTHER YA'AQOV. You are with Yeshua?

ELEAZAR. I guess I am now.

BROTHER YA'AQOV. He is my brother. Can you get his attention for us? It's very important.

ELEAZAR. Of course.

ELEAZAR approaches YESHUA.

YESHUA. Not now, Eleazar, I'm having an important conversation with your sister.

ELEAZAR. But, Rabbi, it's your family.

YESHUA. I know. Not now.

ELEAZAR. All right. (*ELEAZAR goes back to YESHUA's family.*) He can't see you right now.

BROTHER YA'AQOV. Tell him that it's urgent. Something terrible has happened.

ELEAZAR. He was insistent.

BROTHER YA'AQOV. Then tell him that *I'm* insistent!

MOTHER MIRIAM. Ya'aqov, calm down. (*Back to ELEAZAR.*) Sir, tell him that his mother wishes to see him. He's never denied his mother.

ELEAZAR. I'm sure you're right. (*ELEAZAR approaches YESHUA again.*) Rabbi . . .

YESHUA. Don't call me rabbi. I am not your master. No man is your master, except our Father in Heaven, our Abba.

ELEAZAR. Yes, Yeshua. But your mother . . .

YESHUA. I already told you.

ELEAZAR. Excuse me, but your mother is a great woman. Blessed is the womb that bore you, and the breasts that fed you.

YESHUA. Blessed are those that hear the word of God and do it. Tell them to come later. I will speak to them privately then.

BROTHER YA'AQOV. (*Who has approached and heard a good deal of the conversation.*) You selfish ingrate! You'd rather spend your time with these admiring strangers than with your own family!

YESHUA. Who is my family? Who are my brothers, my sisters, my mother? Those who keep my commandments are my family. (*Grabbing MIRIAM's hand and presenting her.*) Behold my brothers, my mother, and my sisters!

MOTHER MIRIAM. Yeshua, you wound me.

YESHUA. You wound me, Mother.

MOTHER MIRIAM. How do I wound you?

YESHUA. You wish again to prevent me from my Father's business.

MOTHER MIRIAM. Never.

YESHUA. I see the fear in your heart. Just as you were afraid when you thought I was lost when I was a boy. You must trust my Abba, and that I am in His care!

BROTHER YA'AQOV. Yes, your Abba, your Abba! Well, my Abba was a carpenter named Yosef and he was the one who raised you well, taught you his profession. You repay his memory by heaping insults and injuries upon his wife and children, while neglecting the trade he taught you by wandering in the wilderness and delivering pointless maxims!

MOTHER MIRIAM. Ya'aqov, don't speak to your brother like that.

BROTHER YA'AQOV. He insults you and still he is preferred. I don't know how to please you, Mother. If this is the son you want to be remembered by, then so be it.

Exit BROTHER YA'AQOV.

MOTHER MIRIAM. Ya'aqov! Ya'aqov . . . (*Then to YESHUA.*) Yeshua, if I have offended you . . .

YESHUA. Mother, I am your sacrifice to lay on the altar. Except there will be no other lamb to replace me. I am the Lamb. (*This effects MOTHER MIRIAM immensely, as she holds back tears of grief, but she nods. YESHUA then comes over and embraces her comfortingly. He then guides her to ELEAZAR.*) Eleazar, thank you for the honor you showed my mother. Would you do me a great favor?

ELEAZAR. After everything you have done for Miriam? Anything.

YESHUA. I want you to get to know the great woman you have defended. Marta, come over here.

MARTA. Yes, Yeshua?

YESHUA. I need someone to accompany my mother back to her home tomorrow. Can you and Eleazar do that for me?

MARTA. Of course.

ELEAZAR. We'll take good care of her.

YESHUA. I knew I could trust both of you.

MOTHER MIRIAM. No, I want to come with you.

YESHUA. Mother, the day will come when you can't come with me, but you'll accompany me to the very brink. The very brink. But I now must be about my Abba's business.

MARTA. What about Miriam?

YESHUA. Miriam will be coming with me.

MARTA. Oh—is that appropriate?

YESHUA. She is my disciple. She must follow me.

MARTA. But why—why Miriam?

> ELEAZAR *and* MARTA *remains with her as* YESHUA *approaches the other newcomers.*

YESHUA. Now, Taddai, come here . . .

TADDAI. Yes, brother.

YESHUA. And your friend as well. Shimon the Zealot.

SHIMON KANAI. How do you know that?

YESHUA. My friends, both of your hearts are right. But you have been misled in many things by political posturers who would manipulate your faith. Such people seek the kingdom of this earth, not the kingdom of heaven.

TADDAI. What would you have us do?

YESHUA. You need to become wise as serpents and harmless as doves. I am calling apostles, those who I will endow with priesthood, keys, and authority. I have already called others. You two shall also be part of that group.

SHIMON KANAI. I am honored—but you hardly know me.

YESHUA. My sheep hear my voice and know me, and I know them.

SHIMON KANAI. Yes—yes.

YESHUA. And you are Yehudah.

YEHUDAH SICARRI. Rabbi, you are well informed.

YESHUA. You don't know how well informed.

    YEHUDAH kneels.

YEHUDAH SICARRI. I have come to serve you. To be your man, if you'll have me.

    YESHUA gives YEHUDAH a long, penetrating look. YEHUDAH is trying to mask his sudden nervousness. YESHUA finally helps YEHUDAH to his feet and silently stares him straight in the eyes. YEHUDAH tries to maintain the gaze, but briefly looks away. YESHUA grabs him gently by the chin and makes him maintain the gaze.

YESHUA. (*Unheard by the others, this is just between him and* YEHUDAH.) I know you, Yehudah Sicarri.

YEHUDAH SICARRI. Sicarri?

YESHUA. Your dagger is beneath your cloak. But you shall not betray me with a dagger.

YEHUDAH SICARRI. I shall not betray you at all. I am your man.

YESHUA. Then what would you do for me, Yehudah?

YEHUDAH SICARRI. I would fight for you, lord. I would sacrifice for you, lord. I would die for you, lord.

YESHUA. Yes, you would. But many come to me and say, lord, lord! I'm telling you right now, Yehudah Sicarri, it is those who do the will of my Father who enter into the Kingdom of Heaven.

YEHUDAH SICARRI. Then I shall do your Father's will.

YESHUA. And Barabba's will?

YEHUDAH SICARRI. Who is Barabba?

YESHUA. Who indeed? His name means son of the Father. I am here to tell you that I am the Son of the Father. I am his Only Begotten. Do you believe me?

YEHUDAH SICARRI. (*Sincere, but rattled.*) Yes. And I believe you can free us!

YESHUA. You want to be free?

YEHUDAH SICARRI. More than anything.

YESHUA. If you continue in my word, then you shall be an apostle and free indeed. The truth will make you free.

YEHUDAH SICARRI. I believe.

YESHUA. Then choose which son of the Father you shall serve. Is it me or Barabba?

YEHUDAH SICARRI. You know my past—my heart . . .

YESHUA. You can't serve God and Mammon . . .

YEHUDAH SICARRI. You! I choose you!

YESHUA. Then come. Follow me.

YEHUDAH SICARRI. I will. To the very end.

> YESHUA *finally turns away from* YEHUDAH *and motions to his sister* RUTH.

YESHUA. And you, Ruth, my dear sister, I—I can't see why you are here. Why did my family even come?

RUTH. Don't you know yet?

YESHUA. Don't I know what?

RUTH. Yeshua, it's our cousin. It's Yochanan . . .

YESHUA. What about him?

RUTH. It was Herod. Herod killed him.

YESHUA. What?

RUTH. He—I am sorry, so sorry. Herod cut off his head.

YESHUA is startled by this, and emotionally confused. He goes off, turning away from the other and addressing his Father.

YESHUA. Abba, you didn't tell me about this—why?

MIRIAM comes to YESHUA tentatively.

MIRIAM. Yeshua, I am so—so very sorry about your cousin. He was loved by all of us . . .

YESHUA. Yochanan was right . . . (*To the group:*) The Baptist was right! Herod is a corrupt leader and we would be wrong to let wickedness go unchallenged!

RUTH. Yeshua, you can't say things like that. Herod killed the Baptist and he would kill you. You must be cautious.

YESHUA. Go tell that old fox that I cast out devils and I cure people today and tomorrow, but the third day I will be perfected! But as for today and tomorrow, he can't harm me: for it can't be that a prophet can perish out of Jerusalem. (*YESHUA stumbles a little from grief. MIRIAM and MOTHER MIRIAM go to him, and hold him up.*) O Jerusalem, O Jersusalem! You kill the prophets and stone them who are sent to you! How often I would have gathered you as a hen gathers her children under her wings and you wouldn't come! And now look! Your house is left to you as a house of desolation! And I'm telling you, you won't see me again until the time comes that you say, "Blessed is he that comes in the name of Adonai!"

YESHUA is unable to contain the emotion any longer and breaks down weeping. MIRIAM embraces him and he accepts the embrace.

MIRIAM. We are here for you, Yeshua.

Lights dim to black.

SCENE 8

The lights raise on the WOMAN OF SAMARIA. *She is at a spot called Ya'aqov's Well, from which she is drawing water.* YESHUA *enters. There is a long silence. The* WOMAN OF SAMARIA *casts her eyes down and is about to take her water and leave, when* YESHUA *speaks:*

YESHUA. Please, give me something to drink. *(The* WOMAN OF SAMARIA *stops. Caught off guard she looks at* YESHUA *with searching eyes and is about to turn away again.)* I mean you no harm. Very much the opposite.

The WOMAN OF SAMARIA *stops again, and then comes back. She puts down the water, draws some for* YESHUA, *but then hesitates before giving it to him.*

WOMAN OF SAMARIA. I don't think you know who I am. I'm a Samaritan.

YESHUA. I know who you are. But I don't believe you know who I Am.

WOMAN OF SAMARIA. I know that you are a Jew. Jews think they are above us, that we are half breeds and apostates. I know that much about you. Jews have no dealing with Samaritans.

YESHUA. If you truly knew me, truly recognized me by the memory of God within you, I wouldn't be the one asking you for water. Instead you would ask water from me. And then I would have given you living water.

WOMAN OF SAMARIA. Sir, you have no jar or rope. The well is deep. How would you give me living water? Are you greater than our father, the great Patriarch Ya'aqov who gave us this well?

YESHUA. If you drink from Ya'aqov's well, the time will come when you will be thirsty again. But if a woman drinks from the water I give her, it will be within her a water springing up to eternal life.

The WOMAN OF SAMARIA *sets aside the water she had drawn, and comes near to* YESHUA.

WOMAN OF SAMARIA. Oh, sir, I have been a thirsty woman all my life.

YESHUA. I know.

WOMAN OF SAMARIA. Give me this water, please, so that I'm quenched. I'm tired of drawing from other men's wells.

YESHUA. Go, call your husband here, so that he can hear, too.

WOMAN OF SAMARIA. I—I don't have a husband.

YESHUA. Yes, that's right. You've had five husbands. And the man you live with now isn't your husband either. Thank you for being honest with me.

WOMAN OF SAMARIA. Sir, how did you..? I see that you are a prophet. (*There is a silence. The* WOMAN OF SAMARIA *then becomes more courageous.*) And, since you are a prophet, I will trust your word. We Samaritans believe that we are the true keepers of the law, the Shamerim. We are descendants of Yisra'el, from Levi and Yosef, Efrayim and Manassah. We are the keepers of the true law which existed before the exile by Babylon.

YESHUA. You want to ask me a question, not give me a history lesson.

WOMAN OF SAMARIA. Sir, it's the great dispute between our peoples— we say that it's here in Mount Gerizim that is the holy place, that it's here that we should worship. It's here that Moses told Yeshua to gather the people. But your people say it's in Jerusalem at your temple that we should worship. You're a holy man, I'll believe your word either way.

YESHUA. Good Lady, do you worship a mountain?

WOMAN OF SAMARIA. No.

YESHUA. Do the Jews worship a temple?

WOMAN OF SAMARIA. No.

YESHUA. You're right, because it's our Father who you worship. And the time will come, when you won't worship the Father here or in

Jerusalem. For I'll send the Spirit of God, and it's through that Spirit that you can worship the Father, wherever you are. That is what will distinguish the true worshippers: the Spirit of God.

WOMAN OF SAMARIA. God is a Spirit?

YESHUA. You don't know who you worship. The Jews know who they worship, and that's why salvation is of them. This is Eternal Life, to know Elohim—and to know Elohim's son.

Something dawns on the WOMAN OF SAMARIA, as she feels this Spirit testify to her.

WOMAN OF SAMARIA. I—I don't want to blaspheme, but—there are stories about the Mashiach. When he comes, it's said that he will tell us all things. I know these stories are true.

YESHUA. I will answer what you already know. What the Spirit has told you. I am he. I am that I Am.

Enter SHIMON CEPHAS, ANDREAS, YOCHANNAN, YA'AQOV, TADDAI, YEHUDDAH SICARRI, SHIMON KANAI, MIRIAM, as well as new apostles, including YA'AQOV ALPHAEUS, MATTAY, PHILLIPOS, BAR'TOLMAY, and TOMA. The Woman of Samaria takes YESHUA's hands, but then pulls them back upon seeing the apostles, afraid of offending YESHUA. YESHUA take her hands back, and she looks up gratefully.

WOMAN OF SAMARIA. The I Am . . .

YESHUA. You understand. You have studied . . .

WOMAN OF SAMARIA. I—I know that a woman is not supposed to . . .

YESHUA. You *are* supposed to. You have the truth, now strengthen those around you.

WOMAN OF SAMARIA. Rabbi?

YESHUA. Bring this man you live with and let him drink. Bring those in your town and let them drink. I'll wait for you.

Thrilled, the WOMAN OF SAMARIA exits, completely forgetting and leaving behind her water pot. The apostles who looked on with some silent shock approach him. YESHUA *offers them some of the water, which they accept.*

SHIMON CEPHAS. Rabbi, who was that?

YESHUA. A Samaritan woman.

The apostles look at each other uncomfortably, except MIRIAM *who is cheered by this, but none of them dare question him further on the subject.* ANDREAS *breaks the awkwardness by bringing forward food they had brought.*

ANDREAS. Rabbi, you must be hungry. This has been a long journey. I have some food. Here, eat.

YESHUA. Thank you, but I'm not hungry.

ANDREAS. Please, I don't know when was the last time I saw you eat.

YESHUA. I have meat you don't know even know I have.

ANDREAS. Miriam, have you been feeding him?

MIRIAM. No.

ANDREAS. Shimon?

SHIMON CEPHAS. No.

YESHUA. So far you have been disciples, students. Now you will be messengers, teachers. I will send you. I am the vine, you will be the branches.

MIRIAM. What shall we teach, Adonai?

YESHUA. Who is your neighbor, Beloved? Is that Samaritan woman your neighbor?

MIRIAM. You tell me, Yeshua.

YESHUA. I love you, as the Father has loved me. Continue in love. This is my commandment, that you love each other, with the kind of love that I have loved you with.

MIRIAM. Then she is my neighbor and I will love her and love all people.

YESHUA. Yes! But, Miriam, what happens when trouble comes?

MIRIAM MAGDALENE. We will continue in love.

YESHUA. Yes! A man can't have greater love than laying down his life for his friends. And you are my friends, if you do what I ask you to do. So you are no longer my servants, or my students. You are my friends. Everything the Father tells me, I'll tell you.

MIRIAM. Then we shall choose you every time, my friend.

YESHUA. You haven't chosen me, Miriam. I have chosen you. So lift up your eyes. You see a town of Samaritans over there. I don't see a town, I see a field. A field which is white and already to harvest. Come, there is the Woman and her friends.

> YESHUA *and* MIRIAM *exit. The remaining apostles look awkwardly at each other.*

SHIMON CEPHAS. I don't know how I feel about this.

YEHUDAH SICARRI. Samaritans.

SHIMON CEPHAS. And the way he acts towards Miriam. Why is she suddenly preferred above us?

THAU'MA. Oh, come on, are we following him or not following him?

MATTAY. I'm with Thau'ma on this one. We did want change, right?

BAR'TOLMAY. Change benefits some of us more than others, Mattay.

MATTAY. What do you mean by that?

BAR'TOLMAY. You were the tax collector, not me. I already had a place at the table.

MATTAY. Yeshua called me. I did not ask for this. Are you or are you not following Yeshua?

BAR'TOLMAY. I don't need to be questioned by you.

ANDREAS. Come on everyone, let's not . . .

PHILLIPOS. I for one am following Yeshua and accepting those who he tells us to accept. You all should know better

THAU'MA. Phillipos, Ya'aqov Alphaeus, Mattay, come on. Let's catch up with Yeshua.

Exit THAU'MA, YA'AQOV ALPHAEUS, PHILLIPOS, *and* MATTAY.

YA'AQOV THE JUST. I'm not sure how I feel about some of these new recruits.

YOCHANNAN. I thought Phillipos would have sided with us Galileans.

ANDREAS. (*Sighs.*) We're already splitting up into factions. And, Shimon, really, speaking that way about Miriam . . .

SHIMON CEPHAS. I don't need any lectures right now, Andreas.

ANDREAS. We'll—we'll work it out. But we're all with Yeshua, right?

SHIMON CEPHAS. Of course we are. Which is why it's important that we are the ones who have the most influence on him.

Exit SHIMON CEPHAS.

ANDREAS. That's not exactly what I meant.

Exit ANDREAS, YOCHANNAN, YA'AQOV THE JUST, *and* BAR'TOLMAY.

TADDAI. This isn't going very well.

YEHUDAH SICARRI. Why do you say that?

SHIMON KANAI. Maybe you didn't see the moment we just did.

YEHUDAH SICARRI. My brothers, if you keep your eyes open you will see what I see.

TADDAI. And what is that?

YEHUDAH SICARRI. Opportunity. I see opportunity everywhere.

Exit YEHUDAH SICARRI. TADDAI *and* SHIMON KANAI *exchange worried glances and then exit as well.*

SCENE 9

A home in Bethany. ELEAZAR *enters with* YESHUA *and* MIRIAM.

ELEAZAR. Marta! I have a wonderful surprise!

MARTA enters. MIRIAM *runs to* MARTA *and impulsively hugs her.* MARTA *extricates herself.*

MARTA. (*Scolding.*) Miriam! What were you doing alone with Yeshua? Did anyone see you?

MIRIAM. Oh, calm down, we just walked a short way over here. The apostles are staying elsewhere. I didn't want to burden you. But I thought—well, the chance to see Yeshua again . . .

MARTA. Of course I want to see Yeshua again. But I wish you would have sent notice! Nothing's prepared. Thoughtless as always, Miriam. Send advance word in the future. Please, Yeshua, pardon the state of my house . . .

YESHUA. Truly, Marta, I don't mind those things. Better a clean inner cup than a clean outer cup. We're all dear friends, aren't we?

MARTA. You need to be careful, Yeshua. Having Miriam travel with your group is bad enough—but to be seen alone with you. A woman's reputation is a fragile thing. I have heard women called prostitutes for the most seemingly benign of actions.

ELEAZAR. Come on, Marta, let's not be unpleasant.

MARTA. You're no better than Yeshua. I don't like that you both encourage her wild notions. We're already reaping gossip on her behalf. There are already those who consider her a sinner . . .

MIRIAM. I haven't done anything wrong.

YESHUA. We all know the quality of Miriam's spirit.

MARTA looks them all over, sighs, and smiles warmly at YESHUA.

MARTA. Well, I'll defer to the men then. But I seriously wonder about my brother sometimes. We'll see to dinner. Come along now, Miriam.

MIRIAM. Wait a moment, Yeshua and I were discussing something.

MARTA. Miriam . . . (*MIRIAM ignores MARTA and turns to the men.*) Eleazar, Yeshua, please tell her . . .

ELEAZAR. Marta, can't that wait? Talk to us.

MARTA. You were raised better than this, Eleazar. Go, talk out your business with Yeshua. That's for the men. Miriam and I have our own place, our own duties.

YESHUA comes over to MARTA and takes her by the hand, which makes her uncomfortable.

YESHUA. Please, Marta, I want to talk to all of you.

MARTA takes her hand away.

MARTA. Please, Yeshua, I must ask that you be more appropriate.

MARTA exits into the kitchen.

ELEAZAR. Excuse her, Yeshua. I don't think she exactly understands who you are yet. What you will mean . . .

MIRIAM. How could she? If she just would sit with him, listen to him, she would know . . .

YESHUA. Don't worry, my friends. It's not so much that she doesn't know who I am—it's that she doesn't yet know who *she* is. But she will prove herself more than you know. Eleazar, how was my mother the last you saw her?

ELEAZAR. A great woman, your mother. She is in good health and good spirits. We got along swimmingly.

YESHUA. You are all now more than my friends. You are my family. You are all now my Beloved family.

ELEAZAR. Yeshua, I have heard that you gave a masterful sermon. Can you share it with us?

YESHUA. Yes, please, sit. You need to hear this.

MIRIAM and ELEAZAR sit at YESHUA's feet.

YESHUA (CONT'D). Listen and ponder these things. This is not my Wisdom, but the Wisdom of our God in Heaven. Blessed are the poor in spirit: for theirs is the kingdom of heaven. Blessed are they that mourn: for they shall be comforted. Blessed are the meek: for they shall inherit the earth. Blessed are they which do hunger and thirst after righteousness: for they shall be filled . . .

MARTA enters and is scandalized to see MIRIAM at Yeshua's feet.

MARTA. Miriam . . .

YESHUA. Blessed are the merciful: for they shall obtain mercy. Blessed are the pure in heart: for they shall see God.

MARTA. Miriam!

MIRIAM. Not now, Marta.

YESHUA. Blessed are the peacemakers: for they shall be called the children of God.

MARTA. We have responsibilities.

ELEAZAR. Oh, let her be, Marta . . .

MARTA. And so I'm supposed to be the one doing all the work? That meal won't prepare itself!

MIRIAM. I'm listening. I'm trying to learn . . .

MARTA. And that's another thing. Look at you, sitting at his feet as if you were one of his disciples.

MIRIAM. I am. I am one of his disciples.

MARTA. As if you were a man who was at liberty to do that kind of thing! It's completely inappropriate.

MIRIAM. Why can't I? Why can't I be like those other men who follow him and devote themselves to him and be his disciples?

MARTA. If you want to help Yeshua with this ministry of his, then come and help me serve him dinner! We can support him in that way!

YESHUA. Marta . . .

MARTA. Is this what you're encouraging, Yeshua? Miriam is not a man, she can't go galloping across the countryside with you.

YESHUA. New wine can't be put into old bottles, Marta.

MARTA. Oh, don't go off into one of your esoteric analogies, Yeshua. I like people to talk straight with me.

YESHUA. You need to have ears to hear . . .

MARTA. Please, Yeshua, I'm asking you to assert your rightful place and tell Miriam to help me!

YESHUA. Marta, Marta, you're worried and upset about many things, but only one thing is needed. Miriam has chosen the better part, and I won't take it away from her.

MARTA is taken back by this.

MARTA. Why do you rebuke me for doing what I need to do?

YESHUA. What I need you to do is sit by your sister and talk with us. We want you here.

MARTA pauses, processing, and then, somewhat reluctantly, she sits.

MARTA. This is madness.

MIRIAM, ecstatic to have Marta sitting with them, takes Marta by the hand and snuggles into her a bit. Marta seems a little uncomfortable from the touch, but endures it stoically.

YESHUA. Blessed are you, when men will revile you, and persecute you, and shall say all manner of evil against you falsely for my sake. Rejoice and be exceedingly glad: for great is your reward in heaven: for so persecuted they the prophets which were before you. You are the light of the world. A city that is set on a hill can't be hid . . .

Lights dim on YESHUA, *etc., although they remain on stage and are very still.*

NICODEMUS *enters.* KAYAFA *enters and reaches* NICODEMUS. *Both characters are Pharisees who are members of the 71 member council of the Sanhedrin, the highest religious and civil authority among the Jews at the time.*

KAYAFA. Nicodemus!

NICODEMUS. Rabbi Kayafa—erm, good to see you.

KAYAFA. I don't blame the coolness in your voice. I know my group of Sadducees were causing trouble today. Always wanting to create a conflict, eh?

NICODEMUS. You're a minority in the council. Without you, they would have no real power.

KAYAFA. That's why I like you Nicodemus. Always level headed and shrewd. Not a reactionary who is likely to cross over into extreme positions. (NICODEMUS *becomes more guarded at this.*) My father-in-law Annas says that you have earned a solid reputation for methodical thinking. This is good, this is good. He likes you very much, you know.

NICODEMUS. I am honored by Annas' good opinion. His former term as the high priest before you was of great service to our people. Of course, his illegal trials and stonings didn't please Rome, did they?

KAYAFA. (*A little angry.*) Of course, Annas still holds a good deal of sway with many other members of the Sanhedrin. But you know this, you know this . . .

NICODEMUS. Yes, your wealth and influence is well known to all of us. Everyone here is so willing to wear everything on the outside.

KAYAFA. (*Indicating* NICODEMUS's *traditional clothing.*) As are you. But that is neither here nor there. Something has been troubling me, Nicodemus, and I was told that you could help me.

NICODEMUS. How so?

KAYAFA. I was told that you have talked to this Yeshua fellow. That you had a very interesting conversation with him.

NICODEMUS. I haven't told anyone such.

KAYAFA. Oh, perhaps I was mistaken then. But this one gentleman said he could have sworn he saw you late at night with this Yeshua person. Even caught snippets of your conversation . . .

NICODEMUS. I'm really in a hurry, Kayafa. Perhaps we can discuss this at another . . . ?

KAYAFA. Of course, of course, but I'll just take a moment more of your time. Nicodemus, you don't need me reminding you of the fragile position we're in right now with our Roman overlords. Barabba and those violent extremists are attracting a lot of attention to our nation—all the wrong kind of attention. The Zealots being hunted by the Romans, and, if we're not careful, we may be next. Then the whole exchanges between Herod and Yochanan the Baptist, well, that didn't do us any favors, did it?

NICODEMUS. No, it didn't.

KAYAFA. We can't have any more fractious groups dividing us. The Romans are tolerating us right now, we are very lucky. We have the temple, we are allowed to practice our religion with some degree of freedom and govern ourselves to a certain extent—our culture is intact. Other cultures have not been so lucky.

NICODEMUS. God has been very good to us.

KAYAFA. Yes, and so have the Romans. Nicodemus, we have been entrusted with the safety of our people. That is a sacred trust.

NICODEMUS. God will protect us, if we do right.

KAYAFA. God protects those who are willing to protect themselves. We have tempted the Empire's hand before when we denied Pilate access to the temple . . .

NICODEMUS. You were brave in that moment, Kayafa.

KAYAFA. Brave or foolish, I could have died that day.

NICODEMUS. Then you would have gone to the bosom of Abraham.

KAYAFA. No! No, I wouldn't have. We Sadducees don't fall for those fairy tales of yours. It is a false hope of an afterlife you Pharisees have built up for yourselves. We are dust, and unto dust we shall return!

NICODEMUS. How can you really believe that?

KAYAFA. God has given us *this* life, Nicodemus, and no fate, no destiny will make anything of it, unless we make something of it ourselves. We must protect our people from any threat that would expose them to the vengeance of Rome. Do you agree with that at least? (*Expectant pause.*) Do you agree?

NICODEMUS. I agree.

KAYAFA. Good. It's best that we leave these fringe elements alone. The Romans have made the Sanhedrin the established authority. We need to teach the people to trust their leaders. These sort of rebels are charismatic, certainly. But when the passions burn out, it will always be the cooler, more experienced heads who prevail. Thank you for your time.

> *KAYAFA goes to leave, until stopped by NICODEMUS's voice.*

NICODEMUS. Kayafa?

KAYAFA. Yes?

NICODEMUS. We have waited for the Mashiach for a long time. We need him now more than ever . . .

KAYAFA. Believe me, Nicodemus, I more than anyone know the need we have of deliverance. But deliverance will not come in the form of a dusty street preacher. If this Mashiach is real—he will need to be mightier than the Empire itself. And can you really say when you look at that dirty man from Galilee that he can overcome the power of Rome?

> *Exit KAYAFA, then NICODEMUS. Lights rise back up on YESHUA, MIRIAM, MARTA, and ELEAZAR.*

YESHUA. Come to me, all of you who work, and carry heavy things. I will give you rest. Take my yoke with you instead, and learn from me, for I am meek, with a lowly heart. Ye shall find rest unto your souls, for my yoke is easy, and my burden is light.

There is an electric pause.

ELEAZAR. So, Marta, are you in such a rush to do your chores now?

MARTA. That was one of the most beautiful things I have ever heard.

MIRIAM snuggles into MARTA even closer and hugs her tightly.

MIRIAM. I told you so.

MARTA. I just have one question, though.

YESHUA. What is it?

MARTA. That "consider the lilies" part—do you really believe that God will just take care of us like that?

YESHUA. The laborer is worthy of his—or her—hire.

MARTA. And what about you? Is God providing for you?

YESHUA. I'm sure of it.

MARTA. Well, as a carpenter who hasn't had much time to work, I'm frankly worried about you. And, as you said, God knows that you have need of food, and shelter, and clothes—well, you know that we are a family of means. Eleazar?

ELEAZAR. I agree, Marta. It's a wonderful idea.

MARTA. You are certainly seeking the kingdom of God and His righteousness. So let us be your food, your shelter, and your raiment. And we can help with your work with the poor. We want to help finance your work. Let us be your patrons.

YESHUA. You are certain about this?

MARTA. Whatever of ours you need, even if it is everything, it is yours.

MIRIAM. Marta, I could kiss you!

MARTA. Please don't.

YESHUA. (*Clearly moved by their sacrifice.*) I met a rich, young man the other day. He told me that he was righteous, that he was keeping all the commandments from his youth. I loved and honored him for that. But then he asked me what more he needed to do. I told him that now he needed to sell all his many goods and give to the poor. He despaired and left me. But you, my Beloved friends, without me even asking you, are willing to do what that good man could not.

MIRIAM *laughs for joy and gives* YESHUA *a huge hug.* YESHUA *laughs in return.* MARTA *looks wryly over at* ELEAZAR.

MARTA. This is wonderful and all, but we do have to do something about all the hugging.

YESHUA. Miriam, I have your new name for you now. You shall be called Magdala.

ELEAZAR. Oh, "tower!" "Fortress!" I would have thought that a more appropriate name for Marta.

MARTA *slaps* ELEAZAR *on the shoulder.*

YESHUA. It also means "elegant, elevated, great, magnificent."

MIRIAM. I don't deserve that name.

MARTA. Yes, you do, dear.

YESHUA. I don't give people new names because the name describes the person, or the person somehow deserves the name. I give a person a new name to transform that person. I will elevate you, Miriam, in ways that you don't understand yet. They called you Mad Miriam, well, now they will call you by the magnificent name of the Magdala. I shall make all things new—I shall make all of *you* new.

SCENE 10

YESHUA's *apostles, as well as* ELEAZAR *and* MIRIAM, *are on the boat. The weather is looking fair at first.* SATAN'EL *walks upon the water and onto the boat. With a smile* SATAN'EL *touches the water one last time, which is when we hear our first peal of thunder and the weather starts to look bleak.*

BAR-TOLMAY. I don't like the look of those clouds.

SHIMON CEPHAS. Nor do I like that thunder. And we're still a long way from the shore.

SATAN'EL smiles, and moves onto YEHUDAH SICARRI, *who is looking darkly contemplative. Throughout the scene, he spurs* YEHUDAH's *thoughts with nudges, whispers, etc.*

YA'AQOV ALPHAEUS. (*To* SHIMON KANAI:) Five thousand—he fed five thousand people! I'm still trying to wrap my head around it.

SHIMON KANAI. All from five loaves and a few fishes. At first I thought he was just some great teacher—but this is something else entirely. What do you think, Yehudah?

YEHUDAH SICARRI. His comments about people eating his flesh— what do you think he meant by that?

YA'AQOV ALPHAEUS. He miraculously feeds five thousand and you care what he *says*?

YEHUDAH SICARRI. What he says is the most important thing, Ya'aqov. Even he would tell you that. I'm here for more than a free meal.

THAU'MA. I thought what he said was interesting, too.

YEHUDAH SICARRI. Interesting isn't quite the word I would use, Thau'ma.

THAU'MA. "I am the living bread which came down from heaven. If any man eat of this bread, he shall live forever: and the bread that I will give is my flesh, which I will give for the life of the world." Yeshua's quite the poet. His figurative language is certainly vivid.

YA'AQOV THE JUST. And you have quite the memory, Thau'ma.

ELEAZAR. I think we'll have to remember these things and try to understand them. They're important. They need to be written down.

MATTAY. Don't worry, some of us have already begun.

MIRIAM. Good.

YEHUDAH SICARRI. You're all idiots! Don't you get it? He's saying hard things, if you'll just open your ears and listen. I've understood everything he's said.

SHIMON CEPHAS. And you don't like what you're hearing, Yehudah? I thought you were with us.

YEHUDAH SICARRI. Yeshua can be the greatest man alive, if he doesn't throw it away. I have more admiration for that man than any of you, for I strive with his words and I see his abilities! But he said that we were going to eat his flesh—that he was going to give his life for the world! He's not being as figurative as you think! How can he do any good for the world, if he's dead?

SHIMON CEPHAS. I won't let that happen. We'll protect him.

YEHUDAH SICARRI. I'm afraid it won't be that easy, Shimon. That man *wants* to be a martyr.

Suddenly the boat is rocked with waves and a ferocious storm begins.

ANDREAS. Whoa! That's no mere breeze!

SHIMON CEPHAS. The sails! Wrap up the sails!

The apostles scramble to prepare the boat against the storm, with SHIMON *and* ANDREAS *directing them. Waves crash, strong winds blow, thunder sounds, lightning flashes, and thick darkness starts to surround them.*

ANDREAS. Shimon, we weren't prepared for this!

SHIMON CEPHAS. Then prepare now!

ANDREAS. I don't think this boat can take this kind of beating! It's not like ours at home . . .

SHIMON CEPHAS. Quite the time to comment on shoddy workmanship!

BAR-TOLMAY. We might not make it through this!

The storm only intensifies, with the darkness becoming blacker and bleaker, when suddenly a bright flash appears on YESHUA *who is walking on the water a distance away from them.*

PHILLIPOS. Ghost!

MATTAY. (*Looking around the boat.*) Did we already lose somebody?

THAU'MA. Don't be ridiculous!

TADDAI. Well, don't *you* see it?

THAU'MA. It's—it's—an optical illusion.

YOCHANNAN. No, don't you see, it's Yeshua!

THAU'MA. Impossible!

YA'AQOV THE JUST. No, he's right—it is Yeshua!

YESHUA *holds up his right hand.*

YESHUA. Peace! Be still!

The storm suddenly stops and the light returns.

THAU'MA. Who is this man that even the waves and wind obey him?

YESHUA. Calm down! It's me.

SHIMON CEPHAS. You're walking on water!

YESHUA. (*With a good humored smile.*) Why, yes, I see that.

SHIMON CEPHAS. Adonai, if it's really you, invite me to come out there with you on the water.

YESHUA. Come.

SHIMON *climbs out of the boat and onto the water. He is not tentative at first, but acts bravely. But then* SATAN'EL, *startled, touches the water and the wind picks up a bit, and* SHIMON *suddenly starts to sink.*

SHIMON CEPHAS. Yeshua, save me!

YESHUA *comes to* SHIMON *and lifts him out of the water.*

YESHUA. Shimon, such little faith. You started out so well—why did you doubt?

YESHUA and SHIMON climb onto the boat. All of them are in awe of YESHUA. YESHUA notes SATAN'EL briefly and, though he can see him, YESHUA generally ignores him.

YEHUDAH SICARRI. Who are you?

YESHUA. Who do people say that I am?

THAU'MA. Some say that you're Eliyahu, or one of the old prophets risen again. You have Herod half convinced that you're the Baptist come back to haunt him.

YESHUA. And who do you say that I am?

SHIMON stands forward at this, certain and strong.

SHIMON CEPHAS. You are the Mashiach. Truly, you are the Son of the living God.

YESHUA. You're blessed for that testimony, Shimon. Flesh and blood hasn't revealed this to you. My Abba has revealed it to you.

SHIMON CEPHAS. Yeshua, I—I feel a—a burning. What is this?

YESHUA. You'll have a new name, my friend. You'll be called Cephas, the Rock, like the Urrim and Thummim of the Tabernacle, like the ancient seer stones of old. And upon this revelatory bedrock, that burning within you now, I will build my Church; and the gates of hell won't prevail against it.

At this SATAN'EL pays rapt attention to SHIMON CEPHAS.

SHIMON CEPHAS. How can I accomplish such a huge job, Adonai?

YESHUA. I will give you keys of the kingdom. With those keys, whatever you seal on earth, will be sealed in heaven, and whatever you loose on earth will be loosed in heaven.

YEHUDAH SICARRI. Then let's tell the whole of Israel! Let's tell the people and they'll unite behind us!

YESHUA. No, Yehudah, you mustn't tell anybody yet.

YEHUDAH SICARRI. What?

YESHUA. My time hasn't come.

YEHUDAH SICARRI. But it will.

YESHUA. Yes. But I must suffer. I must die.

> SATAN'EL *is becoming very anxious about* YEHUDAH *and* SHIMON. *He pushes his tactics with increasing aggressiveness.*

YEHUDAH SICARRI. No . . .

YESHUA. The elders, the scribes, the Sadducees, the Pharisees, they're all conspire against me and they will make me suffer.

YEHUDAH SICARRI. No.

YESHUA. They will kill me, Yehudah. But the temple that is destroyed will be rebuilt on the third day.

YEHUDAH SICARRI. No!

SATAN'EL. (*To* SHIMON CEPHAS.) Speak up, you imbecile! Do you want to see your leader die?

SHIMON CEPHAS. Yehudah is right, Adonai! We won't let this happen to you!

YESHUA. (*Looking squarely at* SATAN'EL.) Get behind me, Satan! You're an offence to me. (SATAN'EL *pauses, unsure, but then exits obediently. Then, without a beat,* YESHUA *turns back to* SHIMON CEPHAS.) Cephas, you don't savor the things of God, but are hungering after the things of man.

SHIMON CEPHAS. Adonai . . .

YESHUA. If any man will come after me, he needs to deny himself. He needs to take up his cross and follow me. For who would save his life, will lose it. And who would lose his life for my sake, will find it.

YEHUDAH SICARRI. What else does a man have, if he doesn't have his life, Yeshua?

YESHUA. What is a man profited, if he gains the whole world, but loses his soul? How much will a man give in exchange for his soul? How much, Yehudah?

YEHUDAH is startled by this and withdraws a bit.

YA'AQOV THE JUST. We're with you, Yeshua. I'll give whatever is required.

YESHUA. Ya'aqov, the Son of man shall come in the glory of his Father; and then he shall reward every man according to his works.

ELEAZAR. Then, to prove our love to you, we'll work.

YESHUA. (*Smiling at* ELEAZAR.) Truly, there are some standing here which won't taste of death until they see the Son of Man coming in his kingdom. (*YESHUA goes to* YEHUDAH, *speaking to him quietly.*) Did this offend you?

YEHUDAH SICARRI. Leave me alone.

YESHUA. No man, putting his hand to the plough, but then looking back is fit for the kingdom of God.

YEHUDAH SICARRI. Shut up!

YEHUDAH exits to the underquarters.

YESHUA. (*To the other apostles.*) Will you go away, too?

SHIMON CEPHAS. Adonai, who would we go to? You have the words of eternal life.

YESHUA. Haven't I chosen you twelve, and one of you is a devil?

ELEAZAR. Yeshua—I'm not feeling so well.

Blackout.

END ACT ONE

Act Two

SCENE 1

SATAN'EL enters, attentive and sharp. He looks over three figures, who are separate: Pontius PILATE, HEROD *Antipas, and* KAYAFA. *They are all attending to various duties attendant with their positions, except perhaps Herod who may be more indolent. They all act out their sections of the scene as if they are in different times, different places, not aware of each other in the least.* SATAN'EL, *however, is aware of each of them individually. Pilate's wife,* CLAUDIA *enters.*

CLAUDIA. Pointius . . .

PILATE. Claudia! How can I help you, dear?

CLAUDIA. Am I interrupting?

PILATE. Please, please, interrupt! Anything to get away from this tedium!

CLAUDIA. Well, I'm glad I can distract you.

CLAUDIA starts giving PILATE *a back rub. Enter* NICODEMUS *to* KAYAFA.

NICODEMUS. You wanted me, Kayafa?

KAYAFA holds up a finger. NICODEMUS *waits patiently. Enter* HERODIAS *to* HEROD.

HERODIAS. You superstitious goat!

HEROD. Good morning, Herodias.

HERODIAS. You are an utter imbecile!

HEROD. Starting at it early this morning, are we?

HERODIAS. Why haven't you killed that Nazarene yet?

HEROD. I already killed one prophet for you—and yet you groan and grind on. Never satisfied.

CLAUDIA. I've been hearing some interesting stories from my Jewish women, Pontius . . .

HERODIAS. Satisfied? Are you satisfied? Are you satisfied by those who challenge your authority?

HEROD. I'm used to it now. You challenge it every day.

CLAUDIA. Are you listening, Pontius?

PILATE. Of course, my dear. Your Jewish women. Go on.

CLAUDIA. I like to hear about their culture, their beliefs. It's all very fascinating.

PILATE. Yes, they seem to have become your little hobby.

CLAUDIA. They've been telling me about a man named . . .

HERODIAS AND CLAUDIA. . . . Yeshua.

HEROD. Yeshua, Yeshua! He's all you ever talk about now. First the Baptist, then Yeshua. Can't you see that you give me ulcers?

PILATE. Yes, I've heard of this man. He's stirring a bit of controversy down there.

SATAN'EL *goes to* HERODIAS *and rubs her shoulders, calming her.*

HERODIAS. I—I know that I harp on this a lot, my dear. I'm sorry.

HEROD. You're—sorry?

CLAUDIA. They tell remarkable stories about him.

HERODIAS. It's just that the stories the people are telling are disturbing.

HEROD. Disturbing—yes, I find them disturbing as well.

SATAN'EL *starts flicking* PILATE *in the ear and in the back of the head, which visibly agitates him.*

PILATE. Yes, I've heard some of these stories as well. The superstitions that run rampant among this people are ridiculous. Why Sejanus assigned me to such a backwater place, I'll never know.

CLAUDIA. Please, don't mention that tyrant . . .

HERODIA starts rubbing HEROD's shoulders, or perhaps his feet.

HERODIAS. I'm sorry if I put you into a sour mood.

HEROD. You're fine, Herodias. I just—well, you'll call me superstitious.

HERODIAS. Try me.

HEROD. I just hadn't heard of this Yeshua until the Baptist's death. What if he—what if he is the Baptist come back from the dead to haunt me? Reincarnated or something like that?

SATAN'EL tickles HERODIAS. She laughs.

HERODIAS. Yes, you were right! I think you *are* superstitious! Oh, Antipas, you silly fool. You're always good for a laugh.

HEROD. Heh, heh, yes. Yes, how silly.

SATAN'EL whispers to HERODIAS, which prompts HERODIAS to kiss HEROD.

HERODIAS. Yes, very silly.

PILATE takes CLAUDIA's hands and has her sit with him.

PONTIUS. I didn't mean to upset you, my dear. You—you've seemed very sad lately.

CLAUDIA. I've been thinking about our dear little Pilo.

PONTIUS. We must come to terms with his condition, Claudia.

CLAUDIA AND HERODIAS. The stories they tell about Yeshua . . .

HEROD. Please, let's get off of the subject, Herodias.

CLAUDIA. They say that he is a healer. (*YESHUA appears, playing out separate scenes on top of what is happening.*) All sorts of sickness, and disease. Even lepers. Even the blind and crippled.

As they speak, YESHUA *heals a* LEPER. *He takes dirt he has spat on and wipes them upon the eyes of a blind man, which heals him. A* MALACH *comes and touches a pool of water (Bethseda) and a* CRIPPLED MAN *appears by it.* YESHUA *tells him quietly to:*

YESHUA. Stand up. Pick up your bed and walk.

The CRIPPLED MAN *does so and is cured.*

HERODIAS. The people are believing these stories, Antipas. They are supporting him.

HEROD. That is precisely why we can't act against him.

HERODIAS. Always conceding to the people does not give you power.

HEROD. Killing their heroes only creates resentment. Haven't we learned that with the Baptist?

HERODIAS. The powerful bear resentment, the weak bear fear. That's the exchange.

HEROD. I didn't want to be feared. I wanted them to love me.

HERODIAS. Love is a fiction! The only real thing is respect.

CLAUDIA. A healer, Pontius. Think about that—a healer.

PILATE. Don't get your hopes up, Claudia.

CLAUDIA. If he can heal a Jewish cripple why can't he heal a Roman cripple? Why can't he heal our son?

HEROD AND PILATE. I've had enough of this . . .

HERODIA. No, don't be angry.

CLAUDIA. Sit with me.

SATAN'EL *stops* KAYAFA's *pen.* SATAN'EL *then raises* KAYAFA's *chin so that his face gazes on* NICODEMUS. KAYAFA *stands.*

KAYAFA. I thought we were in agreement, Nicodemus.

NICODEMUS. What are you referring to, Kayafa?

KAYAFA. The Nazarene. I thought we were in agreement.

NICODEMUS. That's the thing, Kayafa. When you bully everyone to your position, you start thinking that it's what they actually believe.

KAYAFA. You talked to Gamaliel behind my back.

NICODEMUS. I wasn't aware that I needed your permission to speak to him. Great High Priest or not, you are not my master. Gamaliel was very open minded about the stories of Yeshua. And, if there is anyone on the council with more clout than you, Kayafa, it's Gamaliel.

KAYAFA. Do you really believe that I do what I do to fulfill my own vain ambition? Everything I have done has been for the safety of our people.

NICODEMUS. And everything I am doing right now is for the soul of our people. I saw a very remarkable thing the other day, Kayafa.

YESHUA is thronged with people. A WOMAN appears.

KAYAFA. If it's another tall tale about Yeshua . . .

NICODEMUS. A woman had an issue of blood. She had been bleeding from her uterus for 12 years . . .

KAYAFA. Don't talk about such distasteful things!

NICODEMUS. She was trying to get to Yeshua. She had heard of his healing powers. She couldn't get through the crowd.

SATAN'EL touches KAYAFA's hand and KAYAFA withdraws his hand, disgusted and uncomfortable.

KAYAFA. She was in the crowd? But all those people—she was unclean!

NICODEMUS. Listen and you will hear how the Nazarene made her clean.

KAYAFA. Nothing makes an aberration like that clean.

The WOMAN touches the hem of YESHUA's clothing.

NICODEMUS. She touched his clothing. He knew.

YESHUA. Who touched me?

SHIMON CEPHAS. Adonai, we're all around you. We've all touched you.

YESHUA. Who touched me? I felt virtue leave me. (*The* WOMAN *identifies herself by nervously raising her hand.*) Daughter, be comforted. Your faith has made you whole.

The WOMAN *embraces him.*

NICODEMUS. He healed her without even trying.

The crowd disappears.

KAYAFA. You're gullible, Nicodemus.

NICODEMUS. I saw it with my own eyes!

KAYAFA. You don't know what you saw.

CLAUDIA. Pontius?

KAYAFA. He has people helping him.

PONTIUS. Hm?

KAYAFA. Deceivers like himself.

CLAUDIA. Do you believe in the gods?

PONTIUS. If the stories we tell about the gods are true, I'm not sure I *want* to believe in them. I encounter enough of their sort in this life, I don't want to encounter their brutality in the next as well.

CLAUDIA. The Jewish God, he seems different.

PONTIUS. I don't know, Claudia. The Jewish God seems to have a lot of blood on his hands. Have you heard some of those stories?

NICODEMUS. You don't know Yeshua.

KAYAFA. I have no interest in him. He's no better than that rascal Barabba. Sons of the Father, indeed. Blasphemy.

CLAUDIA. How Yeshua has been teaching about Him, though—full of love and mercy. Forgiveness. A Father. The God he teaches about is so different than the ideas we've created for ourselves. And he said something so interesting . . .

KAYAFA. You tell these stories of uplift and miracles. You haven't mentioned his heresies—he breaks the Sabbath, he touches the unclean, he dines with tax collectors and sinners, he is a wine bibber and a sorcerer. If he does miracles, it is by the power of the devil.

NICODEMUS. The lies of his enemies!

KAYAFA. You say I haven't seen him. Well, I have. And I heard him blaspheme to heaven. Blaspheme our very god!

CLAUDIA. As the women described it, I couldn't help but think it was a very remarkable idea. A very beautiful idea . . .

KAYAFA. It was the most idolatrous and wicked thing I have heard any man say:

> YESHUA *is now surrounded by angry* PHARISEES *and* SADDUCEES. KAYAFA *joins the scene.*

PHARISEE #1. How long do you make us doubt? If you claim to be the Mashiach, tell us in plain language!

YESHUA. You don't have ears to hear. I have told you and you haven't believed me.

PHARISEE #2. You speak in parables and shadow. Talk Plainly. Bravely.

YESHUA. Then let this be plain and brave enough: My Father and I are one.

KAYAFA. (*Shocked pause.*) Blasphemy!

YESHUA. As those whom the Father has given me, and obey my commandments, are one in me, and are one in the Father with me.

> *With a gentle, comforting clasp on* KAYAFA'*s shoulder,* SATAN'EL *hands* KAYAFA *a stone.*

KAYAFA. Stone him!

> *The other* PHARISEES *are also given stones by* SATAN'EL.

YESHUA. I've shown you many good works. For which one do you plan on killing me for?

KAYAFA. We don't stone you for good works, evil one. We'll stone you for blasphemy. You're a man, but you make yourself a god.

YESHUA. You don't understand your own immortality, Kayafa. Your own divinity.

KAYAFA. Don't pretend you understand anything about me, Blasphemer.

YESHUA. Is it not written in your law, "Ye are gods?"

NICODEMUS. He quoted the Praises. "Ye are gods, and all of you children of the most high."

KAYAFA. He was blaspheming the scriptures, twisting them to his own perverted purpose!

YESHUA. Is it not written in your law, "Ye are gods?" Well, if the inspired man who wrote those words called all of humankind gods—and this scripture is true and can't be broken—then why do you tell me that I blaspheme when I tell you that I have been sent of our Father and sanctified? Why do you say I blaspheme when I say that I am the Son of God? Look to your own scriptures and they will tell you the truth.

KAYAFA. Are you truly telling us that you believe you are the Son of God?

YESHUA. Does this offend you?

KAYAFA. Is that what you're telling us?

YESHUA. If I honor myself, my honor is nothing. It is my Abba that honors me. Yet you don't know my Abba. But I know him. But if I were to spare your feelings and try and not to offend you, then I would be a liar like you. Your abba Abraham rejoiced to see my day. He saw it and was glad.

PHARISEE #2. You aren't even fifty years old, and you claim to have seen Abraham?

YESHUA. I saw Moses face to face, I loved Abraham, and I am older than them all. My Abba set me over all of you before Adam. Before Abraham was, I Am. I Am that I Am.

SADDUCEE #1. You claim to be . . . ?

PHARISEE #2. Am I hearing this?

PHARISEE #1. You are not Adonai!

KAYAFA. Blasphemy!

NICODEMUS. If you were so affronted, why didn't you stone him?

KAYAFA. We were about to . . . (*YESHUA disappears*) . . . but he went through the temple and got away.

PILATE. I'll say this for the man, he's bold. I like that.

CLAUDIA AND NICODEMUS. I didn't tell you yet . . .

> *YESHUA re-appears at the bedside of a* LITTLE GIRL.

YESHUA. Little girl, I'm talking to you. It's time to get up.

CLAUDIA AND NICODEMUS. . . . he raised a child from the dead.

> *The* LITTLE GIRL *rises from her bed and* YESHUA *exits with her in his arms.*

KAYAFA. Ridiculous.

PILATE. Now let's not get carried away.

CLAUDIA. There are a lot of witnesses.

NICODEMUS. I saw it myself. I saw the girl was dead, and when he was done with her, she was alive again.

KAYAFA. You were deceived.

PILATE. A clever deception, clearly.

NICODEMUS. I know dead when I see it.

CLAUDIA. The women I talked to said they saw her themselves and helped handle the girl's dead, cold, unbreathing body.

KAYAFA. You are in league with him. Get out of here.

NICODEMUS. Gladly. But don't think you can stop this movement, Kayafa. God has set up a light on a hill, and no one can extinguish it.

NICODEMUS exits calmly and then KAYAFA exits in frustration. SATAN'EL helps PILATE to his feet, giving him a manly slap on the back.

PILATE. Claudia, I think you're going a little far with this. These stories-they may give you some sense of hope, but let's remember, we're supposed to be the civilized ones here in this savage land. Let's not indulge too much in the flapping tongues of women and the myths of backward primitives.

PILATE goes to leave, but CLAUDIA stops him with her words.

CLAUDIA. You talk about civilization? Then tell me why our government has been overrun with power hungry killers and our landscapes are littered with crucified carcasses. Don't think I haven't been hearing of your own violent exploits since we came here.

PILATE. Claudia . . .

CLAUDIA. You present yourself as distant and pure and untouched, but you sent our engraved images into their city, and threatened to bring those statues into their temple, which you knew were offensive to them. It was only the act of their offering their own necks to be severed rather than relinquish to your force that finally dissuaded you. But you didn't flinch from their blood when you sent your guards into their temple, taking their sacred funds for our aqueducts and then had them killed to prevent protest. If this is us at the height of "civilization," then perhaps this "Kingdom of Heaven" I hear about is a better alternative.

CLAUDIA exits. PILATE is silent. He's not angry, but somber. SATAN'EL puts his hand on PILATE's shoulder, but PILATE shrugs it off. Exit PILATE. SATAN'EL, somewhat disappointed with these outcomes, goes to his old reliables HEROD and HERODIAS. He kicks back and enjoys himself on their furniture and starts whistling a spritely tune.

HERODIAS. Come now, Antipas, let's not be glum. I feel like some fun.

HEROD. Herodias . . .

HERODIAS. No, really, we fight and then cry, fight and then cry! It's always so much better when we're laughing and making love!

HEROD. Don't you ever get afraid, Herodias?

HERODIAS. Afraid? Afraid of what? We're on top, my love. We're on top!

HEROD. Which makes the precipice all the more precarious.

HERODIAS. Since when did you become a philosopher?

HEROD. We will reap consequences sooner or later.

HERODIAS. Consequences? I don't believe in them. Justice, the Law, the Torah! What nonsense. We will die, that is the only consequence. Until then, let's have some fun. Come to bed with me.

HEROD. I used to enjoy that. It was good once. I used to love you.

HERODIAS. Well, that's odd, because I never loved you. But I do enjoy you, despite your little sad spells and your cowardice. Come now.

SATAN'EL starts whistling his tune again. HEROD laughs.

HEROD. Yes, listen to me! Who chooses grief over pleasure?

HERODIAS. There's my man.

Exit HEROD and HERODIAS. SATAN'EL exits whistling cheerily.

SCENE 2

YESHUA is sitting alone. He looks up to the sky, toward Heaven.

YESHUA. Abba, I feel it. I feel it coming. I thought—I thought I would be very brave. You've prepared me for this. But . . . but . . .

Enter THAU'MA. He sits next to YESHUA.

THAU'MA. Is everything all right?

YESHUA. You've been very quiet today, Thau'ma.

THAU'MA. I've had a lot on my mind.

YESHUA. My thinker, always analyzing, always dissecting the evidence . . .

THAU'MA. I wait. I try to be very patient before I commit myself to choices and beliefs. Early in my life I saw my twin brother make some very impetuous choices without thinking. It got him in a good deal of trouble. There is wisdom in waiting.

YESHUA. Something bothers you. Tell me.

THAU'MA. You told me and the other apostles to cast out devils and heal the sick. When that man who brought us his lunatic son—we couldn't heal him. You rebuked us. I admit, I was a little frustrated. You expect impossible things from us.

YESHUA. But it wasn't impossible, was it?

THAU'MA. No. *You* healed him. Why couldn't we cast out that infirmity?

YESHUA. Because of your unbelief. If you have faith the size of a mustard seed, you can say to that mountain over there, "Remove from here and go over there!" And it will move.

THAU'MA. That's impossible.

YESHUA. Nothing is impossible with prayer, fasting—and faith.

THAU'MA. You make it sound easy.

YESHUA. Oh, it's not easy. Nothing is harder.

Enter YESHUA's apostles.

YOCHANNAN. Yeshua, a messenger came from Miriam and Marta. Eleazer has gotten worse. They think he is going to die. They want you to come to Bethany.

YESHUA. No. We're going into Judea again.

YOCHANNAN. But the condition sounds very serious. With your power you can . . .

YESHUA. I have said what we must do, Yochanan.

SHIMON CEPHAS. Master, your enemies there almost stoned you the last time we were in Judaea. And you want to go again? They'll kill you.

THAU'MA. Then let's all go, that we may die with him.

YESHUA turns to THAU'MA, very moved by this declaration.

YESHUA. With faith like that, my friend, you could have healed that boy.

YESHUA turns and exits, with THAU'MA immediately following him. The other apostles look at each other and firming up their courage, also follow. Lights raise on MARTA and MIRIAM in mourning. There are other mourners with them in the house, coming to comfort MARTA and MIRIAM in their shiva (Jewish mourning practice).

MARTA. I—I keep expecting to hear Eleazar's sandals come up the stairs. They needed repairing, those shoes of his.

MIRIAM. Shhh, my dear. I—I wish . . .

MIRIAM breaks down and can't speak anymore, just simply weeping in grief. Then they suddenly hear a commotion outside. MARTA goes to their window.

MARTA. What now?

MIRIAM. What is it?

MARTA. You! What is going on down there?

VOICE. (*Off Stage.*) It's the Nazarene! Your friend Yeshua! He's come to Bethany again!

MARTA and MIRIAM both visibly react. MARTA goes to the door.

MIRIAM. Marta, what are you doing?

MARTA. He's here!

MIRIAM. We can't go out—we're sitting shiva . . .

MARTA. Aren't you the one who taught me to disregard tradition in favor of truth?

MIRIAM. Not a tradition like this. We're mourning for Eleazar. We can't leave this house!

MARTA. Let me go.

MIRIAM. He's your brother . . .

MARTA. Yes, and it was for our brother that we sent for Yeshua. Why didn't he come?

MIRIAM. I don't know.

MARTA. And so I'm going to find out.

MIRIAM. I'm going to stay here. There is only one who can call me out of the house during shiva . . .

MARTA. Fine, wait here. But I'm going.

> MARTA *descends the stairs from her home and encounters* YESHUA *and his disciples.*

YESHUA. Marta.

MARTA. We sent for you.

YESHUA. I know.

MARTA. You didn't come.

YESHUA. No. I didn't.

MARTA. Adonai, if you would have been here, my brother wouldn't have died.

YESHUA. Your faith is great, Marta. Are you angry with me?

MARTA. Angry?

> *We see* MARTA*'s strong exterior crack for the first time, weeping.*

YESHUA. You still believe.

MARTA. I *know*. I know that even now whatever you ask of God, he will give it to you.

YESHUA. Your brother will rise again.

MARTA. Yes, I know. He will rise again in the resurrection.

YESHUA. I Am resurrection. I Am life. He who believes in me, even though he's dead, yet he will live.

MARTA. Yeshua?

YESHUA. And she who lives and believes in me, she will never die. Do you believe me?

MARTA. Yes. I believe you are the Mashiach, the Son of God which we were told would come to our world.

YESHUA. Go get Miriam.

MARTA. She wouldn't come. She is in shiva.

YESHUA. Tell her that her Lord who loves her calls her from her mourning, and will dry all her tears. I will be with Eleazar.

 YESHUA and his disciples make their way to a tomb, while MARTA goes to MIRIAM.

MARTA. Miriam, he's here and he calls for you.

MIRIAM. Where is he?

MARTA. He's gone to the tomb.

 MIRIAM rises quickly and both she and MARTA rush to the tomb where they see YESHUA. The mourning visitors are confused by this break from protocol, and follow the two sisters to the tomb.

MIRIAM. Yeshua! My Beloved Yeshua.

 MIRIAM falls at his feet.

YESHUA. My Magdala.

MIRIAM. Oh, Yeshua, if you had been here, we would still have Eleazar. And now—why have you called us out of our mourning for him?

MIRIAM weeps, distraught. YESHUA is also overcome by emotion and also weeps. He kneels down to her and touches the tear in her garment, speaking tenderly to her.

YESHUA. Beloved, why is your garment torn?

MIRIAM. Yeshua, you know as well as I do.

YESHUA. Please. Say it.

MIRIAM. We rip it to show how Lazarus is gone from us and that we will never hold him again. We show how our hearts are torn asunder. It is a rip that will never be mended.

YESHUA. My heart is torn, too.

YESHUA tears the front of his garment. MIRIAM embraces him, clutching at him.

MIRIAM. Oh, Yeshua . . .

YESHUA. But I will mend both of our hearts. Tell them to take the stone away.

MARTA. But, Adonai, it's the fourth day. His body is past hope, the spirit is gone. It will stink now.

YESHUA. Didn't I say, Marta, that if you believed, you would see the glory of God today?

MARTA. Move the stone—move the stone!

In utter amazement, some of the crowd move the stone.

YESHUA. Abba, thank you for hearing me. I know that you hear me always, and I say so for the people around me, so they know that it is you who has sent me to save them. (*YESHUA then reaches out to the tomb and calls out in a loud voice:*) Eleazar, Beloved friend, come out!

There is stunned silence as a figure emerges from the tomb. He tears at the death shroud and wrappings that encumber him to reveal ELEAZAR. There is a huge, audible commotion as the crowd erupts in shock and stunned amazement. MARTA and MIRIAM *rush to* ELEAZAR *embracing his equally stunned form. Among all this commotion,* YESHUA *stands quietly by, weeping.*

SCENE 3

SHIMON THE LEPER *(who is no longer a leper) is preparing a table for guests. He is placing some of the plates, etc., most of which are earthenware. One, which he places at the head of the table, is made of a fine metal. Before he places it down, he accidentally glances his reflection and stops, gazing as if he doesn't recognize himself. He touches his smooth, perfect skin.*

SHIMON THE LEPER. A true marvel.

He hears his guest approaching and opens the door. Enters YESHUA, *a number of his apostles, as well as* MIRIAM, MARTA, *and* ELEAZER.

SHIMON THE LEPER (CONT'D). Yeshua—shalom! Please, I want you and your friends to come in! My home is now your home. Miriam, Marta and Eleazer have helped with the meal. Forgive me, it's been so long since I have had company, I didn't know how to make you a proper guest. And here are two other friends of mine. I wanted them to meet you.

Upon seeing them, SHIMON *brings in* PHARISEE #2 *and* CLEOPAS.

PHARISEE #2. I have actually met Yeshua before, Shimon. Many of my fellow Pharisees have their doubts about you, sir. But after hearing about Eleazar being raised from the dead! And now Shimon healed! Well, I have an open mind—I'm willing to see your proof.

YESHUA *all but ignores this man and goes to* CLEOPAS *instead.* PHARISEE #2 *is offended.*

YESHUA. You are Cleopas.

CLEOPAS. Did Shimon already tell you my name?

YESHUA. I know my sheep, as you know me. We must talk more later, all right?

CLEOPAS. All right.

The others go to perform a ritual hand washing, while YESHUA approaches SHIMON again.

YESHUA. Shimon, thank you for having us.

SHIMON THE LEPER. (*Suddenly serious.*) You're thanking me? Yeshua, touch my face again. (*YESHUA does so.*) What do you feel?

YESHUA. The skin that my Father meant for you.

SHIMON THE LEPER. But it is not the skin I had recently, is it? My skin was diseased—it was falling off. I was a leper, and now I am not.

YESHUA. Your faith was great.

SHIMON THE LEPER. (*Becoming emotional.*) No, no, it is you who are great. This meal—I wish I could give you so much more than this meal. I am—I am so grateful. I—I just want to find so many ways to thank you.

YESHUA. You thanked me when nine others I also healed forgot me.

SHIMON THE LEPER. And yet I will forever be in your debt.

YESHUA. I forgive the debts of those who forgive others. If you can do that, then I will be very happy with you.

SHIMON THE LEPER. So be it.

YESHUA and SHIMON go to the meal. YESHUA, caught up with his conversation, didn't wash his hands, either purposely or not purposely, it's not clear. YESHUA lifts up the bread to bless it with a traditional Jewish blessing (but substituting the traditional "Lord" or "Adonai" with "Abba.")

YESHUA. Blessed art thou Abba, King of the Universe, who brings forth bread from the earth.

PHARISEE #2. The bread is unclean—he hasn't washed his hands!

YESHUA. You are right, I haven't.

PHARISEE #2. Is this the respect you show our traditions?

YESHUA. Scribe, Pharisee, hypocrite. You Pharisees make clean the outside of the cup and the platter; but inside the cup is full of ravenous wickedness.

PHARISEE #2. Do you defy our law, sir? Do you defy the law of Adonai?

YESHUA. You don't know who you speak of. I know Adonai's true law, for it is written within me and shall be engraved upon me.

PHARISEE #2. You don't know who you speak to. I'm part of the Sanhedrin. I'm a man of influence who can help you or break you.

YESHUA. You're blind. You need to clean the inside of the cup first, then you can worry about cleaning the outside of the cup.

PHARISEE #2. You're the one with the filthy hands. You are the one who is unclean!

SHIMON THE LEPER. Please, I must insist that you don't speak to Yeshua that way.

PHARISEE #2. We must have pure hearts and clean hands, isn't that the scripture?

YESHUA. You call me unclean, but it's you who are a whitened sepulchre. You look beautiful on the outside, but inside you're full of dead men's bones.

PHARISEE #2. I'm not going to just sit here and be insulted like this. I keep the law, unlike you.

YESHUA. Yes, you tithe of mint, anise, and cummin. But you have omitted the weightier matters of the law. You have forgotten judgment, mercy, and faith. These are the important things which you should have done and left the other things undone. You're a blind guide. You strain your eyes at gnats, but swallow camels.

PHARISEE #2. I was going to give you a chance. I was going to hear you out. But you have proven unworthy of my attention.

CLEOPAS. (*Laughs.*)Yes, so unworthy. He forgot to wash his hands!

PHARISEE #2. Do not mock the law!

YESHUA. I haven't come here to destroy the law—but to fulfill it.

PHARISEE #2. I'm done with you!

ELEAZAR stops him.

ELEAZAR. You wanted proof, sir? Here I am.

PHARISEE #2. A deception. A clever deception.

ELEAZAR. I saw the next world, my friend. You don't want to enter it unprepared.

PHARISEE #2. Oh, I'm prepared.

Exit PHARISEE #2.

SHIMON THE LEPER. Yeshua, before my disease struck, he was my friend . . .

CLEOPAS. But then he abandoned you.

SHIMON THE LEPER. I forgave him for that.

YESHUA. As is right. But will you eat of my bread, Shimon? Do you also think it's unclean? You once called yourself a Pharisee, too.

SHIMON THE LEPER. (*Pause.*) Adonai, you made me clean, so I have no fears about this bread.

SHIMON takes of the bread and eats it. He hands it to the others, all of whom eat of it. After eating, MIRIAM excuses herself and exits momentarily.

ELEAZAR. You are a disciple now, my friend.

YA'AQOV THE JUST. It's not an easy road.

SHIMON THE LEPER. I haven't lived an easy life. I'm not afraid of that.

MIRIAM appears, with an alabaster box of costly spikenard, a fragrant anointing ointment.

MIRIAM. Beloved Yeshua, you are the Mashiach—the anointed one. It's time that we made that literal.

MIRIAM comes to YESHUA and first pours the ointment on his head, anointing him. She then starts rubbing the oil into his feet, bathing the feet also with water and her tears, while wiping them with her hair. She kisses his feet. YESHUA submits to this with a good deal of unrestrained emotion. Some of the disciples, including SHIMON THE LEPER and YEHUDAH SICARRI, seem deeply disturbed by the proceedings. YESHUA suddenly looks up sharply at SHIMON THE LEPER.

YESHUA. That thought was an unworthy of you, Shimon.

SHIMON THE LEPER. Pardon me?

YESHUA. You have said within yourself that if I were prophet that I would know that Miriam is rumored to be a sinner and that I wouldn't let her touch me.

SHIMON THE LEPER. I . . . I . . . Yeshua, it was just a thought.

CLEOPAS. Amazing.

YESHUA. I have something to say to you.

SHIMON THE LEPER. Good teacher, say on.

YESHUA. There was a certain creditor who had two people in debt to him. The one owed one denarii, and the other man owed him fifty denarii. And when they had nothing to pay, he frankly forgave them both. Tell me then which do you think loved him the most?

SHIMON THE LEPER. I suppose the person that had the larger debt forgiven.

YESHUA. You see this woman you have judged, she is beautiful in my eyes. I entered into your house, but it is she who prepared the food that I eat. Why didn't you? You didn't give me water for my feet, but she has not only washed my feet with her tears, but also wiped them with the very hairs of her head. You didn't give me a kiss, but she has not stopped kissing my feet. You didn't provide oil to anoint my head, but she has not only anointed my head, but has anointed my feet. So I'm telling you, her sins, which may have been many and which grieve her still, are forgiven, for she has loved much. But those who have little forgiven of them, love very little as well.

MIRIAM MAGDALENE. And I do love you.

YESHUA. I love you too, Miriam.

CLEOPAS. Can you forgive sins as well?

YESHUA. Why, Cleopas? Do you want a weight lifted?

Suddenly YEHUDAH SICARRI, *unable to contain himself anymore, stands.*

YEHUDAH SICARRI. But, Yeshua, there is something you haven't considered.

YESHUA. Yehudah.

YEHUDAH SICARRI. May I speak?

YESHUA. You are always welcome to speak to me.

YEHUDAH SICARRI. This—this—this woman and her family have great wealth.

YESHUA. Yes. Wealth that they have consecrated to my Father's cause.

YEHUDAH SICARRI. Yes, since you have entrusted me to be the steward over those funds, I know that. But, obviously, she has kept something significant back if she could afford such an expensive ointment! Do you approve of this waste? What purpose does it have?

YESHUA. Why do you accuse her? She has done nothing but kindness to me.

YEHUDAH SICARRI. Do you know how much that spikenard was worth? We could have sold it and given that money to the poor!

YESHUA. You will always have the poor with you, Yehudah. Whenever you want, you can find them and do them good. But you won't always have me. Wherever my good news will be preached, this thing that you've seen Miriam do will be told as memorial to her name.

YEHUDAH SICARRI. A memorial! And what, pray tell, great prophet, has fate proclaimed to be my memorial? How will I be remembered, who am now championing the poor and the destitute?

YESHUA. Do you really want to know the answer to that question, Yehudah?

YEHUDAH SICARRI. What do you mean?

YESHUA. I know your heart.

YEHUDAH SICARRI. You've never known my heart!

YEHUDAH leaves them as all lights blacken, except for those lights on him as he retreats from the group. The lights suggest the same dark, secretive place that Yehuda last met Barabba.

YEHUDAH SICARRI (CONT'D). Barabba! Barabba! Where are you? I was supposed to meet you here, curse you!

Enter TADDAI and SHIMON KANAI.

SHIMON KANAI. Yehudah . . .

YEHUDAH SICARRI. You followed me.

TADDAI. Shalom, Yehudah.

YEHUDAH SICARRI. We say kanai—kanai! We are zealots for the Lord! Have you forgotten your loyalties?

TADDAI. Have you forgotten yours? We serve God first, and it's God who's sent my brother!

YEHUDAH SICARRI. Do you know where Barabba is? We meet here every week.

SHIMON KANAI. Haven't you heard?

YEHUDAH SICARRI. Heard what?

SHIMON KANAI. Barabba was captured.

YEHUDAH SICARRI. What?

SHIMON KANAI. It was during one of his insurrections—the Romans have him.

YEHUDAH SICARRI. No—no! We must rescue him.

SHIMON KANAI. Yehudah, Barabba's way is not our way anymore.

YEHUDAH SICARRI. Barabba is our leader. He will be our salvation as a people.

SHIMON KANAI. The only way to salvation now is Yeshua. He is the way, the truth, and the life.

YEHUDAH SICARRI. Not without Barabba. We were going to bring Yeshua to Barabba. With the influence of Yeshua's words and Barabba's sword—we were going to unite them! That was the plan!

TADDAI. That is not the plan. It never was. That is not the kind of deliverance Yeshua is giving us. His truth has made us free.

YEHUDAH SICARRI. No, no, no! No more allegories, no more homilies, no more maxims! Don't you get it? Yeshua tries to feed us on stories and magic tricks when we have real world problems to deal with. In a world of politics and tyrants, he gives us parables!

TADDAI. Haven't you believed at all, Yehudah? Or were you just trying to manipulate Yeshua for yours and Barabba's plans?

YEHUDAH SICARRI. I thought—I thought he could really make a difference. I thought he could end all of this oppression and heartache and persecution our people have received. We need a person who can feed us, who can arm us, who can lead us!

SHIMON KANAI. Back there when we were eating—you weren't really worried about the poor, were you, Yehudah?

YEHUDAH SICARRI. Of course I was. I always see the suffering of our people before me.

SHIMON KANAI. We've been investigating the record books—you've been embezzling. You've been siphoning that sacred, consecrated money for Barabba, haven't you? Or have you been taking it for yourself?

YEHUDAH SICARRI. You're fools. Idealistic, fuzzy headed fools who don't know exactly how deep we are in this pit. Like Yosef of Egypt thrown into the hole by his brothers.

TADDAI. Who is throwing whom, Yehudah?

YEHUDAH SICARRI. Barabba understood, but now we have lost him. Yeshua could take his place, if he had the guts! But now we're lost! We—we've got to give this people a reason. We must give them a reason to rise up and free themselves.

TADDAI. When you get your priorities straight, come back to us, Yehudah. (*TADDAI goes to exit, but then realizes* SHIMON *isn't following.*) Shimon?

SHIMON KANAI. I understand, Yehudah. I really do. I once thought like you do. But—well, haven't you felt it?

YEHUDAH SICARRI. Right now I feel nothing but despair. Despair and rage.

SHIMON KANAI. And that is all you will ever feel until you discover the peace he has to offer us.

Exit SHIMON *and* YEHUDAH. *Lights fall on* YEHUDAH *and raise on* KAYAFA *and others of the* PHARISEES *who are talking with each other.* SATAN'EL *is there, influencing them subtly.*

PHARISEE #1. Then let's take him now! It's not exactly like he is hiding himself. It would be easy!

PHARISEE #2. No, certainly not now. If we took him during Passover, do you understand the uproar that would cause?

KAYAFA. That's right. We must be very careful about this, my friends. If we act too openly, we could upset a very delicate balance. Every day we deal with the volatile situation we are put against. And every day we find a way to calm the raging waters. We must always find a way.

Enter YEHUDAH SICARRI.

YEHUDAH SICARRI. Excuse me.

KAYAFA. Or the way finds us.

SATAN'EL. This is an interesting development.

KAYAFA. You're one of his followers, aren't you?

Everyone freezes in place except for SATAN'EL *and* YEHUDAH
SICARRI.

SATAN'EL. Are you? His follower?

YEHUDAH SICARRI. Who are you?

SATAN'EL. Someone who can help you.

YEHUDAH SICARRI. No one can help us. I've learned that only too
intimately.

SATAN'EL. Not even your Yeshua? (*YEHUDAH pauses, reluctant to
respond.*) Well?

YEHUDAH SICARRI. Especially not him.

SATAN'EL. Then you must help yourself.

YEHUDAH SICARRI. Yes.

SATAN'EL. You must help your people.

YEHUDAH SICARRI. Yes.

SATAN'EL. He can't save you. You must save yourselves.

YEHUDAH SICARRI. Yes.

There is a flash of darkness and SATAN'EL *is suddenly gone.*

KAYAFA. Well, are you? His follower?

YEHUDAH SICARRI. I want to make an exchange. Find a way to give
us back Barabba, and I will lead you to Yeshua.

KAYAFA. It hardly does much good to exchange one rebel for another,
does it?

YEHUDAH SICARRI. Then I'm sorry I wasted your time.

YEHUDAH goes to exit, but KAYAFA *stops him.*

SATAN'EL. Wait!

YEHUDAH SICARRI. Barabba for Yeshua.

KAYAFA. We can't do that. He's a Roman prisoner. But I know your heart, brave patriot.

YEHUDAH SICARRI. You never knew my heart.

KAYAFA. Don't I? You are a brave man, one who honors his people and his God with such unselfish sacrifices. You are willing to sacrifice yourself for your friends, for your countrymen, to ensure that we throw off the yoke of Caesar and instead become the masters and heroes we were always meant to be.

YEHUDAH SICARRI. Then what are you?

KAYAFA. I am the man who knows what must be done to preserve our nation. I will be the one to sacrifice everything, even his own reputation, to make sure we are safe. You and I are often seemingly against each other—one who wants to liberate, one who wants to stabilize. But our love for our nation is perfect, it is flawless, and on this instance I believe that love converges so that we must help each other. The Nazarene threatens both of our priorities.

YEHUDAH SICARRI. Perhaps he just needs some firm guidance, someone who can show him . . .

KAYAFA. He is more strong minded than that. Stubborn. If you feel like you can mold him, you're a fool. It's more likely that he will mold you. Is that what you want, to lose yourself?

YEHUDAH SICARRI. What good can come of me helping you, if you can't give me Barabba?

KAYAFA. You can prevent Rome from destroying Yeshua's followers—your friends, your people. That is what matters to you, isn't it? Your people? You can save them all. For do you think Rome will be any gentler with this Nazarene than he has been with your Barabba? Both you and I know that Yeshua hasn't the will to wield the power he has gained to his advantage.

YEHUDAH SICARRI. He's still a man, a human being. To just hand him over to you . . .

KAYAFA. It is better for one man to die than for a whole nation to perish.

YEHUDAH considers this.

YEHUDAH SICARRI. Thirty pieces of silver.

KAYAFA. How much?

YEHUDAH SICARRI. I will give you him for thirty pieces of silver.

KAYAFA. Agreed. Yehudah, you will be lauded as a hero for generations.
Blackout.

SCENE 4

YESHUA, his apostles, and his disciples (male and female) have gathered around a dining table. YESHUA is washing their feet, currently MIRIAM's, which some are clearly uncomfortable with. YEHUDAH enters and YESHUA stands. A moment passes between them, but YESHUA motions for YEHUDAH to sit. YEHUDAH, somewhat reluctantly, does so. YESHUA goes to SHIMON CEPHAS and goes to wash his feet. SHIMON CEPHAS resists.

SHIMON CEPHAS. Adonai, how can I let you wash my feet? You?

YESHUA. If you don't let me wash your feet, you have no part with me. (*SHIMON submits and YESHUA washes his feet.*) All of you have often split off from each other and argued which of you will be the greatest in the kingdom of Heaven. This is vanity. The kings of the Gentiles lord over their people, saying they are benefactors. You won't follow their example. The greatest among you shall be a servant.

SHIMON CEPHAS. Adonai, wash my hands and head also, that I may be entirely clean.

YESHUA. When I wash you, you're clean, every part of you. (*YESHUA stands and cleans his hands, preparing for the meal.*) Your heart is clean, Cephas. But not every one of you is clean. (*YESHUA goes back to his place at the table and raises the bread to the sky, addressing his Father:*) Blessed art thou Abba, King of the Universe, who brings forth bread from the earth. (*YESHUA lifts up a goblet of wine to his Father.*) Blessed art thou Abba our God, King of the Universe, Creator of the fruit of the vine. (*YESHUA starts handing out the bread to his disciples.*) This is my body which is given for you. Do this in remembrance of me. (*YESHUA hands the wine to his disciples.*) This cup is the new testament in my blood, which is shed for you. (*As they eat and drink, a Jewish hymn is sung.*) One of you will betray me tonight.

There is a shocked pause and then a general outcry. Yeshua calms them all, except SHIMON CEPHAS, *who is desperate.*

SHIMON CEPHAS. Not I, Yeshua.

YESHUA. Shimon, Shimon, Satan desires you even now, that he may sift you as wheat. But I have prayed for you, that you won't fail. And when you are truly converted, strengthen those around you.

SHIMON CEPHAS. Why do you show such a lack of faith in me, Adonai? I am ready to go with you, into prison, into death.

YESHUA. Cephas, the rooster won't crow this day before you deny that you know me three times.

SHIMON CEPHAS. Here are two swords, we will defend you!

YESHUA. Enough!

TADDAI. Adonai, am I to betray you?

A number of the apostles/disciples gather around him asking, "Is it I?"

MIRIAM. Adonai, are any of our family to betray you?

YESHUA. Miriam, I love you, Marta, and Eleazar. You have already served me, anointed me, washed my feet. You are true to me. No, it is one of the Twelve that dip in this dish with me. The Son of Man goes as prophesied and written, but woe unto the man who betrays him! It would have been better for that man that he was never born.

They all eat in uncomfortable silence for a moment. MIRIAM *leans upon* YESHUA *as they eat.* SHIMON CEPHAS *leans over to* ELEAZAR.

SHIMON CEPHAS. Eleazer, it's obvious. He favors your family. He'll tell you who will betray him.

ELEAZAR. Maybe not me—but Miriam.

SHIMON CEPHAS nods and ELEZAR leans over to MIRIAM, whispering to her. MIRIAM hesitates, but then nods and addresses YESHUA privately.

MIRIAM. Yeshua, who will betray you?

YESHUA. (*Whispering back:*) Who I give this bread to after I dip it is the one who betrays me.

YESHUA dips the bread and then leans over, handing it to YEHUDAH.

YEHUDAH SICARRI. (*Quietly, like a confession:*) It is I.

YESHUA. (*Quietly, only to YEHUDAH:*) You said it. (*YEHUDAH looks frightened for a moment, until YESHUA says:*) The thing you are going to do, now is the time to do it. Quickly.

YEHUDAH gives YESHUA a searching expression, but not able to read him, he rises and then exits. Blackout.

SCENE 5

YESHUA is praying in the Garden of Gethsemene. A ways off SHIMON CEPHAS, YOCHANAN, and YA'AQOV lay sleeping. ELEAZAR is with them, but still awake. YESHUA wanders over to ELEAZAR for a moment. ELEAZAR is wearing very little besides a linen cloth and some undergarments.

ELEAZAR. I tried to wake them, especially after your last visit, but . . .

YESHUA. It's all right now. Why are you wearing so little? It's a cold night.

ELEAZAR. Ever since—ever since you woke me up, I have an awful fear of being wrapped up when I'm sleeping.

YESHUA. I—I need to keep praying.

ELEAZAR. I understand.

YESHUA goes back to his prayers, as ELEAZAR wanders a ways off.

YESHUA. Abba—Abba, if you are willing—if it is your will—please, please—I am growing so afraid. I didn't expect to be so afraid. I didn't expect to feel so much sorrow.

SATAN'EL enters.

SATAN'EL. Dear Yeshua . . .

YESHUA notes SATAN'EL's entrance, but then tries to ignore him and focus on his prayer.

YESHUA. Abba . . .

SATAN'EL. I know you think that I don't care about you.

YESHUA. Abba, help me focus . . .

SATAN'EL. But you don't understand. This "Abba" of ours, this distant Being you so admire—he doesn't deserve your devotion.

YESHUA. Abba! If it is your will, let this cup pass from me!

SATAN'EL. He didn't deserve my devotion either. Don't you see how sadistic this whole life is? He demands from you sacrifice and death and pain and anguish and sorrow and grief—what kind of loving father would do that to his son?

YESHUA. If it is your will—please, let it be your will . . .

SATAN'EL. It's his will that we suffer. He says there is no other way. I don't believe him.

YESHUA. Abba, all things are possible to you . . .

SATAN'EL. That's what I say. All things are possible to him! If this world is wicked, whose fault is that? If we erred, who didn't stop us when he had the chance? He has such power and he just stands by. As if he didn't even care! We've been abandoned. Cast out. Yes, even you are abandoned.

YESHUA. Please, answer me . . .

SATAN'EL. You already know his answer. You know the set up, you know the requirement. But there *is* another way. Come. Join me and we'll find another way. You love these people of yours? Then let's find a way which is more compassionate, that has no bloodlust. Let's lead them by the hand, take their burdens . . .

YESHUA. I am taking their burdens! I will be pressed for their sins! Agh!

YESHUA's anguish increases.

SATAN'EL. No! Not like that, not by HIS terms! Listen, Yeshua, listen, it's not too late. We don't have to let him win. You know the cost his so-called freedom requires. Taking up a cross, that's his way—that's not mine! I have a different way. Life can be a delight, it can be a joy—we can give your friends, your loved ones pleasures they never imagined. Help them forget . . .

In great pain, YESHUA desperately looks into SATAN'EL's eyes for just a moment, but then firms up his courage.

YESHUA. I can't forget! I will never forget what is required!

SATAN'EL. Required by whom? Him!

YESHUA. Abba, if it's your will, let this cup pass from me . . .

SATAN'EL. You know his answer, you already know his answer!

YESHUA. Then not my will, but yours be done! I am required. My love is required. My sacrifice is required! I can save them—I will take their sins!

SATAN'EL *cries out in anguish, as does* YESHUA. SATAN'EL *retreats or disappears.* YESHUA *continues to suffer physically, mentally and spiritually, so that his sweat is mingled with blood. He collapses. A female* HEAVENLY FIGURE *appears and comes to* YESHUA, *embracing him and comforting him.* YESHUA's *cries into the* HEAVENLY FIGURE's *lap, almost as if he were a child.*

HEAVENLY FIGURE. Your Abba loves you. Feel his love.

YESHUA *looks at the* HEAVENLY FIGURE, *kisses her cheek, and rises.*

HEAVENLY FIGURE. Your Abba is pleased. We both are.

The HEAVENLY FIGURE *exits or disappears.* YESHUA *looks up to Heaven.*

YESHUA. Abba, thank you for not leaving me alone.

YESHUA *walks over to* SHIMON CEPHAS, YOCHANAN, YA'AQOV, *and* ELEAZAR. *He gently wakes them.* ELEAZAR *is asleep this time as well.*

YA'AQOV THE JUST. Yeshua—oh, Yeshua, you told us to stay awake! We're so sorry.

ELEAZAR. I fell asleep as well. I'm so sorry . . .

SHIMON CEPHAS. Please, forgive us . . .

YESHUA. It doesn't matter now, it's enough. You took your rest and you'll need it now. The hour is here. Rise up and look, the Son of Man is betrayed into the hands of sinners. Here's Yehudah.

The apostles rise to their feet as YEHUDAH *approaches them, accompanied by* TEMPLE GUARDS.

YEHUDAH SICARRI. (*Quietly to the guards.*) The others might try to claim to be him or fight for him. The man that I kiss, he's the one. Take him and get him out of here.

YESHUA. Who do you seek?

TEMPLE GUARD. Yeshua of Nazareth.

YESHUA. I am Yeshua of Nazareth. Do you come against me, as if I were a thief, with swords and staves? When I was with you every day in the temple, you didn't come against me. But now this is your hour, cloaked in the power of darkness. *(The* TEMPLE GUARDS *hesitate, waiting for* YEHUDAH's *cue.)* I have told you that I am him. If you seek me, take me, but let these men go their way.

YEHUDAH goes to YESHUA *and kisses him on the cheek.*

YEHUDAH SICARRI. Rabbi.

YESHUA. Ah. Now I know. You betrayed me with a kiss.

The TEMPLE GUARDS *go to seize* YESHUA *and his disciples, but* SHIMON CEPHAS *leaps into the fray and fights the guards, culminating in him cutting off one of the guard's ears.*

SHIMON CEPHAS. Run, Adonai! We will hold them!

YESHUA. Stop!

SHIMON CEPHAS. I will protect you!

YESHUA. Put it away, Shimon . . .

SHIMON CEPHAS. Yeshua, shouldn't we fight for you?

YESHUA. Those who live by the sword, die by the sword. This is the cup which our Abba has given me. Shouldn't I drink it?

YESHUA goes to the TEMPLE GUARD's *whose ear was cut off, takes the ear, and touches it to the area it belongs to. It heals instantly. The* TEMPLE GUARD *looks at him with amazement. With the exception of the one who was healed, the other* GUARDS *pounce and try to take them again, while* YOCHANNA *and* YA'AQOV *scatter and exit. They try and grab* ELEAZAR, *but they only get his outer covering, which he abandons and exits.* YESHUA *quietly and bravely presents himself to the guards. They hesitate, but he presents himself again, so they seize him and carry him off.* YEHUDAH *just stands there stunned, until Shimon rises and grabs him by the front of his shirt.*

SHIMON CEPHAS. Coward! Traitor!

YEHUDAH SICARRI. What have I done, Shimon?

Disgusted, SHIMON CEPHAS *throws* YEHUDAH *aside and runs after the* TEMPLE GUARDS. YEHUDAH *cries out in grief and tears his garment.*

SCENE 6

MIRIAM, MARTA, *and* MOTHER MIRIAM *are together when* ELEAZAR *rushes in.*

ELEAZAR. They have Yeshua.

MIRIAM. What? Who has Yeshua?

ELEAZAR. The Sanhedrin!

MOTHER MIRIAM *stumbles and* MIRIAM *supports her.*

MIRIAM. Are you all right, Mother?

ELEAZAR. We have to go to him!

MARTA. You're not going anywhere. The Sanhedrin want to kill you nearly as much as they want to kill Yeshua.

MIRIAM. Nobody's being killed!

MOTHER MIRIAM. Bring me to him.

MARTA. No, no, we've got to think this through.

MOTHER MIRIAM. Bring me to him!

ELEAZAR. I'll take you.

MIRIAM. Then I will go, too.

MARTA. All right, then I will as well.

ELEAZAR. No. Stay here in case the others come back.

MARTA. I'm not staying behind again . . .

ELEAZAR. We need you to. If we're killed . . .

MARTA. No one's getting killed . . .

ELEAZAR. We need you to do this . . .

MARTA. Why must I always be the one left behind? Why can't I be a disciple too?

MIRIAM. Marta, you *are* a disciple. You are the one we trust if something goes wrong. You are the most steady and reliable of all of us.

MARTA. (*Pause.*) All right. Go then.

MIRIAM. We'll come back when we know what's happened.

MARTA. All right, but . . .

MIRIAM. Yes?

MARTA. Please. Be careful.

> *MIRIAM embraces MARTA.*

MIRIAM. Shalom.

MARTA. Shalom.

ELEAZAR. They've brought him to the palace of Kayafa. I know someone in his household. I think I can get us in.

> *MIRIAM, ELEAZAR, and MOTHER MIRIAM all exit. Lights fall on MARTA, who begins to pray. Lights rise on YEHUDAH who approaches KAYAFA and other PHARISEES.*

KAYAFA. Yehudah the hero! Well done!

YEHUDAH SICARRI. No, no, I have made a mistake!

KAYAFA. A mistake?

YEHUDAH SICARRI. He's an innocent man. I have betrayed innocent blood!

PHARISEE #1. What is that to us? See to that yourself.

YEHUDAH SICARRI. I am trying to see to it! He is a man of peace. I can testify of his innocence!

PHARISEE #2. We can't use your testimony. It's against our law to use the testimony of an accomplice.

YEHUDAH SICARRI. Then on what basis have you arrested him, if not my testimony?

KAYAFA. Yehudah, go home. We'll take care of this matter. You have been a good citizen and this is our affair now.

YEHUDAH SICARRI. No, no, you must understand . . .

KAYAFA. Go home.

YEHUDAH SICARRI. Home? I have no home.

KAYAFA. Here is your money.

> *KAYAFA hands YEHUDAH the bag with 30 pieces of silver. Exit KAYAFA and the PHARISEES. YEHUDAH looks mutely at the money and then exits in despair. SHIMON CEPHAS enters and sees YESHUA carried in and brought in to be arraigned. A large group of people have gathered, including KAYAFA and the HIGH COUNCIL. SHIMON CEPHAS sees the ELEAZAR, MIRIAM, and MOTHER MIRIAM approach KAYAFA'S MAN.*

KAYAFA'S MAN. Eleazar, what are you doing here? Are you crazy, they have your leader arraigned up in there for trial!

ELEAZAR. We need to get in.

KAYAFA'S MAN. No. If Kayafa found out that I let you . . .

ELEAZAR. Please. You have heard what he did for me.

KAYAFA'S MAN. It's true then?

ELEAZAR. Every word.

KAYAFA'S MAN. Oh, I could get in so much trouble . . .

> *ACCUSING WOMAN comes out.*

ACCUSING WOMAN. I've seen her. She's the Nazarene's mother. You can't let them in here.

ELEAZAR. Hold your tongue. She is *my* mother.

KAYAFA'S MAN. It's all right, I know these people. Please, come in. It's happening down the hall.

SHIMON CEPHAS approaches them.

ELEAZAR. Cephas! (*Back to KAYAFA'S MAN.*) He's with us . . .

KAYAFA'S MAN. Yes, yes, come in, all of you. Down the hall.

ELEAZAR, MIRIAM, MOTHER MIRIAM, and SHIMON CEPHAS go to where YESHUA is being arraigned. KAYAFA and other members of the SANHEDRIN, including NICODE-MUS, and PHARISEES #1 and #2, all of whom have gathered, watched by a tumultuous crowd.

NICODEMUS. What is happening here, Kayafa? I have to hear second hand that you're having a trial? At night? You know that people have to be accused during the day. And you're doing this on the eve of the Sabbath, during Passover! Why is this happening in your palace, and not in the official courtroom?

KAYAFA. These are extenuating circumstances, Nicodemus. If we draw too much attention, we'll have a riot on our hands . . .

NICODEMUS. Isn't it you who's always harping on the importance of the law!

The ACCUSING WOMAN has been watching SHIMON CEPHAS and leans over to KAYAFA'S MAN. This overlaps with the scene between, KAYAFA, NICODEMUS, and the SANHEDRIN.

ACCUSING WOMAN. I think I know that man sitting over there . . .

KAYAFA'S MAN. Stay out of it. It's none of our business.

ACCUSING WOMAN. None of our business? Don't we serve the Great High Priest?

KAYAFA. Nicodemus! I know what I'm doing . . .

NICODEMUS. Which condemns you all the more.

The ACCUSING WOMAN approaches SHIMON CEPHAS.

ACCUSING WOMAN. Weren't you with Yeshua, the Galilean?

SHIMON CEPHAS. I don't know what you're talking about. Get away from me.

ACCUSING WOMAN. You are him. I know it.

SHIMON CEPHAS. I don't know him, I was just curious . . .

PHARISEE #2. Nicodemus, let's get on with this . . .

NICODEMUS. Get on with this? What is this? It's certainly not a legal trial!

PHARISEE #2. He's already been brought before Annas. Annas approves of this . . .

NICODEMUS. Arraigned before trial? To Annas? Annas is no longer part of this council—is it Annas's illegal trials you're basing this farce on?

PHARISEE #1. Be careful, my friend, Annas is still very influential . . .

NICODEMUS. Annas is no longer high priest!

KAYAFA. No, he isn't. I am.

The ACCUSING WOMAN *comes back to* SHIMON CEPHAS *to badger him.*

ACCUSING WOMAN. I'm not stupid, you know him! More than that, you're his disciple!

SHIMON CEPHAS. You're crazy . . .

ACCUSING WOMAN. This man was with the Gallilean!

KAYAFA. What is going on over there?

SHIMON CEPHAS. Shut up! I swear to you, I don't know him.

SHIMON escapes to the outer court where some men have set up a fire. He joins them.

NICODEMUS. Where is Gamaliel? Where is Yosef of Arimethea? Do we even have half of the Sanhedrin?

KAYAFA. We have a quorum.

NICODEMUS. Yes, one filled with this man's most intent enemies. The law requires an unbiased judgment, it requires someone to advocate this man's cause . . .

KAYAFA. Which you seem to be doing eloquently. Are you saying that I'm not fair?

NICODEMUS. Show me that you're fair! You are going to condemn an innocent man.

KAYAFA. If he is innocent, then let his blood be upon us and this nation—but he is not innocent.

NICODEMUS. No! His blood will not be on our nation, it will be on your guilty hands! You may think that you speak for all our people, Kayafa, but that's not true!

KAYAFA. I am the high priest! I am this people's voice!

NICODEMUS. You are not my voice! What you say is not what our people say! You can't cast your sins upon our pure nation! I am of Yehudah as well, and I say that your curses are your own to inherit, not ours!

KAYAFA. Enough! Get this man out of here, he insults me!

NICODEMUS. You don't decide our fate! We each have our own voice!

KAYAFA. Get him out!

NICODEMUS. Your sins will be answered on your own head!

The TEMPLE GUARDS *take* NICODEMUS *out.*

PHARISEE #2. Let's get on with this. Bring in the witnesses.

Audience attention is diverted to SHIMON CEPHAS *and the group around the fire.* ACCUSING MAN *rises and re-sits himself next to* SHIMON CEPHAS.

ACCUSING MAN. I recognize you.

SHIMON CEPHAS. I don't see how. I'm a stranger here, just curious about politics.

ACCUSING MAN. Yes, your accent is different. It betrays you. You sound—Galilean.

WITNESS #1, #2, and #3, have arrived.

WITNESS #1. I heard him say that he would destroy the temple.

WITNESS #2. No, he said that the temple would be destroyed, not that he would destroy it . . .

WITNESS #3. No, he said he was "able to" destroy it—that's not a threat, only a declaration of capacity. And he also said that he would raise it again after three days!

PHARISEE #2. Kayafa, are these really the only accusers we have? They contradict each other. We need at least two solid witnesses that agree with each other—we need to make a solid case of this!

KAYAFA. The Galilean will make our case.

PHARISEE #2. He's not supposed to be a witness against himself . . .

KAYAFA. He'll be our greatest witness, won't you, Yeshua? (*YESHUA is silent.*) No answer? Don't you know what these men accuse you of? You are going against the most beloved and established institutions of our people by threatening the temple. You are going against not only us and our most revered traditions, but Rome, by destroying the peace of its vassals. Isn't that right? (*YESHUA doesn't answer.*) No, it's more than that. You know we wait for our Mashiach. You take advantage of that. But you have made it worse than that—instead of trying to be the deliverer that we need, you have heaped blasphemy upon the prophecy by calling yourself the Mashiach—by calling yourself the Son of God. What have you been teaching our people? (*Then to the witnesses.*) What heresies has he taught?

YESHUA. I spoke openly to the world. I often taught in the synagogue, and in the temple, where our people are. Why do you ask these people what I teach? They know what I said. You know what I said. I haven't taught in secret.

PHARISEE #1 slaps YESHUA.

PHARISEE #1. Is this how you answer the high priest?

YESHUA. If I speak false things, tell me what they are. But if I speak true things, why do you hit me?

PHARISEE #2. Let's keep our composure here, all right?

KAYAFA. (*Confronting* YESHUA *directly.*) I adjure you by the living God, that you tell us whether you are the Mashiach, the Son of God.

YESHUA. You have said it. And I tell you now, you shall yet see the Son of Man sitting on the right hand of power, and coming in the clouds of heaven.

> KAYAFA *screams loudly and rends his outer garment.*

PHARISEE #2. Kayafa, what are you doing? You'll discredit the entire thing!

KAYAFA. No, it's not against the law to tear my garment when the so-called defendant is guilty of blasphemy! And, once again, this Galilean has made a man into God!

PHARISEE #2. Kayafa . . .

KAYAFA. He's spoken blasphemy! Do we need more need witnesses after this? You all have heard his blasphemy for yourselves! We are all witnesses! (*The Sanhedrin and the crowd go into an uproar.*) What do you all think?

PHARISEE #1. He is guilty of death!

> *The Sanhedrin voice agreement.* MIRIAM, MOTHER MIRIAM, *and* ELEAZAR, *who have stood by shocked and mournful this whole time, follow as* YESHUA *is pushed out by the Sanhedrin into the outer court where* SHIMON CEPHAS *still sits with the other men by the fire.*

ACCUSING MAN. (*To* SHIMON CEPHAS:) You don't know who you've been lying to. I was with those who arrested the Nazarene. You cut off my cousin's ear.

SHIMON CEPHAS. He healed his ear!

ACCUSING MAN. So you admit it! You were with the Magician!

SHIMON CEPHAS. No! I swear by God and all that is holy, I don't know the man!

SHIMON CEPHAS turns to see that YESHUA has come out being pushed along by the Sanhedrin, YESHUA having distinctly heard the denial. Their eyes connect and SHIMON is immediately wracked with guilt. A rooster crows.

ACCUSING MAN. You are his man!

SHIMON CEPHAS. Adonai . . .

YESHUA is pushed along and exits with the crowd. SHIMON CEPHAS yells out in grief and exits.

YEHUDAH SICARRI enters with a rope. YEHUDAH ties it onto a tree, makes a noose, and puts it around his neck. As he is about to jump and hang himself, the lights go black, but we hear the sound of the rope tightening, and a gentle swinging of a body. We also hear the spilling of money, thirty pieces of silver.

SCENE 7

Lights rise on CLAUDIA, who awakes from bed, screaming. PILATE enters and rushes to her.

PILATE. Claudia! What's wrong?

CLAUDIA rises, washing her face.

CLAUDIA. Yeshua.

PILATE. The Nazarene? How did you know . . . ?

CLAUDIA. Know? Know what?

PILATE. I've been with the Sanhedrin for hours—they even refused to enter the judgment hall, so that they wouldn't become "defiled" by our home—that thing about leaven. It was all an awful headache. They wanted me to judge the man—this Yeshua.

CLAUDIA. Pontius, have nothing to do with that man!

PILATE. That what was my thinking, too. Normally, they judge their own people, but with cases like his . . .

CLAUDIA. Cases like his . . .

PILATE. I thought that being here for their feasts would engender me to them . . . We should have taken that holiday. In fact, we should never have left Caesarea.

CLAUDIA. What do you mean cases like his?

PILATE. They want me to execute him. Rome has reserved that privilege for the State. They can't kill him without my approval.

CLAUDIA. Oh, Pontius . . .

PILATE. What's wrong?

CLAUDIA. I had a dream about him. It was full of blood and torture and traitors and—and that poor man. It was an omen.

PILATE. Let's not be superstitious.

CLAUDIA. It was an omen!

PILATE. Shhh, it's all right.

CLAUDIA. What was he like?

PILATE. He was rather magnificent. On first glance you wouldn't think he was anything special, but—but I've never had one of them look me in the eye like that, as if he was—unafraid of me. (*YESHUA appears, and PILATE relives the memory.*) Their accusation against you is treason and insurrection. They say you're setting yourself up as the King of the Jews. (*YESHUA doesn't answer, but looks at PILATE steadily.*) It's a pretty serious charge, if it's true. There can be no king but Caesar.

YESHUA. I render to Caesar what is Caesar's and to God what is God's.

PILATE. Astute answer. But it doesn't get to the heart of the matter. Are you the King of the Jews?

YESHUA. Do you say this of yourself or do did others give this definition of me?

PILATE. What?

YESHUA. The Roman definition of a king and the Jewish definition of the King are very different . . .

PILATE. Am I a Jew? Your own leaders have delivered you to me— your own people! What have you done?

YESHUA. My kingdom is not of this world. If my kingdom were of this world, then my servants would have fought before they let me be delivered to the Sanhedrin. But their charges are wrong—my kingdom is not from here.

PILATE. Are you a king?

YESHUA. You say that I am a king. This was the reason I was born, and for this cause came I into the world, that I should bear witness of the Truth.

PILATE. Truth! What is truth?

YESHUA. Every one that is of the Truth hears my voice.

    YESHUA *fades out, and it's just* PILATE *and* CLAUDIA *again.*

CLAUDIA. And did you?

PILATE. Did I what?

CLAUDIA. Hear the voice?

PILATE. Claudia, sometimes your gullibility astounds me.

CLAUDIA. I hear it. Very clearly.

PILATE. You're strained. Go back to bed. We don't have to worry about it. Yeshua is from Galilee, so he's Antipas's jurisdiction. I told them to let Herod handle it.

Lights go down on PILATE *and rise up on* YESHUA *again, this time surrounded by* HEROD, HERODIAS, *a* ROMAN CAPTAIN, *etc.*

HEROD. Yeshua! *The* Yeshua! You have a common name, my friend, but from what I hear you are not a common man! (YESHUA *looks directly at* HEROD, *but says nothing.*) Now don't be shy, I'm not here to hurt you. In fact, I'm thrilled!

HERODIAS. Don't make a fool of yourself again.

HEROD. Enough of your sharp tongue, woman, I'm sick of it! This man is a special guest, give him our best robes! Suited for a king. (HEROD'S SERVANTS *arraign* YESHUA *in royal garments.*) I can get you out of this mess, Yeshua. But I want you to do me a favor first. The stories I hear—oh, the stories I hear! Your miracles: water to wine, walking on water, feeding five thousand with just a few loaves and fishes! And your friend: Eleazar! Oh my. Risen from the dead. I—I want to believe in these miracles. Give me a reason to believe, Yeshua! Show me some little sign, some little miracle, and I'll make this nightmare of yours go away. Will you do that for me? (YESHUA *doesn't answer, but continues to look at him in contempt.*) I'm here to help you. (YESHUA *still doesn't answer.*) Don't you know who I am? What power I have over your life in this moment? Ask the Baptist what sort of power I had over his life!

YESHUA simply looks away, refusing to acknowledge him with even that much respect anymore. HERODIAS *laughs.*

HERODIAS. A fool! He's brought to be judged by you, and he makes you the fool!

HEROD. I could have helped you. But I already have killed one prophet—I dare not kill you, too. (*To a* ROMAN CAPTAIN.) Tell the Sanhedrin I'm not going to be a puppet in their game. Send him back to Pilate.

The lights blackout on Herod's court. The sound of whips are heard and the crying out of YESHUA's *voice in extreme pain.*

Gradually, lights appear on CLAUDIA, *once again in her bed. She shifts, crying out some. She starts up.*

CLAUDIA. Yeshua!

She rises and goes to her bowl again, washing off the sweat. She sits to gather her breath. Still in terror, she exits the room. PILATE *enters in a separate section, where a* ROMAN CAPTAIN *enters.*

CAPTAIN. My lord, we've done as you asked. We've whipped and punished him.

PILATE. Severely?

CAPTAIN. The cat of nine tails is as severe instrument as we have, before you ascend a cross.

PILATE. It must be convincing. If we're going to save this man's life, then they must be convinced that he's suffered enough for his supposed sins.

Enter CLAUDIA *to their section.*

CLAUDIA. Pontius . . .

PILATE. (*To the* CAPTAIN.) Bring Yeshua to me.

CLAUDIA. Yeshua! I thought you sent him to Herod.

PILATE. Claudia, I can't have you here right now.

CLAUDIA. You can't do this!

PILATE. Herod sent him back. There is insurrection brewing. You've said it before, they hate me. I pushed them too hard, and I've paid for that with their resentment—now they have cooked up a perfect revenge. Best case scenario, they denounce me to Caesar for letting an insurrectionist go. Worst case scenario, complete rebellion and bloodshed.

CLAUDIA. You have to be brave and do the right thing.

PILATE. I'm trying to find a third path. Placate them.

CLAUDIA. With what?

The ROMAN CAPTAIN brings in YESHUA, who is violently and grotesquely bloodied from being beaten and then whipped with a cat of nine tails, a whip that has glass, metal, etc. attached to it. He also wears a crown of thornes. CLAUDIA gasps and tears up at the sight.

PILATE. Why is he wearing those thornes?

CAPTAIN. I believe it was the soldiers' idea of a joke, sir.

PILATE. Have them reprimanded.

CAPTAIN. Yes, sir.

Exit CAPTAIN.

CLAUDIA. Pontius, what have you done?

PILATE, in a confused and torn state, stands and looks at YESHUA.

PILATE. I'm sorry.

Exit PILATE. CLAUDIA approaches YESHUA.

CLAUDIA. Your face—it's exactly as I saw it in my dream.

YESHUA. You are a child of truth. You hear my voice.

Suddenly CLAUDIA is taken away, while the CAPTAIN re-enters to present YESHUA to the audience. PILATE enters, and directs himself towards the audience. Amongst the audience, in the aisles, etc. a number of the cast stand, creating the "crowd." Certain among the crowd are chanting, yelling, etc. PILATE is shouting above them, desperate. SATAN'EL is among the crowd, influencing them with subtle touches, and also whispering things to the audience. Certain of YESHUA's disciples and other compassionate Jews are also there, trying to be heard, but are having difficulty getting their voices above the fray.

PILATE. Isn't he your king? Do you want me to crucify your king?! (*The crowd continues to yell, etc.*) Look at him! I have chastised him! Is this not enough punishment? (*The crowd continues. Pilate motions*

374

to the CAPTAIN, *who brings out a chained* BARABBA.) Your people and I have created a custom the past several years. A custom of mercy. I will release one prisoner to you in recognition of your Passover. Here is Barabba! Barabba is a known insurrectionist, an enemy of Rome and of this people! The blood he has spilled has been great! And here is Yeshua, in whom I find no fault. They are both sons of your God, but which one do you choose to accept among you?

PHARISEE #1. Give us Barabba!

Some of the crowd starts chanting "Barabba!" while those who try to shout "Yeshua!" are either shouted down or silenced by others. Hearing the cries for Barabba, PILATE *is clearly discouraged, but releases Barabba to the crowd.* BARABBA *shouts in rejoicing, but not before he makes eye contact with* YESHUA. BARABBA *looks away disturbed and exits into the crowd.*

PILATE. And what should I do with Yeshua of Galilee?

KAYAFA. Crucify him!

The crowd picks up on this, and start chanting "Crucify him!" PILATE *is drained of energy and motions to the* CAPTAIN, *who brings him a bowl of water.* PILATE *washes his hands in the water and then motions to the* CAPTAIN *before he walks away. The* CAPTAIN *grabs* YESHUA, *who goes without a struggle. The masts of the boat have turned into crosses and one of the crosses comes down.* YESHUA *is brought down onto the cross, where it is presented that nails are driven into his hands, wrists and feet.* YESHUA *cries out in extreme pain.*

YESHUA. Abba, forgive them! They don't know what they're doing!

The cross is brought back up with YESHUA *hanging upon it. The crowd has dispersed, with only a small group under the cross, including* MIRIAM, MOTHER MIRIAM, ELEAZAR, KAYAFA, PHARISEES #1 *and* #2, *the* ROMAN CAPATAIN, *some* GUARDS, *and perhaps a few other spectators. A quiet, lonely wind blows.* SATAN'EL *arrives below the cross.*

SATAN'EL. You couldn't leave it alone.

The ROMAN CAPTAIN *tries to feed* YESHUA *sour vinegar.* YESHUA *refuses to drink it.*

CAPTAIN. Just drink. It will help deaden the pain.

YESHUA *still refuses.*

SATAN'EL. You *want* to feel every tortured nerve, every bleeding gash? Then feel it, Yeshua, son of man, feel it and despair! I would have given you wealth, I would have given you comfort, I would have given you life! And what is this, what is this that your precious "Abba" has given you? (*The* CAPTAIN *start to throw lots to divide up* YESHUA's *garments among the* GUARDS.) And there is that fine garment that Herod gave to you. The guards seem to think it's pretty special. That was a trinket compared to what you could have had! Following your Abba—where does it lead you? Tortured upon a cross! This is what you agreed to!

MOTHER MIRIAM, MIRIAM, *and* ELEAZAR *draw closer.*

MOTHER MIRIAM. My little boy—oh, what are they doing to my little boy?

YESHUA. Mother, I am the Lamb. But for your sacrifice God has raised up for you another son. (*Indicating* ELEAZAR.) Dear Woman, behold your son ... (*Indicating* MOTHER MIRIAM.) Beloved friend, behold your mother!

ELEAZAR. Yes, Adonai.

YESHUA. (*To* MIRIAM.) Magdala. Beloved Magdala ...

Suddenly YESHUA *feels intense pain, first physical, then spiritual.*

SATAN'EL. You feel it, don't you? He's left you on your own to endure this. I told you He would abandon you. I know that feeling, Yeshua! I remember that feeling!

YESHUA. Eloi, Eloi, lama sabachthani? My God, my God, why have you forsaken me!

YESHUA yells in grief and pain, which is more than MOTHER MIRIAM, MIRIAM, and ELEAZAR can bear, as they weep and cry out for him. SATAN'EL touches KAYAFA's shoulder, with a pitying look at YESHUA.

KAYAFA. He saved others—but he can't save himself! If he is the King of Yisra'el, if comes down from the cross, then we'll believe him. He trusted in Elohim—let Elohim deliver him now! Didn't he tell us that he was the Son of God?

YESHUA. I thirst.

The CAPTAIN give him fresh vinegar to drink from a sponge affixed on a pole.

SATAN'EL. Even the fresh vinegar is sour, isn't it, Yeshua? If a man asks for bread, does a loving father give him a stone? If a man asks for water, does a loving father give him vinegar?

MIRIAM suddenly sees SATAN'EL. She approaches him, defiant, and then turns back to YESHUA.

MIRIAM. Yeshua, we're here for you, as you were there for us!

YESHUA looks down at MIRIAM, moved.

SATAN'EL. No, no, you think they mean anything? You think once you're dead, they will have changed at all? They'll be right back where they started!

MIRIAM. I accept your sacrifice, Yeshua!

SATAN'EL. Feel the pain, Yeshua, feel the anguish—if you are indeed their Mashiach, surely you can save yourself and them without this shadow show!

MIRIAM. Redeemer, you have saved my soul!

YESHUA. It is finished! Abba, Abba, into your hands I commend my spirit!

YESHUA cries out in death, SATAN'EL cries out in rage, and MIRIAM cries out in grief. There is the sound of an earthquake as the lights blackout in an eclipse, all which culminates in the sound of a tearing sheet.

SCENE 8

Lights raise on the tomb, with two ROMAN GUARDS *by it.*

GUARD #1. A lot of fuss.

GUARD #2. Did you hear the noise the Sanhedrin made about the inscription Pilate put above his head?

GUARD #1. "King of the Jews." Not much of a people to be king of, if you ask me.

GUARD #2. I don't know. I've seen them be very brave. You weren't there when they defied Pilate about the images he brought into Jerusalem—they exposed their necks and were willing to have their heads cut off before they let him do that. I don't know if I've ever believed in anything enough to be willing to die for it. Have you?

GUARD #1. By Jove, no! What else do we have, if not our life?

GUARD #2. (*Indicating* YESHUA.) Apparently this fellow thought there was something more.

GUARD #1. Not that it helped him in the end. This "king" is as dead as any peasant.

Suddenly there are the sounds of an earthquake, and two MALACHIM *appear, one male and one female. The two* ROMAN GUARDS *fall to the ground in fear. The* MALACHIM *looms over them and one waves its hand, and the guards fall to the ground unconscious. The* MALACHIM *motion towards the stone covering the tomb, and it rolls away. Light pours from the tomb as* YESHUA *steps out. The* MALACHIM *sit atop of the tombstone, almost casually, while* YESHUA *touches both of the soldiers foreheads before he exits. The* SOLDIERS *awake,*

astounded, and run away. The light changes, suggesting morn-
ing. MIRIAM, MARTA, MOTHER MIRIAM, *and other women*
enter, carrying spices and ointments for the body of YESHUA.
They're talking soberly and quietly until they reach the tomb
and see the MALACHIM, *at which they are shocked and afraid.*
The MALACHIM *reassure them:*

MALACHIM #1. Don't be afraid. We know you're here to anoint the body. You seek for him who was crucified, but he isn't here. Come, see where they laid him.

The women step into the tomb to see.

MOTHER MIRIAM. His body—my boy's body is gone.

MALACHIM #2. Go quickly. Tell the other disciples that he's risen from the dead. He goes before you to Galilee. You shall see him. It will be as we told you.

The MALACHIM *climb the stairs and are gone. The women run*
and exit, all except MIRIAM *who stumbles in grief.*

MIRIAM. How can I dare believe this? My heart wants to, but—oh, I miss him!

MIRIAM begins to weep. YESHUA *enters and approaches her,*
although his face is shadowed at first.

YESHUA. Dear Woman, why do you cry?

MIRIAM. Sir, are you the gardener here? If you've taken his body, tell me where you put him and I'll take his body myself.

YESHUA steps into the light.

YESHUA. Miriam.

MIRIAM. Rabbi!

MIRIAM stands and rushes to YESHUA, *ready to embrace him,*
but YESHUA *holds his hand out to fend her off.*

YESHUA. You can't hold me yet, Miriam. I haven't yet ascended to my Abba, and your Abba. My God, and your God.

MIRIAM. Yeshua, I—I love . . .

YESHUA. You are my Beloved.

> YESHUA *ascends up the stairs and, in joy,* MIRIAM *exits.* MOTHER MIRIAM, MARTA, *and the other women re-enter, rushing.*

MOTHER MIRIAM. (*Catching her breath.*) Wait, wait! I'm not a young woman anymore!

MARTA. Are we dreaming? Can this possibly be true?

> YESHUA *appears.*

YESHUA. You know it's true, Marta, my disciple, my friend. The Spirit in your heart tells you so.

MARTA. Yeshua!

YESHUA. (*Laughs.*) Hello! All of you, hello. (*They all crowd in around* YESHUA, *crying, laughing, etc., although, as with* MIRIAM, *he wards off their touch.*) You don't have to be afraid anymore. Go, tell my brethren in Galilee that it's there that they shall see me also.

MARTA. Why have you come to us first?

YESHUA. Your faith brought me to you. Now go.

> *Exit* YESHUA *and the women. The male disciples are seen gathering.*

ANDREAS. Why have the women called us all to meet? Not exactly protocol.

ELEAZAR. It sounded urgent.

SHIMON CEPHAS. Aren't we all tired now? Do we have to keep talking about it? It's over.

PHILLIPOS. Shimon . . .

SHIMON CEPHAS. What else is there to do? He's gone!

TADDAI. Where is Thau'ma?

SHIMON KANAI. I couldn't find him.

Enter MIRIAM, MARTA, MOTHER MIRIAM, *etc.*

SHIMON CEPHAS. What is this about?

MOTHER MIRIAM. It's a miracle, Shimon. I have never been so happy in my whole life!

SHIMON CEPHAS. After what we've all been through you can claim to be happy?

MARTA. You don't understand, Shimon. Watch your tone.

SHIMON CEPHAS. Don't you tell me to watch my tone! Will any of us truly get over this grief? How can any of us ever be the same?

MIRIAM MAGDALENE. Now that is where you're right. We won't ever be the same.

SHIMON CEPHAS. Leave me alone, Miriam.

MIRIAM MAGDALENE. Now listen, Shimon. All of you, listen. You were called and set apart as teachers. But now you must be taught.

SHIMON CEPHAS. By you? By what authority do you have to claim to teach us?

MIRIAM MAGDALENE. Yeshua's. He sent us to give you the good news.

SHIMON CEPHAS. Yeshua! Ha!

There is a tense silence.

ELEAZAR. Miriam, what are you talking about?

MIRIAM MAGDALENE. It's so wonderful, Eleazar. I saw him.

ELEAZAR. What do you mean you saw him? A vision?

MIRIAM MAGDALENE. No, I saw him. I *saw* him! He's risen from the dead. He wants us to go to Galilee to meet him.

SHIMON CEPHAS. She's insane again. Mad Miriam!

MARTA. Don't you ever call her that again, Shimon. We all saw him.

ELEAZAR. All of you?

MOTHER MIRIAM. All of us.

SHIMON CEPHAS. What's going on here? What are you up to?

MIRIAM. You don't believe us, Shimon?

SHIMON CEPHAS. How can I?

ELEAZAR. I can. Out of anyone, I can.

SHIMON CEPHAS. But—oh, I want to believe.

MIRIAM. Then go see for yourself. His tomb is empty.

> At this both SHIMON CEPHAS and the ELEAZAR bolt out of
> the room, while the other disciples crowd around the women,
> anxious to ask questions. Lights dim on them and rise on SHI-
> MON CEPHAS and ELEAZAR as they reach the empty tomb.

SHIMON CEPHAS. Can it really be true, Eleazar? Can it really be true!

ELEAZAR. He said three days—he would raise up this temple in three days. *His* temple!

> ELEAZAR exits joyously as SHIMON CEPHAS sits there in
> shock.

SHIMON CEPHAS. It's true.

> YESHUA appears to SHIMON CEPHAS.

YESHUA. Shimon.

SHIMON CEPHAS. Adonai.

YESHUA. Why did you not believe the women who I sent to you to testify of me?

SHIMON CEPHAS. I . . . I . . .

YESHUA. Shimon, son of Yona, do you love me?

SHIMON CEPHAS. Yes, Adonai, you know that I love you.

YESHUA. Feed my lambs. Shimon, son of Yona, do you love me?

SHIMON CEPHAS. Yes, Adonai, you know that I love you.

YESHUA. Feed my sheep. Shimon, son of Yona, do you love me?

SHIMON CEPHAS. Adonai, you know all things! You know that I love you.

YESHUA. Feed my sheep.

SHIMON CEPHAS. Yeshua! Why do you ask me so many times?

YESHUA. Three times for three denials.

This strikes SHIMON CEPHAS *hard, but then he nods and looks up into* YESHUA's *gaze.*

SHIMON CEPHAS. I will feed your sheep.

Lights blackout on them and rise on CLEOPAS *and* SHIMON THE LEPER, *walking to Emmaus.* YESHUA, *his face hidden by a hood, is following close behind them.*

CLEOPAS. What are we to believe?

SHIMON THE LEPER. Have you ever known any of those women to lie to us?

CLEOPAS. No, of course not. But perhaps—perhaps they saw all of the despair, all of the hopelessness we were feeling. Perhaps they saw all that and decided it was time that we had some—hope.

SHIMON THE LEPER. Lying to us to make us feel better?

CLEOPAS. It makes sense to me.

SHIMON THE LEPER. No. I would prefer to wail in the truth, than to be pacified by lies. I can't think that of them. Yeshua told me himself the respect and love he held for Miriam Magdala. I trust her. And you can you imagine Yeshua's mother uttering such a falsehood about her own son?

CLEOPAS. Then what?

SHIMON THE LEPER. Maybe the impossible has happened. Haven't we seen the impossible again and again with him?

CLEOPAS. But risen from the dead!

SHIMON THE LEPER. Eleazar was dead, too.

CLEOPAS. Yes. (*Pause.*) Wouldn't it be marvelous?

YESHUA catches up with them.

YESHUA. I apologize, but I could hear parts of your conversation and was curious. What kind of things are you discussing? They seem remarkable. And why are you so sad?

CLEOPAS. Are you a stranger in Jerusalem? Don't you know the things that have been happening here?

YESHUA. Tell me.

CLEOPAS. My name is Cleopas. This is Shimon. We were fortunate to have a great prophet with us—Yeshua of Nazareth. He performed miracles, taught us great truths, taught us to love each other. But our rulers condemned him and crucified him. We thought it was going to be he who would redeem Yisra'el.

YESHUA. But you said something about him being—raised from the dead?

SHIMON THE LEPER. There are women among our group who claim to have seen him since his death.

YESHUA. And do you believe these women?

CLEOPAS. Hope can be difficult to muster after so many disappointments.

YESHUA. Why are you so slow of heart to believe what the prophets have spoken?

CLEOPAS. The prophets?

YESHUA. Didn't Yeshayahu say, "Therefore I will give him a portion among the great, and he will divide the spoils with the strong, because he poured out his life unto death, and was numbered with the transgressors. For he bore the sin of many, and made intercession for the transgressors." Doesn't this sound like your Yeshua? "He is despised and rejected of men; a man of sorrows, and acquainted with grief: and we hid as it were our faces from him; he was despised, and we esteemed him not." Wasn't his suffering meant to be part of your redemption?

SHIMON CEPHAS. You are acquainted with the scriptures, sir.

YESHUA. "Who is this coming from Edom, from Bozrah, with his garments stained crimson? Who is this, robed in splendor, striding forward in the greatness of his strength? 'It is I, speaking in righteousness, mighty to save.' Why are your garments red, like those of one treading the winepress? 'I have trodden the winepress alone; from the nations no one was with me.'"

CLEOPAS. Sir, we are at my house. Please, come eat with us. Your views are—enlightening.

YESHUA. I still have much to do . . .

SHIMON THE LEPER. Please. Eat with us.

YESHUA. Yes. I would like to eat with you.

SHIMON CEPHAS. (*Aside to* CLEOPAS.) I almost dare not hope—but don't you recognize his voice?

CLEOPAS. It can't be. Can it?

They sit to eat bread.

SHIMON CEPHAS. Tell us more—rabbi.

YESHUA. Was he not betrayed? The Praises say, "Even my close friend, whom I trusted, he who shared my bread, has lifted up his heel against me." Was he not from many places—Bethlehem, Egypt, Galilee? "When Yisra'el was a child, I loved him, and out of Egypt I called my son." "But you, Bethlehem Ephrathah, though you are small among the clans of Yehudah, out of you will come for me one who will be ruler over Yisra'el, whose origins are from of old, from ancient times." "But in the future he will honor Galilee of the Gentiles, by the way of the sea, along the Jordan—The people walking in darkness have seen a great light; on those living in the land of the shadow of death a light has dawned."

SHIMON CEPHAS. How do you know all of this about Yeshua?

YESHUA. What were his last words?

SHIMON CEPHAS. He said . . .

YESHUA. The Praises say, "My God, my God, why have you forsaken me? Why are you so far from saving me, so far from the words of my groaning?" And then: "Into your hands I commit my spirit!"

SHIMON CEPHAS. You say the truth.

YESHUA. Your Mashiach, this Yeshua, is written all across your prophecies. The Praises, Mikha, Yirmyahu, Zekharya, Devarim, Mala'khi, and the great Yeshayahu. Search them all and you will see the handwriting of God telling you all these things.

CLEOPAS. Please, Rabbi, will you bless our bread for us?

YESHUA *lifts the bread to the sky, in a similar fashion as he has done previously in the play.*

YESHUA. Blessed art thou Abba, King of the Universe, who brings forth bread from the earth. (*Giving the bread to them.*) This is my body which is given for you. Do this in remembrance of me.

SHIMON THE LEPER. Yeshua, it is you!

CLEOPAS. Adonai!

The lights flash and then blackout. The lights raise again on the other disciples gathered again. THAU'MA *is upset, as the others are gathered around him.*

THAU'MA. Have you all gone insane?

SHIMON CEPHAS. Every word these women have told you is true, Thau'ma. I didn't believe at first either, but he has appeared to me as well!

THAU'MA. What, do you think that I'm not rational? That I can't tell fact from fairy tale?

MIRIAM. Thau'ma, please, you must listen . . .

THAU'MA. I did listen, Miriam, although I think all that I heard was gibberish. I don't know what game you all are playing at. Is this some kind of play for power?

MOTHER MIRIAM. Do you think that I would play so idly with the death of my son, Thau'ma?

THAU'MA. Then maybe all of you have been deceived. Maybe Rome, or the Sanhedrin, or some opportunists are taking advantage of our grief . . .

SHIMON CEPHAS. I would know our Savior from a fraud.

THAU'MA. I don't know, I don't know, I don't know! I just know that dead men don't come back alive!

ELEAZAR. I would beg to differ.

THAU'MA. I'm not sure what to think of that supposed event either! How do we know that you were really dead? What is going on here?

Enter CLEOPAS and SHIMON THE LEPER.

CLEOPAS. We have seen him! We have seen him! Yeshua is alive!

ELEAZAR. See, Thau'ma? We have all seen him now.

THAU'MA. Everyone but me, and—well, look! Look, look, look, unless I see in his hands the print of the nails, and put my finger into those prints, and thrust my hand in his side, I won't believe!

Suddenly YESHUA is in their midst. They are astonished. YESHUA approaches THAU'MA.

YESHUA. Thau'ma . . .

THAU'MA. Yeshua?

YESHUA. Bring your hands here. Here are my hands. Here is my side. Do you feel that? Be not faithless, but believing.

THAU'MA. My Adonai. My God.

YESHUA. Thau'ma, you're blessed for believing after you saw. More blessed are those who haven't seen and still believed.

MIRIAM. Yeshua, we are all here now.

YESHUA. Peace on all of you. Don't be terrified. A spirit doesn't have flesh and bones like I do. Nor does a spirit eat. (*YESHUA goes over to the meal on the table and eats some fish and honeycomb.*) So let's eat together, as friends eat.

They hesitate, but then they all sit at the table and begin eating. They start smiling, talking, laughing, enjoying each other's company. Lights dim to blackout.

POST SCRIPT

There is no curtain call, rather two of the MALACHIM *appear in light and address the audience.*

MALACH #1. You people of _____, why do you sit there gazing upon this stage for actors to bow? This same Yeshua, which was taken up from you into heaven, shall not be found here, but shall come in a similar manner as he was seen going into heaven. As you wait for his return, keep his commandments and love one another.

Lights fade to black.

THE END

Acknowledgements

"Are we not all beggars?" In my writing, I am in debt to so many people, that I will never be able to name them all. But here are a few.

My wife Anne Ogden Stewart is my best support, my best editor, and my best friend. As a former English teacher, her mad-ninja editing skills were put to good use once again. She was an excellent proof reader and my most thorough critic. She never let me get away with any of my sloppy nonsense. More than that, though, she continues to believe in the work I do, despite the many years of hardship and wandering in the wilderness we have both had to endure. I love her more than I can ever adequately express.

I am deeply indebted to the many directors, designers, crew members, and actors who have contributed to these plays. The extra layers of interpretation and life that they give to my words and characters are always a delight to see unfold. They truly give my imagination flesh and blood.

I am grateful to Zarahemla Books' publisher Christopher Bigelow, for once again believing in my work enough to publish it. I am also grateful to Marny Parkin for her beautiful layout of the interior of the book. I also love how Jason Robinson took my original poster design for *A Roof Overhead* and made such a nice cover with it. The art of bookmaking always intrigues me, and Zarahemla Books' team always does a compelling job.

I'm grateful for all the critics and readers who refined these plays, both solicited and unsolicited. Tricia Harris Evanson, Hillary Sterling, Kayela Seegmiller, Scott Hales, James Goldberg, Guillermo Reyes, Philip Taylor, Gitta Honneger, James Arrington, my MFA Playwriting cohort at Arizona State University, William Taysom, Liz Lund Oppelt, Tiffany Smith, JoAnna MacKay Stewart, Sarah Stewart, Russell Warne, and so many more people—they all did so much to help polish these particular plays. It is such a blessing to have such a support system for me and my work.

As these are a group of religious plays, I would of course be amiss in failing to recognize my Heavenly Father, my Heavenly Mother, and my Savior Jesus Christ. In gratitude, these are for you.

www.ingramcontent.com/pod-product-compliance
Lightning Source LLC
Chambersburg PA
CBHW031943090426